FOR CLUB, KING AND COUNTRY

THE STORY OF THE GLOUCESTERSHIRE COUNTY CRICKETERS AND THE GLOUCESTER RUGBY CLUB PLAYERS AS SOLDIERS OF GLOUCESTERSHIRE IN THE GREAT WAR, 1914-1918

MARTIN AND TERESA DAVIES

THE SOLDIERS OF GLOUCESTERSHIRE MUSEUM

This book is dedicated to all the players of the Gloucestershire County Cricket Club and the Gloucester Rugby Club who fought for their country in the British Armed Forces during the Great War, 1914-1918

"Do we remember? Why of course we do"

Captain A.F. Barnes, MC, 2/5th Gloucesters, writing in 1930

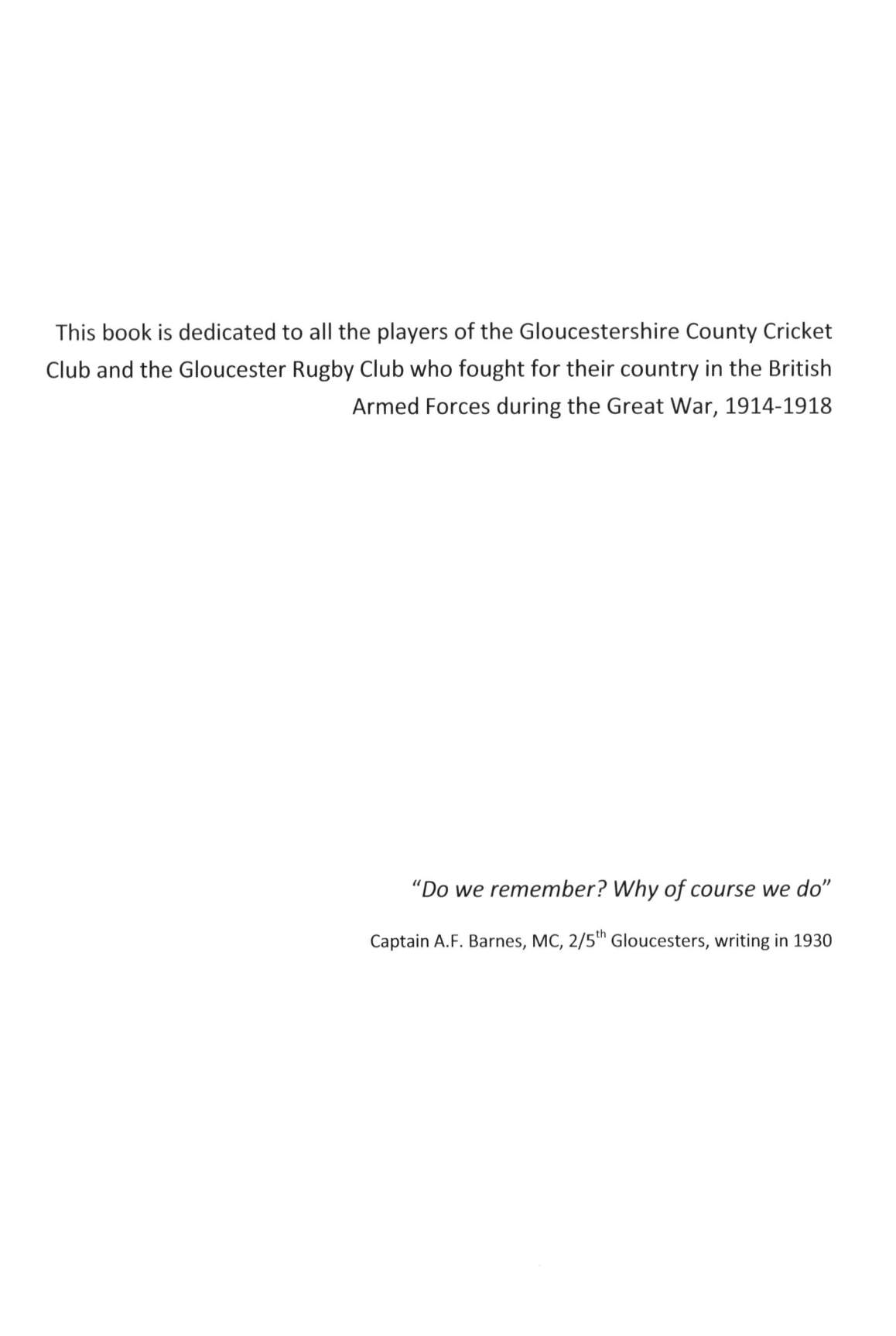

To Rachael, Hannah, Finley ('Finn'), Neil and Dave

First published 2014

© Martin Davies and Teresa Davies 2014

Copyright declaration. The right of Martin Davies and Teresa Davies to be identified as the Authors of this work has been asserted in accordance with the Copyrights, Designs and Patents Act 1988.

All rights reserved. No part of this book may be reprinted or reproduced or utilised in any form or by any electronic, mechanical or other means, now known or hereafter invented, including photocopying and recording, or in any information storage or retrieval system, without permission in writing from the authors.

British Library Cataloguing in Publication Data

A Catalogue Record for this book is available from the British Library

ISBN 978-0-9929100-1-5

Jacket design by Martin Davies

Printed in Great Britain by MWL Print Group (Pontypool)

CONTENTS

Foreword Jack Russell, MBE, FRSA (former Gloucestershire County Cricket Club and England wicket-keeper)

Foreword Mike Teague (former Gloucester Rugby Football Club, England and British Lions wing forward)

	Preface	
	Introduction	1
1	1914: For King and Country and a Great Adventure	5
2	1915: Truly a First World War	39
3	1916: Industrialised Modern Warfare. The Real Cost	65
4	1917: Death and Glory	91
5	1918: The End of the Great Adventure	105
6	1919 and Beyond: The Aftermath	121
7	The Roll of Honour	135
8	Appendices	183
	A. Exhibition at the Soldiers of Gloucestershire Museum	183
	B. Explanatory Notes	183
	C. Gallantry Awards	186
	D. Statistics	187
	E. Snippets	189
	F. The Soldiers of Gloucestershire Museum (*written by Ralph Stephenson, Trustee Soldiers of Gloucestershire Museum*)	190
	G. Gloucestershire County Cricket Club (*written by Roger Gibbons, Executive Committee Member and Honorary Archivist, Gloucestershire County Cricket Club*)	190
	H. Gloucester Rugby Football Club (*written by Simon Devereux, former Gloucester Rugby Football Club player and Broadcaster*)	192
	I. Maps	195
	Bibliography	201
	Index	203

FOREWORDS

Jack Russell MBE (Gloucestershire County Cricket Club and England)

For many it must have felt like a great adventure. A "quick contest" and "all over by Christmas", followed by a heroes return back to the playing fields of England. If only!

Like the uncertainty of sport (only more deadly) little did they know that for many of them there was never to be a return. This account of the sportsmen of Gloucestershire gives a vivid story of their experiences.

Amidst the horror, during their moments of reflection, I wonder how many of them longed for the sweet smell of cut grass, or to throw a ball around and enjoy that nervous excitement of a sporting contest, followed by a shake of hands and a drink with the opposition. A far cry from death and destruction.

Having stood in the very Flanders field where my great great Uncle was killed with his Gloucestershire pals, I can only try to imagine what they really went through. What was overwhelming as I travelled the battlefields of the Great War was the scale of the carnage. Fortunately, my sporting generation has never had to go through such an experience on that scale. We can only be thankful that our sporting lives have not been cut short, unlike the men who you will read about in the pages to come.

Mike Teague (Gloucestershire Rugby Football Club, England and the British Lions)

Every team player knows how important it is to support and remain loyal to your fellow players; so was it with the young men of Gloucester Rugby Club who volunteered to serve their country in August 1914. The country expected the young to step forward and defeat the 'Hun' and return before Christmas; the Club players, the 'celebrities' of their time, did exactly this. Many, of course, did not return and many were injured, either physically or mentally.

This book gives a comprehensive story to their military service as well as their contribution to the Club and it puts a life behind the names that are carved on our own War Memorial. The rugby team of the 5th Gloucester's – the local Territorial Battalion, had many Club players and most of these played for their Division, the 48th (South Midland) Division, winning cups and trophies. Throughout the grim time spent in the trenches, sport was an important means of forgetting the horror and rebuilding moral.

I was lucky enough to meet Tom Voyce in the winter of his life. He came to give an inspirational speech to all the players at Gloucester myself included; I was just starting my career. He simply said "The fifteen men that walk out on the field for Gloucester represent GRFC, at that moment in history you are the Club" I am also reminded of another one of his quotes "Never take a backward step" something, I'm sure, adopted from his experiences in the first world war.

At this Centenary of the outbreak of the First World War it is good that we, the directors and officials, as well as the players and supporters, of the Club remember their service and sacrifice. Read these pages and reflect on how they served their Club, their King and their Country.

ACKNOWLEDGMENTS

Throughout the research for this book various individuals have been of enormous help providing information, photographs and memorabilia. Although the list is probably not exhaustive and apologies to anybody overlooked, we would like to thank: Mike Barford (Honorary Curator, Christ's Hospital Museum, London), Jill Barlow (Cheltenham College), David and Jackie Brown (Jackie is the granddaughter of Francis Potter who married Violet 'Vi' Simmons who was previously the wife of Percy Simmons, GRFC, prior to his death in 1918), Tony Brown (Gloucestershire County Cricket Club), Lieutenant Colonel Rollo Clifford, Chris Collier (Gloucester Rugby Football Club Community Heritage Project), James Corsan, Roger Deeks (F.W. Harvey Society), Andrew Dennis (Assistant Curator, Royal Air Force Museum), Lavinia Drake (Museum Manager, Soldiers of Gloucestershire Museum), David Drinkwater, Roger Gibbons (Executive Board Member and Honorary Archivist, Gloucestershire County Cricket Club), Graham Gordon (Soldiers of Gloucestershire Museum), Roger Hiam (great nephew of Alfred White), Malc King (Gloucester Rugby Football Club Community Heritage Project), Gwen Johns, Kelli-Louise Johnson (MWL Print Group), Mike Kean-Price (grandson of John Price, GRFC), Sharon Potts (Rossall School, Lancashire), David Read (Collections Manager, Soldiers of Gloucestershire Museum), Clive Reade (grandson of Charles Cook, GRFC), Marjorie Reade (daughter of Charles Cook, GRFC), Catherine Roberts (Wycliffe College, Gloucestershire), Colin Sexstone (Gloucestershire County Cricket Club), Terry Short (grandson of Albert Cook, GRFC), Alison Steere (Glamorgan Cricket Archives), Lieutenant Colonel Ralph Stephenson TD (Trustee, Soldiers of Gloucestershire Museum), Andy Sysum (first cousin twice removed of Sidney Sysum, GRFC), John Theyers (Gloucester Rugby Football Club Community Heritage Project), Brian Ward, Dick Williams (Gloucester Rugby Football Club Community Heritage Project).

Special thanks to David Drinkwater for diligently trawling through the local newspapers and to Ralph Stephenson for assistance in the editing of the manuscript. Also to Roger Gibbons (Executive Board Member and Honorary Archivist, the Gloucestershire County Cricket Club) for his cricketing knowledge, the tracking down and provision of photographs pertaining to the county cricket players and for his contribution on the history of the Cricket Club and to Simon Devereux (Gloucester Rugby Football Club player, 1990-1999) for his contribution regarding the Gloucester Rugby Football Club.

Photographs: The sources of the photographs or the memorabilia are acknowledged (in brackets) within the photograph captions as follows: *CCGG, Cheltenham Chronicle and Gloucestershire Graphic* (reproduced with permission of the Gloucestershire Archives); *SOGM*, The Soldiers of Gloucestershire Museum – the reference includes the museum's catalogue number; *GRHP*, The Gloucester Rugby Football Club Community Heritage Project at the Gloucestershire Archives; *www.xxxxxxx*, Internet website reference; private and public collections from David and Jackie Brown, Roger Gibbons, Roger Hiam, Gwen Johns, Mike Kean-Price, Malc King, Andy Sysum and Wycliffe College and the Library of Congress, Washington, USA; *Author*, authors' personal collection. Throughout work was undertaken to establish copyright and ownership and apologies if there any errors or omissions. All of the photographs attributed to the Soldiers of Gloucestershire Museum are available for purchase through the museum's on-line shop at www.glosters.org.uk.

PREFACE

The majority of military studies of soldiers of the Great War have often been based on Army units or villages and towns, but researching sporting institutions provides a unique opportunity for studying the players before, during and after the war. This approach enables an understanding of how their lives were affected by what was the then biggest war that Great Britain had been involved in and certainly the closest to its borders since the Napoleonic wars one hundred years previously.

The Information used in this book has been gathered primarily from sources available at the Gloucestershire Archives and the Soldiers of Gloucestershire Museum, supplementing where necessary with information from The National Archives, from institutions which played a part in the players' lives and from descendants of the players. The information in this book cannot be claimed as a *fait accompli*, and in reality it is just a stage of an actively on-going project as new information is unearthed. It would be appreciated if any new information or corrections to existing information regarding the players included or on players who should be included chould be emailed to *martin191418@hotmail.co.uk*.

The players were well known throughout Bristol, Gloucester and Gloucestershire and were regarded as local celebrities. Despite the absence of radio, television and the Internet these men were publically recognisable and were often stopped on their streets by club supporters to discuss the latest game and the prospects for the next one. The local newspapers carried the news of their involvement in the Great War from their enlistment to their demobilisation, from their training to their battlefield experiences and tragically in a number of cases their demise. During their playing careers the local population celebrated their on-field sporting glories and it hoped that through this book they will not forgotten and that their memory will live on not just as great sportsmen but also as defenders of Great Britain.

Martin and Teresa Davies

September 2014,

Woolaston, Gloucestershire

Martin and Teresa Davies are the authors of '*They played for Gloucester and fought for their country. Gloucester Rugby Football Club: A Place in Military History*' published in 2013 by the Gloucester Rugby Football Club Community Heritage Project at the Gloucestershire Archives.

INTRODUCTION

The Gloucestershire County Cricket Club started life in 1846 as a merger between the Mangotsfield Cricket Club and the West Gloucestershire Cricket Club, with the new club adopting the latter name. In 1867 the club changed its name to the now familiar Gloucestershire County Cricket Club [GCCC] and three years later played its first First Class match against Surrey before joining the then unofficial County Championship in 1870. In contrast, the Gloucester Football Club was not formed until 1873 following a meeting at the Spread Eagle Hotel, Northgate Street, after it was recognised that a club was needed to bring structure to the local game.[1] By the summer of 1914 both Clubs were well established in the sporting and social life of the people of Bristol, Gloucester and Gloucestershire but across Europe political tensions would soon escalate and severely impact on both the clubs, their players and supporters.

The catalyst for the escalation came on 28 June 1914 when Archduke Franz Ferdinand, the heir presumptive to the Austro-Hungarian throne, was assassinated in Sarajevo by Gavrilo Princip. Frantic diplomatic messages criss-crossed Europe between Great Britain, France, Germany, Austro-Hungary, Belgium, Serbia and Russia. On 28 July Austro-Hungary invaded Serbia and amidst a cascade of recriminations and accusations, war became inevitable. Germany threatened to support her ally, Austro-Hungary, while Russia mobilised its armed forces (30 July) in support of its ally, Serbia. Germany swiftly followed by France mobilised their armies on 1 August with subsequent declarations of war. At 11.00 am on 4 August Great Britain issued an ultimatum to Germany regarding the violation of Belgian sovereignty. At 11.00 pm on 4 August as Big Ben tolled out the final note, the deadline for the British ultimatum passed and Great Britain declared war on Germany and the order to mobilise its army was issued by King George V.[2] On the following day, Lord Horatio Kitchener home on leave from the Army in Egypt, and now as the newly appointed Secretary of State for War, addressed the British Cabinet and informed it that the conflict would last for three years and would need an unprecedented army of one million men. Great Britain, unlike its friend, France, and its foe, Germany, had never introduced conscription and as such its army was relatively small and made up of professional soldiers and part-time volunteers, the latter, since 1908, known as the Territorial Force [TF]. In August 1914 both Germany and France were able to mobilise trained and equipped armies of between three to four million men apiece; Britain had, in contrast, 733,514

---

[1] The Gloucester rugby club in 1914 was known as the Gloucester Football Club [GFC] although the name soon evolved to the more familiar Gloucester Rugby Football Club [GRFC].
[2] The war declaration was at midnight German time. Despite the time deadline set in the ultimatum Great Britain began the mobilisation of its regular forces at 4.30 pm on the afternoon of 4 August.

soldiers although only 247,000 were Regular soldiers, the majority of which were scattered across the globe on British Empire garrison duties.[3]

With fighting between France and Germany already in progress the British Expeditionary Force [BEF] started to cross the Channel within ten days of the declaration and by the end of August the Germany Army of 3,800,000 men faced the French Army of 3,720,000 men supported by the 100,000 men of '...*the contemptible little army*...*"* of their British Allies.[4] The opening exchanges in Alsace-Lorraine and in Belgium at Mons witnessed the destruction of the opposing forces on a scale which weeks earlier would have seemed unimaginable but over the next four years industrialised total warfare would sweep across the World (see Map 2). Britain was ill-prepared for such a war although in reality neither France nor Germany were ready for what was to come!

A review of the British Army in 1907 had resulted in the Haldane Reforms which led to the creation the BEF and the TF. The BEF, about 160,000 men strong, was intended as a mobile force for rapid deployment to deal with situations arising in the British Empire. It was envisaged that it would fight a decisive battle, win and subsequently withdraw to leave a garrison of regular British soldiers supported by local troops to maintain the ensuing peace.[5,6] The TF, in contrast, consisted of part-time soldiers numbering about 272,000 in 1914, was specially designed for home defence and not for overseas deployment. Neither the BEF nor the TF were designed for modern industrialised warfare. With a credible threat of a German invasion of mainland Britain, only 100,000 soldiers of the BEF were sent to France with the remainder deployed in mainland Britain to assist the understrength TF before new recruits could be trained to bring it to a sufficient strength capable of sustaining home defence.

On 23 August approximately 70,000 men of the BEF engaged the German First Army, the largest of the German armies with 160,000 men at the Belgium town of Mons. Although the BEF's professional training enabled it to inflict a disproportionate number of casualties on the Germans, the sheer weight of numbers was too great to be contained and by 24 August the BEF was in full retreat even though rear guard actions continued to cause high casualty rates amongst the pursuing Germans. With the BEF and French Armies, the latter having begun to retreat on 22 August, falling back along the whole of the front and with Paris vulnerable, the German commanders made a serious tactical error in sweeping across the rear of the retreating Allies which rendered their armies

---

[3] Official Government statistics published after the war (*The Citizen* 20 August 1919)

[4] The smallness of the British Army lead Kaiser Wilhelm II to utter his insult regarding Britain's '*contemptible little army*' although the soldiers would turn this into an 'honour' and hence the men who fought in 1914 came to be known as the '*Old Contemptibles*'

[5] The BEF had been created on the basis of Major-General Sir James M. Grierson's strategic analysis which concluded that there were five situations which the army could get involved in, namely (1) a war against France (2) an Anglo-French war against Germany (3) a war against Russia in defence of India (4) a war against the USA in defence of Canada and (5) a third South African war against the Boers. The special army order issued by the War Office on 12 January 1907 did not envisage that the army would have primarily a Continental role. On 13 August 1914 Major General Grierson would travel to France as a Corps Commander with the BEF but died of heart failure on 17 August.

[6] This British 'way of warfare' implies a short decisive battle and encouraged the '*over by Christmas*' notion. Further implicit in the design of the BEF is that the Army is not trained for Continental industrial warfare and is certainly not designed for the static trench warfare characteristic of the Great War in general and the Western Front in particular. The BEF is however designed for mobile warfare with the artillery firing over open sights; the latter implies that the artillery gunners can see their target and fire by sighting along the barrel of the gun – in the trench warfare that developed targets in general cannot be seen and at the start of the war the artillery had to 'guess where their target was until suitable methods of detection were developed.

vulnerable to an Allied counterattack along their exposed flank. On the Marne (7-10 September) and the Aisne (12-15 September) Allied counter-attacks forced the Germans back to pre-prepared defensive positions of sufficient strength to force the Allies to dig in opposite the German positions rather than engage in costly frontal assaults. After some frantic action in Northern France and Belgium a stalemate situation ensued and Britain, France and German dug in; thus was born the trench system that would become known as the Western Front, the most strategically important theatre of the Great War. Other theatres would become active as the Great War spread across the globe.

The creation of the 'stand-off' trench system allowed the combatants sufficient time for a degree of consolidation. In Britain Lord Kitchener's call for volunteers was sounded across the land and men rushed either to join existing TF units to bring them up to strength or to join Kitchener's New Army which formed additional 'Service' Battalions attached to existing regiments.[7] The Gloucestershire Regiment, for instance, had six battalions on the outbreak of war but by end of 1914 it had expanded to sixteen battalions with a further four battalions added in 1915. By the end of August 1914 80-90% of the Territorial soldiers had volunteered for overseas service although there would be a delay before they saw active service as the battalions needed to be brought up to strength with untrained recruits.[8]

The call for volunteers echoed across the country and in Bristol and Gloucestershire ordinary men would flock to recruiting stations in towns and villages.[9] Amongst the men who answered the call were those who were not as anonymous as the vast majority of the recruits - these were the men from the Gloucester Rugby Club and the Gloucestershire County Cricket Club.[10] The men were well known locally and reports on their sporting activities were regularly published in local newspapers including in *The Citizen*, the *Gloucester Journal*, the *Cheltenham Chronicle and Gloucestershire Graphic* and the *Western Daily Press*. Although they were sportsmen first and soldiers second, the cricketers and the rugby players generally came from different social backgrounds and age groups and as a result in 1914 the average age of the soldier-cricketers was 32 years with 35% being officers compared with 27 years and 8% officers for the soldier-rugby players.[11,12] As soldiers however they shared common fates as warfare did not differentiate between social status or age - both groups of men suffered, either through losing their lives or being seriously wounded. Both won their fair share of gallantry awards. Amazingly few of the rugby players and cricketers actually served together although there were exceptions, none more so than the first cricketer and first rugby player to be killed in action in October 1914.

---

[7] These battalions were 'for service during the hostilities' after which they would be disbanded.
[8] Under the terms of their service Territorial soldiers were for home defence only and could not be deployed overseas without individuals' agreement.
[9] Bristol was granted County status in 1373 and hence is a separate administrative area to Gloucestershire.
[10] Throughout this text the inclusion of players is based on the match statistics recorded either on the Cricket Archive website (www.cricketarchive.com) or on the Gloucester Rugby Football Club Community Heritage Project website (www.gloucesterrugbyheritage.org.uk). The inclusion of names is not dependent on the number of matches played.
[11] See Appendix D: Statistics, Tables 1 and 2
[12] The higher percentage of officers amongst the cricketers in 1914 compared with the rugby players showed that a military career was a favoured profession for the former sportsmen; there were more manual workers amongst the rugby players with a large proportion of those employed by the Gloucester Railway Carriage and Wagon Works Limited.

Although much has been written about the young men of the Great War generation it is still truly difficult to comprehend how they came so rapidly to submerge themselves in the great killing machine. Men who were reflecting either on a cricket season just finished or a rugby season about to start could have had little comprehension of what their life would be like over the next four years, provided of course that they lived that long! The spirit and discipline of the men and their unquestioning willingness to go '*over the top*' defied comprehension and was amply demonstrated by the cricketers and rugby players who climbed out of the trenches on the Somme on the 2 and 3 July 1916 after witnessing the carnage of the previous day whilst they were in support. For sportsmen the winning mentality of the sports field readily transferred to the battlefields as witnessed in their letters home and although most would question why they were fighting, there was still a stoic acceptance of their fate which was flippantly captured in the words of the well-known soldiers' marching song from the era "*We're here because we're here because we're here*".[13]

Despite the harsh environment of the Great War, through training and subsequent battlefield experiences a new 'team spirit' developed based on loyalty to one's comrades and the need to 'look after' one another. Social historians have concluded that this loyalty functioned best at the Section level where small groups of ten to twelve men survived as 'family' units; but there was also considerable loyalty at battalion level. With the sportsmen there was already a loyalty to team mates, to look after each on the sporting field and it is probable that this carried over into the Great War, especially for the men of the Gloucester Rugby Club as the majority served together in the same units/platoons; for the men from the Gloucester Rugby Club the 5th Battalion, the Gloucestershire Regiment would become the equivalent of a Pals Battalion.[14] There was however no similar experience for the cricketers who generally served in different regiments with little contact with pre-war team mates.

This is the story of men who loved to play cricket and rugby in Gloucestershire but through political machinations across Europe were forced to participate in a greater game for which there would be no friendly drinks in a bar after the final whistle and no discussions on how they would change their approach for the next time.[15]

---

[13] This song was sung to the tune of Auld Lang Syne and became more prevalent as a marching song especially as the war dragged on.

[14] So called Pals Battalions were formed to encourage men from local communities to enlist together in the same units with the promise that they would serve together. The first Pals Battalion formed on the 29 August 1914, was the 17th (Service) Battalion, The King's (Liverpool Regiment) (www.1914-1919.net). This undoubtedly helped the recruitment drive but when these units suffered badly whole communities were affected back home and became decimated as the local young men were killed or wounded *en masse*.

[15] The story of the men from the Gloucester Rugby Club has recently been told in greater detail in Martin and Teresa Davies, *They played for Gloucester and fought for their country. Gloucester Rugby Football Club: A Place in Military History*, (Gloucestershire Archives, 2013) (Available through Gloucester Rugby shop and Hudson's Sports, Northgate Street, Gloucester)

1

1914: FOR KING, COUNTRY AND A GREAT ADVENTURE

"…the prospects for the next season were exceeding bright and given good weather and as successful a team as last years, the Club should experience another good time…"
W. H. Worth, Treasurer, GRFC, Commenting on prospect for forthcoming season
The Citizen 13 June 1914

"The Great War Begins"
A common headline in the local newspapers

"…another great crowd [sang] the 'Marseillaise', the Russian Hymn and English national airs…"
Report of recruitment meeting at Cheltenham
Cheltenham Chronicle and Gloucestershire Graphic 12 September 1914

"Take care of your health: remember your friends at home; and stick to it!"
Advice given by Captain S.S. Champion, in charge of the 5/Gloucesters Depot, to the new recruits

In June 1914 despite worrying reports in the national newspapers the British population were unaware of the true nature of the situation developing across Europe. The sporting public in Bristol and Gloucestershire were enjoying the end of the cricket season and looking forward to the start of the rugby season with hardly a break in between. The cricketers were reflecting on their rapidly-ending disastrous season while the rugby players were anticipating the new season which was scheduled to start on 12 September against Stroud. But after the 4 August declaration the country was plunged into an unimaginable reality which would optimistically be a *'great adventure'* which *'would be over by Christmas'* and would, for a period, provide relief from the hardship of everyday life and a chance, perhaps the only one, to see the world.

June-July-August:

The Gloucester Football Club at its annual general meeting at the Kingsholm Ground on 12 June announced the fixture list for the forthcoming 1914-15 season although the availability of returning players would not become apparent until just before the trial matches normally scheduled for early September. In the 1912-13 season the Club had declared a financial deficit of £60 3s 9d but with a grant from the County Union (£40) and *The Citizen*'s Shilling Fund (£50 14s 6d) and a healthier set of gate receipts, the Club now posted a positive balance of £203 5s 7d.[16] Despite this volatile financial climate the Treasurer, Mr W. H. Worth reported on what was the largest financial balance ever declared by the Club and optimistically predicted that,

> "...the prospects for the next season were exceeding bright and given good weather and as successful a team as last years, the Club should experience another good time..."[17]

Photograph 1. Gloucester Football Club: Gloucester First XV 1913-14: Players left to right. Standing: R.A. Clarke, S. Smart, A. Saunders, J.F. Lawson, S. Millard, A. Cook and W. Parham. Seated: F. Ayliffe, N. Hayes, A. Hall, F. Webb, G. Halford (captain), L. Hamblin, W. Washbourne, S. Sysum and C. Cook. On Ground: A. Lewis and J. Baker. This unique photograph has been water-damaged. This would be the last team photograph until the start of the 1919-1920 season. (*Andy Sysum*)

The new Committee members were voted for and amongst others elected were the players **Arthur Hudson** (wing), **W.A. 'Billy' Johns** (front row), **Fred Pegler** (front row) and **George Romans** (full back);[18] none of them would take up their duties after the end of August. The AGM came sixteen days before the assassination of Archduke Franz Ferdinand but speculation still continued regarding the team throughout July. For instance **Fred Webb** (GRFC) "*...the brilliant threequarter...*" would not

---

[16] A Shilling Fund, often set up by local newspapers, tried to get as many subscribers as possible to donate the reasonable amount of at least one shilling to a particular cause.
[17] *The Citizen* 13 June 1914
[18] George Romans, a full back, played 268 games for GRFC between 1899 and 1907 and as a right-handed batsman played 11 matches for GCCC between 1899 and 1903.

be available for the 1914-15 season because as an employee of GWR Goods Staff he had been transferred to Newport and as a consequence would be turning out for Gloucester's fierce rivals.[19]

Photograph 2. Gloucester Football Club: Gloucester A 1913-14: Players left to right. Standing: A. Comley, W. Cromwell, C. Mumford, F. Hayward, J. Harris, F. Lewis, F. Osbourne and W. Dovey. Seated: T. Powell, W.Wilkes, H. Kingscott, F. Bloxsome (captain), C. Staunton, T. Miller and J. Webb. On Ground: E. Wootton and T. Burns. (*GRHP*)

Meanwhile the newspapers' journalists were busy compiling their assessment of the Gloucestershire County Cricket Club's disastrous 1914 season with only one victory and four draws out of twenty-two matches; the season ended on 31 August 1914.[20] The situation for the Club was not much better off the field as it was in considerable financial difficulties. At the last Annual Meeting before the war on 29 January 1914 the Club reported a debt to the bank of £671 14s 5d and that the previous seasons' gate receipt had fallen to £1,560 while the expenses had risen to £3,040. The *Gloucestershire Chronicle*'s Shilling Fund appeal which closed in May raising nearly £1,000, alleviated the situation but this was offset by a fall in the income from gate receipts which for the 1914 season amounted to just £760.[21] This dire situation was unsustainable and the future of the Club was in doubt to the extent that the Committee arranged a meeting for October to decide on the Club's future.

---

[19] *The Citizen* 28 July 1914
[20] *Gloucester Journal* 5 September 1914
[21] From 1900-08 the average gate receipts had been £2,000 per annum but this figure had subsequently fallen to £1,230 per annum between 1909 and 1913. For the 1914 season the figure had dropped to an all-time low of £760 (*Western Daily Press* 28 October 1914).

Photograph 3. The Gloucestershire County Cricket Club squad versus Warwickshire, 3 July 1913: Players left to right. Standing: C.W.L. Parker, T. Langdon, F.B. Roberts, E.G. Clarke, T.H. Gange and A.E. Dipper. Seated: W.M. Brownlee, D.C. Robinson, C.O.H. Sewell, G.L. Jessop and J.W.W. Nason. On ground: E.G. Dennett and H. Smith. All bar E.G. Clarke fought in the Great War and three died (F.B. Roberts, W.M. Brownlee and J.W.W. Nason). (*Roger Gibbons*)

Since 1889 the Ashley Down ground in Bristol (now known as the County Cricket Ground) had been the principal home of the Club. The majority of the games were played there although Cheltenham College regularly hosted the Club at the annual Cheltenham Cricket Festival which normally generated a significant amount of revenue for the Club.[22] In 1914 the Committee took the decision, despite the war, to continue with the tournament scheduled for 10-18 August, mainly with the intention of easing the Club's financial predicament. This business-as-usual decision reflected the attitude of most institutions across the country; this attitude was shaped by the experiences of the Boer War (1899-1902) and to a certain extent current reports in the local newspaper. Following the reporting of the assassination on 28 June there was subsequently little news other than a few references regarding the prospect of an Austro-Hungary-Serbian war with the newspapers concentrating on the more immediate domestic matters of the Suffragette activities, industrial

---

[22] The ownership of the Ashley Down ground has changed several times; the Gloucestershire County Cricket Club first bought it in 1933

unrest, Ulster Home Rule and to a lesser extent Welsh Home Rule. It was not until the 27 July, a week before the declaration of war, that an article appeared in *The Citizen* under the headline '*Grave News*' which suggested that a '*European War*' was a distinct possibility.[23] This was followed a day later by the statement which declared "*the outlook, both abroad and at home, is decidedly more hopeful...*",[24] and although an inevitable slide towards war began the British involvement seemed only to become a public probability on 3 August. On 5 August the early editions of *The Citizen* carried the headline "*War Declared. By Great Britain on Germany*" and the Mayor of Gloucester, James Bruton appealed to the people of Gloucester "*...to meet the existing position in a calm and trustful manner.*[25]

Photograph 4. The Gloucestershire County Cricket Club squad 1914: Players from left to right. Standing: H.Smith, T.Langdon, T.H. Gange, E.G. Dennett, A.E. Dipper and F.E. Ellis. Seated: W. St C Grant, M.A. Green, C.O.H. Sewell, T. Miller and C.W.L. Parker. All bar T. Langdon fought in the Great War: William St C Grant would be killed in action. (*Roger Gibbons*)

But the legacy of the Boer War still influenced local thinking. In October 1899 volunteer part-time soldiers were called up to bring the 2nd Battalion, Gloucestershire Regiment up to strength to go to

---

[23] *The Citizen* 27 July 1914
[24] *The Citizen* 28 July 1914
[25] *The Citizen* 5 August 1914

South Africa after the 1st Battalion had suffered a serious 'reverse' at Nicholson's Nek.[26] This created the illusion that warfare was always fought in far-off lands across the Empire by professional soldiers who were supported by part-time civilian-soldiers if an emergency arose. In Gloucester two rugby players, **Arthur Mills** (front row) and **Fred Goulding** (back row) joined the 2nd Battalion, Gloucestershire Regiment while **Alec Spence** (back row) volunteered for the 3rd (Gloucestershire) Company, 1st Battalion, Imperial Yeomanry. Alec Spence would never return from South Africa and died from enteric fever on 16 June 1901 at Harrismith.[27] Similarly, **Frank Townsend** (GCCC), the brother of **Charles Townsend** (GCCC), had volunteered for the 19th Battalion (Paget's Horse), Imperial Yeomanry and had landed in South Africa in the autumn of 1900. Within seven months on 25 May 1901 he also died from enteric fever at Kimberley.[28] **William Woof** (GCCC) fought in South Africa but was taken prisoner and served some of his time as the cricket coach at St Andrew's College in Grahamstown.[29] There were a number of soldiers who had fought in that war and subsequently joined the clubs. These included **Harry Berry** (GRFC), 4th and 2nd Gloucesters, **Harry Collins** (GRFC), 1/Gloucesters, **George Dennett** (GCCC), 2/Somerset Light Infantry, **Arthur Du Boulay** (GCCC), Royal Engineers, **Ernest English** (GCCC), King's Shropshire Light Infantry, **George Griffiths** (GRFC), 1/Gloucesters and **Fred Pegler** (GRFC), 1/Gloucesters.[30] In the event the number of part-time soldier-players called to the Colours was relatively small and there was no impact on the playing ability of their respective clubs; this seemingly 'negligible' effect would underpin the approach of the sporting institutions in 1914.[31] But stirring tales, worthy of *"The Boy's Own Paper"* emerged from the Boer War which romanticised the nature of warfare and reduced it to a *'great adventure'*. All of these factors combined to ensure that the rugby and cricket clubs embarked on a business-as-usual financially-driven approach while their players, and the general population, would enlist for a four months-long *'over by Christmas' 'great adventure'* as they enthusiastically answered Kitchener's call. However the *'Great Adventure'* and *'over by Christmas'* approach was not universally supported and men such as Kitchener and Winston Churchill, the latter as early as August 1911, had recognised that *this* war would be different to any that had gone before.

On 4 August the War Office with Royal Approval had ordered the mobilisation of the Regular Armed Forces and the subsequent recall of Reservists, with all units proceeding to their designated

---

[26] Throughout this book references to particular battalions and regiment, where appropriate, will use the following short-hand nomenclature, the 1st Battalion, Gloucestershire Regiment will become 1/Gloucesters, the 2nd Battalion, Welsh Regiment will become 2/ Welsh and so forth. This will apply to all regiments.

[27] **Alec Spence** (1875-1901), a back row forward played sixteen games for the Gloucester Rugby Club between 1899 and 1901 before he cut short his career and answered Lord Robert's call for 5,000 volunteers for the Imperial Yeomanry.

[28] **Frank Norton Townsend** (1875-1901), a right-handed batsman, played twelve matches for the Gloucestershire County Cricket Club between 1896 and 1900 before volunteering for the Imperial Yeomanry.

[29] **William Albert Woof** (1858-1937), a right-handed batsman and a slow left-arm orthodox and left-arm fast bowler played 160 matches for the Gloucestershire County Cricket Club between 1878 and 1902.

[30] If it is not apparent from the context whether a soldier is a rugby player or cricketer, immediately after his name will be placed (GRFC) to indicate he is a rugby player and (GCCC) to indicate he is a cricketer.

[31] As a comparison and although casualty rates statistics are notoriously unreliable, the local newspapers (*The Citizen* 4 September 1902) reported on information supplied by the British Parliament which showed that Britain mobilised 448,435 troops in the Boer War and that 7,999 died by enemy action; rate = 1.8%. In the Great War 8,905,000 men of the British Empire were mobilised and 908,371 died by enemy action; rate = 10.2%. The figures for Great Britain alone in the Great War are 5,397,000 troops mobilised with 702,410 killed by enemy action; rate = 13.0%. This difference in scale would become evident to the military authorities, the Government and the general population alike even by the end of 1914.

war stations.[32] The 1/Gloucesters was on brigade exercises at its annual battle camp at Rushmoor Bottom (Aldershot) but on 1 August, before the declaration, orders came through to abandon the exercise, strike camp and proceed to its war station at Bordon (Hampshire).[33,34,35] The Cardwell Reforms of 1881 had resulted in British regiments consisting of two active service battalions (1st and 2nd) which usually alternated with one stationed overseas and the other on home duty. For economic reasons the overseas battalion was maintained at strength while the other acted as a reserve. Both battalions could not be stationed on active service without recalling former soldiers who were part of the Army Reserve. As a consequence the 1/Gloucesters, as the home battalion, was understrength and required an additional seven subalterns and 600 men to bring it up to a strength sufficient for going to war; hence at 4.30 pm on 4 August the War Office issued the order to mobilise the Reservists.[36] On 6 August the Reservists in Gloucester who arrived home after a long day in their civilian occupations received telegrams containing the following order,

> "Members of the National Reserve will parade at the Guildhall, Eastgate Street on Friday [7 August] morning at 7 a.m, and will march to the Midland Station en route for Bristol – J.R. Bibby, Acting Captain for Major Knowles"[37,38]

As a result, and with less than one day's notice, **Harry Barnes** (GRFC), **Harry Berry** (GRFC), **George Halford** (GRFC), **Walter Hancock** (GRFC), **Frank Smith** (GRFC) and **Claude Mackay** (GCCC) left their families, peacetime homes and employment and proceeded ultimately to the Depot at Bordon.[39] It is difficult to appreciate the change in the lives of the Reservists as in less than twelve hours they changed from civilians to soldiers preparing to go into battle. There would have been very little time to settle affairs or say proper farewells to their families! The return to army life for the Reservists would have been a surprise as the only precedent they had was the Boer War when the Reservists had been mobilised but only after the regular forces had suffered serious reverses. By 11 August, with all its Reservists re-called, following a well rehearsed Army practise, all equipment issued and all forms filled, the 1/Gloucesters entrained for Southampton and crossed the channel in SS *Gloucester Castle*, together with the 1/South Wales Borderers, and landed at Le Havre at midnight on 12 August; in less than six days the Reservists had gone from civilians on the peaceful streets of Britain to soldiers in a war zone! The war however got off to a hesitant start for the 1/Gloucesters as the unloading of the men and animals immediately hit a snag. Although ramps were provided to bring out the horses there were no mats to prevent them slipping and as a consequence the animals

---

[32] The British professional soldier of the regular army signed up for seven years active service followed by five years in the Reserve, although there were variations of these time periods. The men of the Reserve were liable to a re-call to the Colours in the event of a national crisis.

[33] During the summer months of July and August both regular army and TF units were engaged in exercises at summer camps and hence with the declaration of war these camps were cancelled and the units ordered to return to their war stations where they would be readied for active service.

[34] The yearly routine of Army battalions consisted of physical exercises, route marches, bayonet fighting, musketry, signalling and scouting in the winter months, unit training in the spring and brigade and divisional exercises in the summer. (Wyrall, *The Gloucestershire Regiment in the War 1914-1918*, p.1)

[35] Everard Wyrall, *The Gloucestershire Regiment in the War 1914-1918* (London: Methuen, 1931), p.7 (Reprinted by The Naval and Military Press)

[36] Wyrall, *The Gloucestershire Regiment in the War 1914-1918*, p.3

[37] *Gloucestershire Chronicle* 8 August 1914

[38] This situation would be repeated in the homes of all Reservists across the country

[39] **Claude Mackay** (GCCC), 3rd (Reserve) Battalion, Gloucestershire Regiment was mobilised but did not proceed to France until November 1914.

were unloaded using cargo slings, a time consuming process; the men were forced to spend an uncomfortable night in a dock-side shed before moving off at 6.00 am to No.1 Rest Camp five miles away.[40]

Meanwhile the 2nd Battalion of the Gloucestershire Regiment had been enjoying life as a garrison force in Tientsin, China, when it was re-called in September and sailed back to Britain uneventfully on board the SS *Arcadia* despite running the gauntlet of the threat posed by the German cruiser, SMS *Embden*.[41] The Battalion arrived back at Southampton on 8 November and proceeded to Winchester where it was brought up to strength and readied for war; it crossed the Channel and landed at Le Havre on 18 December.[42]

A similar situation applied to the Gloucestershire Regiment's Territorial Battalions, the 4th (City of Bristol) (HQ, Queen's Road, Bristol), 5th (HQ, The Barracks, Gloucester) and 6th (HQ, St Michael's Hill, Bristol). The 4th and 6th Battalions summer camp at Minehead began on Sunday 26 July but they were ordered to return to Bristol the following day.[43] However despite this the 5th Battalion travelled to its annual two week-long summer camp at Marlow the following week on Sunday 2 August but at 3.00 am Monday morning was re-called. By 5.00 am the camp had been struck although due to a lack of trains the Battalion did not arrive back at the Great Western Station in Gloucester until 4.30 pm.[44] On 5 August the A, B, C and D Companies assembled at the Drill Hall, Brunswick Street with the E, F, G and H Companies at Barrack Square for medical examinations; well over 800 men were examined and only six were failed. The advance guard left at midnight on the same day for the Battalion's War Station at Parkhurst on the Isle of Wight; the remainder of the men including Captain **Gilbert Collett** (GRFC and GCCC), Sergeant **James Meadows** (GRFC) and Lance Corporal **Trevor Powell** (GRFC) paraded at the Gloucester Drill Hall on 6 August and at 6.30 pm marched via Clarence Street and Station Road to the Midland Station to join the advance guard (see Photograph 5).[45]

After a few days the Battalion was relieved and moved to Swindon where it joined its sister Territorial Battalions, the 4th and 6th Battalions at their war stations. On 16 August seventy-eight special trains took almost twenty-four hours to move the 5th Battalion and two other battalions and their equipment to the training camp at Chelmsford while the 4th and 6th Battalions moved to training camps at Maldon, Essex.[46]. The men had been asked to waive their legal right and volunteer

---

[40] Battalion War Diary, *1st Battalion, Gloucestershire Regiment 11 August 1914*, TNA WO 95/1278

[41] The German cruiser, SMS *Embden*, had evaded the Royal Navy after the declaration of war and for over three months sailed the Pacific Ocean sinking or capturing twenty-five merchant and naval ships before being sunk by HMAS *Sydney* on 9 November 1914.

[42] The 2/Gloucesters as the 'abroad' battalion was at establishment strength but this was a nominal strength and with sick and injured men would have needed Reservists before it could enter a theatre of war.

[43] Everard Wyrall, *The Gloucestershire Regiment in the War 1914-1918*, p.60

[44] The men of the TF were expected to attend regularly the weekly drills and musketry practice, in addition to, and probably the highlight of their year, an eight- or fifteen-day attendance at the annual two week-long summer camp. In 1914 the men attending for the second week only were expected to leave home on Saturday 8 August. The weekly drill was usually on Saturday evening and as a consequence the men of the TF were referred to disparagingly by the regulars as 'Saturday night soldiers'.

[45] These men now included Captain **Gilbert Collett** (GRFC) a pre-war Territorial who had resigned two months previously owing to work commitments but had not yet been gazetted out and hence he immediately re-joined the battalion (*Cheltenham Chronicle and Gloucestershire Graphic* 8 August 1914)

[46] Although the 4th, 5th and 6th Battalions were all within the 48th (South Midland) Division, the 4th and 6th were part of the 144 Brigade while the 5th Battalion were part of the 145th Brigade and hence trained separately.

for overseas service - across the land 86% of the Territorial volunteers came forward with the 5/Gloucesters reflecting the national trend as all of the officers and 886 Other Ranks volunteered for foreign service.[47] These TF units would spend the next eight months, after receiving new recruits to bring them up to strength, in training ready for their active deployment.

Photograph 5. 1/5th Battalion, Gloucestershire Regiment. The Battalion marching along a street in Gloucester in 1914. This postcard sent by Private Walter Middlecote whilst in training at Chelmsford to his home in Gloucester. (*SoGM, GLRRM:04782.3*)

With the battalions at their war stations and training camps the Colours were left behind for safekeeping, usually with the local mayor. At 11.00 am on 8 August the Mayor of Bristol received the Colours from the 4/Gloucesters and at 12.15 pm from the 6/Gloucesters in front of a large crowd.[48,49] For those unable to attend the ceremony, it was captured on news reel footage and on 10 August the Zetland Picture House advertised the film of the ceremony as one of its featured attractions.

For sporting institutions and employers the re-call of Reservists and the deployment of the TF to war stations were considered to have little impact on their activities as Reservists and TF soldiers only represented a small proportion of the playing squads or the employees. The loss of these few men was seen as nothing more than an *'inconvenience', as everybody knew*, they would only have to do without their services until Christmas; the true nature of this war had yet to become apparent.

---

[47] *The Citizen* 19 August 1914
[48] *Western Daily Press* 8 August 1914
[49] The tradition had been that the Colours were usually carried onto the battlefield to act as a rallying point but the nature of modern warfare spread over large tracts of land gave the Colours a more symbolic role. As soon as the war finished in 1918 Colour Parties were immediately despatched to Britain to bring the Colours across to the battlefields to be paraded.

For the Gloucester Football Club at the end of May **George Halford** had been unanimously re-elected as the captain of the First XV, with **Lionel Hamblin** as the vice-captain, but as a Reservist the former had been re-called to the Colours on 6 August. On 22 August after a Club Committee meeting it was decided that Lionel Hamblin should now be elevated to the captaincy with **Sid Smart** as the vice-captain with the expectation that the first game against Stroud, only three weeks away on 12 September, would proceed as usual.[50]

On 5 August, Lord Horatio Kitchener, as Secretary of State for War pronounced that the war would last at least three years and would require a British Army of one million men. Supported by Churchill, the Cabinet permitted Kitchener to call initially for 100,000 volunteers aged between 18 and 38 years (*'Your Country Needs You!'*) on 11 August.[51,52,53] This 'Call to Arms' would completely change the nature of the situation although this was not immediately apparent as the Gloucestershire CCC decided to embark on its annual Cheltenham Cricket Festival, the opening of which coincided with Kitchener's 'Call to Arms' which elicited a massive response from the general population who stayed away from the Festival; after the first day The Citizen reported that,[54,55]

> "*The cricket festival at Cheltenham began on Monday under the depressing influence of the war. The weather was beautifully fine, but neither this nor the promise of a good day's play was sufficient to attract anything like the usual crowds seen on the College Ground on the first days………*"[56]

Subsequent reports indicated that the situation got progressively worse throughout the nine days of the Festival despite lowering the admission prices.[57] This situation exacerbated the Club's already perilous financial situation and challenged the long term viability of the Club,[58] but bizarrely the war would save the club from possible financial ruin and extinction as in the absence of games its expenses bill would become markedly reduced. Beside the 'Call to Arms', the situation in Cheltenham had not been helped by the much publicised fact that following the declaration of war on 4 August the Club's renowned big hitter <u>and</u> 'crowd puller', **Gilbert Jessop**, despite a previous promise, decided not to play in any of the remaining five county matches or to participate in the Cheltenham Festival.[59] On 21 December 1914 Gilbert obtained a commission in the 14/Manchesters and would play a great deal of Army cricket throughout 1915 whilst in training at Lichfield although

---

[50] *The Citizen* 23 August 1914
[51] On 13 August 1911 Winston Churchill sent a memorandum to the Committee of Imperial Defence [CID] which predicted that the coming war would be of a long duration; his views were dismissed and derided by Sir Henry Wilson, Director of Military Operations (1910-1914)
[52] For an explanation of the criteria for voluntary enlistment and subsequent requirements during conscription see Append B Note 3:
[53] The first 100,000 men were designated as Kitchener's Army or K1. Further calls for volunteers issued after the beginning of September resulted in the formation of K2, K3, K4 and a Fifth New Army before the end of December 1914
[54] The Cheltenham Cricket Festival played in August at the Cheltenham College ground had started in 1872.
[55] In 1914 the Cheltenham Cricket Festival was played at the College Ground between 10 and 18 August.
[56] *The Citizen* 10 August 1914
[57] *The Citizen* 11 August 1914
[58] The staging of the Cheltenham Cricket Festival away from GCCC's home at the County Ground in Bristol attracted additional costs which were normally covered through the revenue generated by the gate receipts.
[59] Gerald Brodribb, *The Croucher. A Biography of Gilbert Jessop* (London: London Magazines Editions, 1974), pp.177-79

the Army realised his potential as a national figure and used him on recruiting drives across Northern England.

In the middle of the Cheltenham Festival, the MCC had passed a resolution which was indicative of the prevailing mood of the country,

"Owing to the war, and realising that every sound man of England will be performing some kind of duty on behalf of his country, it has been decided that no cricket shall be played at Lord's during September. No county game is affected by this decision but as a rule a large number of club matches are played at headquarters during September. With Lord's and the Oval not available, it is uncertain whether the match, Champion County v. Rest of England will be carried through."[60]

The end of the cricket season gave some respite to the GCCC's difficulties but it was now the rugby club's turn to come to terms with reality. On 28 August at a recruitment meeting at Shire Hall the Officer Commanding the 5/Gloucesters, Major John Henry Collett, had called for additional volunteers to bring the battalion up to establishment strength (i.e. battle strength). The Gloucester players, **Sid Smart** (second row, Gloucester and England), **Lionel Hamblin** (centre, Gloucester captain), **Albert Cook** (back row) and **William Washbourne** (wing), stepped forward to be greeted by "...*a tremendous cheer*..." of recognition and a jubilant throng of 300-400 men rushed the stage with the crush being so great that the dignitaries on the stage who had hoped to whip up *some* enthusiasm for the Army were forced to retire until calm was restored.[61] The Rugby Club Committee would now come under severe pressure with the disruption of the financially vital income from gate receipts, a situation all too familiar to the County Cricket Committee.

The rush to the recruiting stations was encouraged by both the general population and employers although the idea of a 'home front' had yet to materialise. In Bristol the specially formed Bristol Citizen's Recruiting Committee, chaired by Sir Herbert Ashman, which met for the first time on 12 August, decided to raise a special city battalion, an idea that came to fruition after permission was granted by the War Council. This became the 12th (Service) Battalion (Bristol's Own), Gloucestershire Regiment on 30 August. Both **Hugh Jones** (GCCC) **Frank Wicks** (GCCC) and **Solomon Levy** (GCCC) enlisted as Privates in the new battalion, however only Solomon went to France within its ranks on 21 November 1915, Hugh Jones having gained a commissioned on 28 February 1915 landed in France on 4 March 1916 with the 13/Gloucesters while Frank Wicks gained a commission in the 22/Manchesters. Similarly employers keen to demonstrate their patriotic nature encouraged their employees to enlist with promises that their jobs would be waiting for them on their return in a few months' time despite the increasing signs that something extraordinary was happening across the channel.

On 23 August at Mons in Belgium, the BEF had engaged the enemy, the German First Army, for the first time. On 28 August the newspapers carried reports of the first batch of thirty wounded British soldiers arriving at Folkestone from Boulogne; also on board the ship were eighty wounded Belgian soldiers.[62] On 1 September the *Western Daily Press* reported that 300 wounded men had arrived in London, 100 in Plymouth and 140 at Bishop Stortford and two days later 130 arrived at Bristol. These casualty reports were full of bravado of Germans being mown down by British rifle fire

---

[60] *The Citizen* 15 August 1914
[61] *The Citizen* 29 August 1914
[62] *Exeter and Plymouth Gazette* 28 August 1914

and with all the wounded men hoping "...*that they would soon be at the front again.*"[63] Within days casualty lists with names and regiments of the killed, wounded and missing were published, a practice that would continue throughout the war with the number of column inches devoted to them an indication of how the war was going! Within a month it would become commonplace to publish daily information on wounded British, French and Belgian soldiers who were transferred to British hospitals for further treatment; these soldiers were frequently moved to the local Red Cross Voluntary Aid [VA] Hospitals for nursing care and recuperation and became a common sight in towns and villages across the country.[64] Reports also soon appeared regarding Belgian refugees, mainly women, children and old men who had fled from the German advance through Belgium. The refugees were welcomed into British society and local committees were sent up to provide support usually in the form of shelter, food, clothing and jobs; appeals for money were published in the local papers.

September:

The 1 September edition of *The Citizen* carried the Gloucestershire County Cricket Club scores for the match against Surrey at the Kennington Oval which Gloucestershire lost by an inning and thirty-six runs. This would be GCCC's last match for five years while two days later the newspaper declared that for the duration of the war no reports of any matches of any sport played would be carried in its columns. The newspaper, echoing the sentiments of the whole country, felt that fit young athletes were needed more on the battlefields than on the sports fields. The same view had been expressed the day before by the Gloucester Football Club which now accepted reality and announced the cancellation of the entire 1914-15 fixture list due in part to the crisis facing the country but mainly as a result of the loss of the squad which almost to a man had enlisted in the British Armed Forces, mainly the Army and mainly the Gloucestershire Regiment and predominantly its 5th Battalion.[65] Although the Gloucester Football Club in contrast to the cricket club had made a net profit of £112 11s 6d in the previous season there was a tacit acceptance that a lack of income from gate receipts which accounted for more than 70% of the Club's income would result in a severe financial situation.[66,67] The Committee's statement, which was fully supported by *The Citizen*'s editor, read,

> "...*practically the whole of the playing members have enlisted but in any case the Committee would not have felt justified in fulfilling the fixtures even if the players were available owing to the rapid change of the situation in connection with the war.*"[68]

---

[63] *Western Times* 3 September 1914
[64] The Voluntary Aid Detachment [VAD] organisation was set up in 1908 after it was recognised that there would be a lack of basic medical support in the event of war. The VAD nurses, both women and men, were part-time volunteers who provided the medical support in the VA Hospitals under the supervision of a doctor and a fully qualified nursing sister. The VA Hospitals themselves were set up for the duration of war in suitable buildings ranging from private mansions to town halls.
[65] GRFC's last match had been played on 18 April 1914 – a ten points to three victory over Bath. Although the rugby club would be encouraged to stage morale boosting games at the end of 1916 to raise money for local hospitals, it would be over five years before regular club rugby returned to Gloucester.
[66] *The Citizen* 12 June 1914
[67] Although the Gloucester Football Club had made a profit at the end of 1913-14 season, the previous season had seen it experience of deficit of £60 3s 9d. As a consequence the Club was 'baled out' with a grant from the County Union (£40) and a Shilling Fund set up by *The Citizen* (£50 14s 6d). Hence prior to the war financial stability for the Gloucester Football Club was not necessarily guaranteed.
[68] *The Citizen* 3 September 1914

The financial pressure on the Rugby Committee had been exacerbated after it received a letter from Buckingham Palace on 23 August requesting a "...*subscription*..." to the Prince of Wales National Relief Fund.[69,70] The Committee which included the newly elected player members, had initially decided to accommodate this request by allocating the gate receipts from the local derby against Stroud scheduled for 12 September but with the abandonment of the fixture list the Committee urged its supporters to continue to purchase tickets for a now non-existent game; by 3 October the Club had donated £50 to the Prince of Wales National Relief Fund.[71]

In general all the sporting institutions abandoned their regular fixtures lists and while some clubs closed for the duration of the war, others which included the Cheltenham Association Football Club gave notice of their intention to organise matches from time to time to raise money for War Relief Funds.[72,73] By Christmas 1916 the Gloucester Football Club would also follow this latter approach usually raising funds for the local Red Cross Voluntary Aid Hospitals. In 1914 despite questions raised in Parliament regarding the playing of sporting fixtures, the Prime Minister, Herbert Asquith, and the Government left it as a matter of conscience whilst urging clubs to encourage supporters to enlist. The last major football (aka soccer) event of the war was the 1915 FA Cup Final in which Sheffield United beat Chelsea by three goals to nil; it was known as the 'Khaki Final' owing to the large numbers of supporters wearing Army uniform.

In Bristol, **Alfred Dipper** (GCCC) and **Thomas Gange** (GCCC) were the first of the professional cricketers to enlist in D Squadron, Royal Gloucestershire Hussars and the Royal Garrison Artillery, respectively. The *Western Daily Press* hoped that "*...their example would be followed by cricketers and footballers across the country*",[74] while *The Citizen* echoed these sentiments and urged that the,

> "...hundreds of supporters of the game might reasonably follow the good example of so many of the players themselves, and respond to the urgent call for men to serve the country in a fight...of life and death to our native land."[75]

The Gloucester Football and Athletic Ground Company Limited, the company formed specifically for the purchase and subsequent management of the Kingsholm Ground, also became aware of the likely reduction in income. Despite the previous year's profit of £113 9s 10d the Directors decided not to issue any dividends to the shareholders including the Gloucester Football Club which held 1,011 of the 3,150 shares. The Directors took the decision that in the face of the "*...present terrible and disastrous war, little or no football is likely to be played on the ground...*" and hence no revenue would be generated to meet any forthcoming costs.[76]

---

[69] *The Citizen* 25 August 1914
[70] In this context a 'subscription' is a donation.
[71] The £50 compared favourably with estimated average gate receipt for a first team game of £32 16s for the 1913-14 season and was equivalent to half the Club's annual profit.
[72] *The Citizen* 3 September 1914
[73] Professional Football (soccer) continued for a considerable period despite concerns being raised in Parliament and requests for the Prime Minister, Herbert Asquith, to legislate against the games. The introduction of conscription in January 1916 would resolve the issue. The last FA Cup Final was played on 24 April 1915 at Old Trafford between Sheffield United and Chelsea with the former winning by 3 goals to nil. This match would be known as the 'Khaki Cup Final' with majority of the crowd wearing the Army's khaki uniform.
[74] *Western Daily Press* 29 August 1914
[75] *The Citizen* 3 September 1914
[76] *Gloucester Journal* 10 October 1914

Kitchener's 'Call to Arms', for a one million strong army, would require one in thirty of the population to come forward. The local Gloucester newspapers calculated that with a population estimated at 60,000, Gloucester could expect 2,000 volunteers. However over the weeks leading up to 12 September the *Gloucester Journal* had published the names of almost 3,000 enlisted men with a figure that should be revised to 4,000 when Regulars, Reservists and Territorials were included; this equated to almost twice the national average.[77,78] Figures published for Bristol showed that 10,664 men had enlisted from the Bristol and Greater Bristol area which had a total of 400,000 inhabitants.[79]

Photograph 6. Parade of New Recruits: Newly enlisted in the Gloucestershire Regiment in civilian clothes for the last time before leaving for the training camps, *circa* 1914. (*SoGM, GLRRM:02557.45*). The occasion has been identified as first battalion strength parade of the 12/Gloucesters at the Artillery Grounds, White Ladies Road on 22 September 1914 (Dean Marks, *Bristol's Own*, p.25)

Great crowds had flocked to recruiting rallies which were held in towns and villages across the county and sang patriotic songs which, in a show of Allied solidarity, included tunes from France and Russia and Britain, and was all part of the '*great adventure*'. At a meeting held at the Clarence Street Lamp in Cheltenham stirring speeches excited the boisterous crowd which sang the '*Marseillaise*',

---

[77] Gloucester Journal 12 September 1914
[78] The lists of names published in the *Gloucester Journal* in early September 1914 are invaluable for modern day researchers supplying name, rank, service number, unit and often the marital status, the home address and the employer of the enlisted men. These lists would continue to be published until December 1915 when the Government realised that such lists would also be invaluable to the enemy and their publication was banned under the Defence of the Realm Act [DORA].
[79] *Western Daily Press* 9 September 1914

the Russian hymn and the British National Anthem, although only fifteen new recruits came forward;[80] this was probably a sign of the number and frequency of the meetings held in different locations all over Bristol and Gloucestershire and indeed the country in general. For the majority of the male population in 1914 the prospect of travel away from Bristol and Gloucestershire became part of that 'great adventure'.

Photograph 7. Barrack Room No.2 Co. B.B.: The barrack room of the 12th (Service) Battalion (Bristol's Own), Gloucestershire Regiment *circa* 1914-1915. The newly commissioned barrack room ready to receive its first intake of recruits following its formation on 30 August 1914. (*SoGM, GLRRM:02557.17*)

Released from the constraints of home life, often with hardship and routine, there would be the twin 'perils' of alcohol and women which they would have to cope with although the British Army from hundreds of years of experience would instil in the new recruits the inherent dangers not only in pursuing these perils but also the consequences both socially and under military law. However, for the rugby and cricket players travelling from home was quite commonplace. In the regular season both clubs travelled across Britain. The Rugby Club regularly travelled to destinations including London (London Welsh, Harlequins), Northampton, Forest of Dean, Oxford, South Wales (especially Newport, Cardiff, Swansea and Llanelly), Leicester, Bristol, Devon and Cheltenham. The County cricketers were probably more widely travelled, facing opposition from Surrey, Warwickshire, Somerset, Yorkshire, Lancashire, Sussex, Northamptonshire and Kent. There were players who also

---

[80] *Cheltenham Chronicle and Gloucestershire Graphic* 12 September 1914

travelled abroad with their Clubs, the England Cricket XI, the England national rugby team and in some instances the British Isles ('British Lions') rugby team.

Photograph 8. Barrack Room No.2 Co. B.B.: The barrack room of the 12th (Service) Battalion (Bristol's Own), Gloucestershire Regiment *circa* 1914-1915. The new barrack room shows the new recruits in their khaki uniforms posing for a recruitment 'publicity' picture. (*SoGM, GLRRM:02557.44*)

The Gloucester Football Club had twice ventured into France to play Toulouse on 28 February 1911 and Stade Français, Paris, on 14 March 1912 with Gloucester winning both games by eighteen points to thirteen and fifteen points to three, respectively. The teams had included **Charles Cook**, **Arthur Hudson, Harry Barnes, James Hamblin, William Washbourne, William Dix, Willy Hall, Fred Pegler, Gordon Vears, Billy Johns**, **George Halford, Fred Yates, Harry Berry, George Griffiths** and **Allen Lodge**, three of whom would be killed in action in the Great War.[81]

Internationally for the Five Nations Championship some of the rugby players had travelled to France representing England – **Arthur Hudson** (1906 and 1910), **Billy Johns** (1910) and **Sidney Smart** (April 1914); it is interesting to think that Sid Smart would have thought that if his form held he could be back in France with England two years later. He went back to France dressed in khaki in less than a year. At a British level **Frank Stout** (GRFC) had travelled with British Isles rugby team ('British

---

[81] These were official club games but there is evidence that 'unofficial' games not sanctioned by the Club also took place amongst players who had retired from Gloucester. These included games against Perpignan on 25 and 29 December 1913 and featured George Griffiths, James Hamblin and Willie Hall (Personal Communication: Malc King and Dick Williams, Gloucester Rugby Football Club Community Heritage Project).

Lions') to Australia (1899) and South Africa (1903) and was joined on the latter tour by **Gilbert Collett** (GRFC and GCCC). While for the 'professional' game (Northern Union) both **John Robinson** (GRFC) and **Dave Holland** (GRFC) were touring New Zealand and Australia with the Great Britain side when war was declared in 1914.[82]

Internationally **Gilbert Jessop** (GCCC) had played cricket for England in Australia in 1901-02 while, and as a sign of how the situation in Europe had deteriorated, **Oswald Wreford-Brown** (GCCC) had played football ('soccer') for the Football Association XI (*aka* England) in the first ever match in Berlin against Germany in November 1899; he would now take up arms against the same country.

Other players had experienced life in foreign countries albeit sometimes under traumatic conditions. **Fred Goulding** (GRFC), **Harry Berry** (GRFC), **Harry Collins** (GRFC), **Fred Pegler** (GRFC), **George Dennett** (GCCC), **Arthur Du Boulay** (GCCC) and **Ernest English** (GCCC) had fought in South Africa during the Boer War while Harry Berry and **George Griffiths** (GRFC) had also served in India and Ceylon. **Frank** and **Percy Stout** (GRFC) had worked for fourteen years in Egypt while **Cornelius Carleton** (GRFC) had been stationed in Egypt and Nigeria with the army. **Lindsay Vears** (GRFC) worked on a plantation in the Federated Malay States for at least ten years and apart from war services and frequent trips to Britain remained there for the rest of his life. **John Williams** (GCCC) moved to New Zealand to work in the mining industry in 1910 and on the outbreak of war he joined the New Zealand Expeditionary Force. There were also a number of the cricketers, because their fathers were serving in the army, who were born abroad including from India **Basil Clarke**, **William Grant**, **Claude MacKay**, **Edmund Marsden**, **Francis Roberts**, **Frank Troup** and **Walter Troup**, from South Africa **Charles Edwards**, **Cyril Sewell** and **Thomas Gange** with **James Horlick** (USA), **Thomas Miller** (Cape Verde Islands), **Donald Morgan** (China) and **Alison White** (Australia).[83] There were also a large number of professional soldiers amongst the cricketers who were variously stationed abroad including, **Claude Bateman-Champain**, **Hugh Bateman-Champain**, **Edgar Chester Master**, **Basil Clarke**, **Eric Crankshaw**, **Arthur Du Boulay**, **Charles Edwards**, **Ernest English**, **Michael Green**, **James Horlick**, **Edmund Marsden**, **Andrew Pope**, **Douglas Robinson**, **Percy Robinson**, **Alison White** and **William Yalland**.

In September 1914 a significant difference between the rugby players and the cricketers emerged in that the majority of the former enlisted together in the same regiment, the Gloucestershire Regiment, with the preponderance of those in the same battalion, the 5th Battalion, the Territorial Battalion from Gloucester and the surrounding area. As a consequence they went off to war together, trained and became soldiers together; the comradeship and friendships developed on the rugby field were taken with them through the training camps and ultimately on to the battlefields. Statistically for the rugby players 95% were local men and as such 75% joined the local Gloucestershire Regiment although eleven other regiments and units boasted Gloucester rugby players in their ranks.[84] In contrast the cricketers were a more diverse group of men – only 54% were born locally while 17% were not born in Great Britain. Their service records show that they served in thirty-five different regiments or units although the greatest representation, 21%, was in

---

[82] The Northern Union was the forerunner of Rugby League and many of the basic rules, e.g. thirteen players per team, were introduced under its auspices. The Northern Union operated a 'broken time' situation whereby any shortfall in players' wages from their full-time employers incurred owing to rugby commitments was made up by the Northern Union itself.

[83] See Appendix D: Statistics, Table 3

[84] 'Born locally' refers to men born in Gloucestershire and Bristol, including the Forest of Dean

the Gloucestershire Regiment.[85] These differences would reflect in the experiences of the men and would have dire consequences particularly on 23 July 1916 at Pozières (see Map 2).[86]

The speed with which the Reservists were sent to their units was now matched by the civilian volunteers who were sent off in batches to their respective training camps. On 1 September the first batch of 350 Kitchener's New Army men left Gloucester from the Midland Station bound for Horfield Barracks with a send-off which included many local dignitaries, amongst whom was Mr J.J. Steinitz from the Gloucester Railway Carriage and Wagon Works Limited who promised them that their jobs would be left open for them ready for their return.[87] Previously Mr Steinitz had sent off the Reservists and Territorials with the same promises although he had added that,

> "...any man filling the place of another who is...called away must understand that his appointment is only a temporary one"

Mr Steinitz would continue with this promise as other batches left Gloucester.[88] Thirty minutes later eighty-four Territorial recruits left the Great Western Station for Chelmsford to join the 5/Gloucesters. On 3 September another 260 Kitchener's Men and 254 Territorial recruits left Gloucester. As the Territorials assembled at the Barracks Mr E.J. Palmer, a local tailor, began measuring them for their khaki uniforms while the Depot Captain, S.S. Champion, offered the advice, *"Take care of your health: remember your friends at home; and stick to it!"*

On 5 September the final ten recruits needed to bring the 5/Gloucesters up to strength left Gloucester under the command of Lance-Corporal **Trevor Powell** (GRFC), a peace-time Territorial soldier;[89] for Messrs **Smart**, **Hamblin**, **Washbourne** and **Cook** and the other rugby players only eight days had elapsed between being a civilian and being a soldier.[90]

On 7 September men destined for the Royal Gloucestershire Hussars Yeomanry [RGHY] left for Newbury in what was generally agreed to be one of the smartest contingents to have yet left Gloucester. The Lord Bishop of the Diocese, Dr E.C.S. Gibson addressed the assembled men and urged them "*...to do their duty and keep up the good name of the regiment.*" The detachment, with **Alfred Dipper** (GCCC) in its ranks, was destined to take the place of existing pre-war yeoman who had not volunteered for overseas service or were passed as unfit by the doctors; they marched from the Barracks to the GWR Station headed by the regimental band.[91] **Hugo Charteris** (Lord Elcho) (GCCC) was already with the RGHY at its war station.

The following day another 189 recruits left Gloucester. They had assembled at 9.00 am under the illusion that, as was their choice, they had enlisted in the Gloucestershire Regiment but at 11.00 am the Mayor, Councillor James Bruton informed them that the Gloucesters was at full strength and they were being sent to the Worcestershire Regiment. The disgruntled men, including **John Price** (GRFC), entrained for Worcester from the Midland Station.[92,93] Although the volunteers, up to the

---

[85] See Appendix D, Tables 3 and 4
[86] Key locations on the Western Front throughout this book are shown on Map 2
[87] *Dean Forest Mercury* 4 September 1914
[88] *Cheltenham Chronicle and Gloucestershire Graphic* 8 August 1914
[89] *The Citizen* 5 September 1914
[90] There was concern amongst the men that their wives and families would struggle to survive but the Government had made provision for them (see Appendix B, Note 5)
[91] *Cheltenham Chronicle and Gloucestershire Graphic* 12 September 1914
[92] *Cheltenham Chronicle and Gloucestershire Graphic* 12 September 1914
[93] By the summer 1915 3,500 men volunteered to join the 5/Gloucesters and of these about 1,200 were selected to bring the 1/5th Battalion up to strength, create the 2/5th Battalion and train in the 5th (Reserve)

end of 1915, had in theory the choice of which regiment they could join, there was a 'greater need' that prevented this happening in all instances and the men would be sent to bring battalions in other regiments up to strength. The same edition of the newspaper carried reports that *another* batch of eighty-nine wounded men had now arrived in Cheltenham from Southampton. Within weeks the newspapers would start publishing photographs from the training camps of groups of men trench digging, bayonet fighting or simply posing for the camera (see Photographs 9 and 10).

Photograph 9. Trench Digging: G Company, 1/5th Battalion, Gloucestershire Regiment digging practice trenches at Chelmsford in November 1914. The men would become all too familiar with this activity especially as one and three-quarters miles of trenches could be dug in three days. (*CCGG*)

The speed with which the enlisted men sped off to their training camps was only matched by the speed with which ships reached Southampton loaded with wounded soldiers who were initially taken by train to major hospitals including the Gloucester Royal Infirmary and, in Bristol, Southmead Hospital, for specialised treatment;[94] with urgent cases it was not unknown for trains to stop whilst an operation was performed in a specially fitted coach.[95] After the wounds were sufficiently recovered the soldiers were transferred to the Red Cross Voluntary Aid [VA] Hospitals for nursing

---

Battalion; the remaining men were generally sent to the Gloucesters' Service Battalions. (*Gloucestershire Chronicle* 4 October 1919).
[94] Frequently hospital ships loaded with wounded soldiers would sail directly from France to Bristol, along the River Avon, to facilitate the transfer of the men to Southmead Hospital.
[95] *Western Daily Press* 2 October 1914

care and convalescence.[96] On 1 September as 350 Kitchener's Men left Gloucester, 120 soldiers wounded at Mons arrived at Southampton; the newspapers reported that "...*about 20 already had legs amputated while others had arms missing and heads bandaged.*"[97]

Soon news reached Gloucester and the player-recruits of the first player to become a casualty. Lieutenant **Cornelius Carleton** (GRFC), 2/Welsh, had been on a reconnaissance mission with two men,

"I was hit when out on a little reconnoitring show with two men. They caught us going across a turnip field at dusk, when it was jolly hard to see anything stationary. It must have been under 100 yards as they got two of us with three shots; the other man luckily got away, and about two hours later rolled up with the stretcher-bearers. During the wait a patrol of Germans wandered past, but I kept as quiet as a mouse, and they did not see me. The other man died on the way in..."

Cornelius became renowned within the Battalion for his daring during reconnaissance missions and it was shortly reported that he had been awarded the Distinguished Service Order [DSO] for his work. His citation read,

"For daring and successful reconnaissance on severely occasions, on the last of which, on 15th September, he was severely wounded."[98]

Although the men had joined their battalions in batches the numbers arriving at the training camps over a short period were immense and created a logistical nightmare in terms of living quarters, kit and equipment; the camps were frequently full and the additional men had to be billeted with the local population. But the training was a major issue and advertisements appeared in the local newspapers requesting ex-NCOs to give up some of their spare time to train the men and although some had already come forward greater numbers were desperately needed.[99] This situation was in contrast to Germany and France where a large body of men had already had compulsory military training and would require comparatively little additional drilling to make them battle-ready, such were the benefits of both countries' legal conscription requirement. There seems to have been a lack of awareness or naivety in Britain which expected that the transformation of civilians into soldiers could be achieved overnight. The War Office, acutely aware of the crisis, justified the active recruitment of civilians on the basis that the war was now officially seen as a much longer undertaking and would result in high numbers of casualties. The War Office now no longer believed that the war would be '*over by Christmas*', a view shared by the front line soldiers, but for the majority of the home front population this attitude still prevailed although it would rapidly fade, as letters from the front were published from ordinary soldiers who soon knew that they were engaged in a war of attrition,

---

[96] In 1909 it was apparent that the military medical services would be inadequate in the event of a war. As a consequence the British Red Cross and the Order of St John set up a voluntary scheme with each volunteer known as a Voluntary Aid Detachment [VAD] given basic nursing skills. In the Great War groups of VADs staffed temporary hospitals (VA Hospitals) which provided basic nursing care for wounded soldiers after they had received major treatment at the larger hospitals.
[97] *The Citizen* 2 September 1914
[98] *London Gazette* 9 December 1914
[99] *Western Daily Press* 10 September 1914

"...it's absolutely certainly a war of 'attrition' as somebody said here the other day, and we got to stick to it longer than the other side and go producing men, money and material until they cry quits and that's about it, as far as I can see..."[100]

Locally however employers still vied with each other to show that their company had done its patriotic duty and there were the promises that jobs held open for a war which would be *'over by Christmas'*. For instance, at the end of September Sergeant-Major Tomlins the Attendance Officer for District C of the Gloucester Education Committee had been summoned to the Colours and the Committee announced that it would be *"..pleased to reinstate him on his return..."* and temporarily appointed **Arthur Paish** the GCCC professional to cover for him.[101]

Photograph 10. Trench Digging: D Company, 1/5th Battalion, Gloucestershire Regiment digging practice trenches at Epping Forest in 1914. The soldier standing on the left has been identified as Private Alfred White, scorer of one of D Company's tries in the 1915 1/5th Gloucestershire Regiment's Inter Company Rugby Competition final. (*SoGM, GLRRM:04925.2*)

Across the county in 1914 employers were keen to show that they were supporting the war effort and the local newspapers published lists of employee-volunteers supplied by various companies. In the *Gloucestershire Chronicle* over a two week period lists from 117 Gloucester companies were published.[102] In shows of *one-upmanship* submitted articles were published under various but similar

---

[100] Captain G.B. Pollard quoted in Paul Fussell, *The Great War and Modern Memory* (Oxford: Oxford University Press, 1975), p.9
[101] *Gloucester Journal* 26 September 1914
[102] Gloucester Chronicle published the employee lists for editions published on 5, 12 and 19 September 1914

headlines which proclaimed *'Patriotism in the Printing Trade'* and *'Tobacconists for the Front'*.[103] In 1919 when the men did return the situation had radically changed and many returning soldiers would find it difficult to find any job let alone return to their old job. However in late 1914 the common belief still persisted that the war would be over within a matter of weeks or months despite the mounting evidence to the contrary. The contribution of employers throughout the war remained the subject of many newspaper articles. In 1917 the local Military Tribunal which dealt with people requesting exemption for war service commented on *"...Messrs E.S. and A. Robinson's fine record..."*[104,105] Fewer than ten employees had been granted an exemption and Second Lieutenant **Foster Robinson** (GCCC), 3/City of Bristol Volunteer Regiment,[106] representing the company stated that of the 793 employees of military age, 655 had enlisted and in order to support their families during the men's absence grants were awarded by the company at a cost of £14,000 a year. Foster Robinson remained in Bristol throughout the war although from July 1915 he worked part-time as a Special Constable in C Division alongside **William Brown** (GCCC); the latter eventually went to France in January 1917 with the 5th North Staffords.[107]

Towns and villages were also keen to stress that they were making significant contributions to the patriotic effort and numbers of enlisted men were published under such diverse headings as *'Call to Arms at Cirencester'*, *'More recruits from Winchcombe'* and *'More from Winchcombe'*, *'342 from St Peter's Parish'* and *'Hinton's Fine Record'*.[108]

By mid-September the numbers of Belgian refugees had increased to a level that an organisation was need to systematically house, feed them and find them jobs. The Bristol branch of the War Refugee Committee was formed with **Foster Robinson** (GCCC) acting as honorary secretary and a fund – The Belgian Refugees in Bristol Fund – was specifically initiated to deal with the issue locally and was independent of the national Belgian Relief Fund. It would become clear that Foster although destined to remain at home would involve himself in many of the war time committees set up in Bristol.[109]

---

[103] *Cheltenham Chronicle and Gloucestershire Graphic* 12 September 1914
[104] *Western Daily Press* 2 February 1917
[105] E.S. and A. Robinson Limited is the family business of **Percy** and **Foster Robinson** (GCCC); after the war they would become joint Managing Directors
[106] Late in 1914, men ineligible for the Army formed contingents across the country known as Volunteer Training Corps (VTC) for home defence and to relieve regular soldiers for overseas service. Although the Government was at first reluctant to accept the services of the VTC, in September 1915 it was officially recognised and affiliated to the relevant County Regiment. In Gloucestershire the VTC contingents belonged to the Gloucestershire Volunteer Regiment which was affiliated to the Gloucestershire Regiment.
[107] Western Daily Press 5 July 1915
[108] Patriotic articles with the words *'Gloucester'* or *'Bristol'* in the headline are too numerous to mention
[109] **Foster Robinson** (GCCC) worked for the family business E.S. and A. Robinson (Manufacturing Stationers and Printers). Although not generally appreciated one of the reasons for the eventual success of the British Army on the battlefield would be the ability to mobilise the printing industry not only to print pamphlets but also to prints millions of maps following the work of the Ordnance Survey. By end of 1917 every Private has his own copy of a map of the enemy trenches annotated with the attack's objectives and importantly was trained to understand it; in 1915 there was on average one trench map for every ten Lieutenants and with the death of those officers, the attacks frequently failed to follow the proper course and objectives were not captured.

October:

A significant number of cricketers (39%) with no military background who had enlisted as Privates, rapidly gained commissions and began officer training courses. By 10 October it was reported that **Francis Bateman-Champain** (GCCC), Worcestershire Regiment, had not only gained his Lance-Corporal's stripe but also gained a commission as a Second Lieutenant in the 9th (Service) Battalion, Rifle Brigade which was in camp at Aldershot.[110,111]

The pitch at the Kingsholm ground, prepared by the groundsman for the 1914-15 season, was not wasted as on 3 October A and B Companies of the 2/5th Gloucesters now in training at Gloucester, played each other in front of a "...*good crowd of spectators...*" in aid of the Soldiers' and Sailors' Home Fund; B Company were victorious by seventeen points to three.[112,113,114]

On 27 October the GCCC Committee, meeting at the Grand Hotel, Broad Street, Bristol, to discuss the Club's future, acknowledged that proceeding with the Cheltenham Cricket Festival in August had been a financially costly mistake! The already severe financial problems of the Cricket Club had been exacerbated as gate receipts did not cover the staging costs of the festival. The Committee concluded that,

> "...*the failure at Cheltenham...was in large measure due to the war, and it would have been much better for the county if they had suspended operations as soon as war broke out* [and while there were serious financial problems the Committee was] *strongly of the opinion that they could not recommend the winding up of the club at the present time, though they equally strongly advised that no fixtures should be made for next season*"[115,116]

The *Western Daily Press* in another column applauded the Committee's decision to abstain from county cricket in 1915, a decision the newspaper felt had to have been greatly influenced by the fact that a number of key players including **Cyril Sewell**, **Thomas Miller**, **Francis Bateman-Champain**, **Michael Green**, **Gerald Deloe**, **Alfred Dipper** and **Thomas Gange** had either, as professional soldiers, been mobilised with their regiments or, as volunteers, were now in training in camps across the country.

One of the volunteers, **William Methven Brownlee** (GCCC) became the first cricketer recorded as a casualty of the war and as a man who "...*was quite prepared to take his place in the ranks...*" had initially enlisted as a Private in 6th Battalion, Gloucestershire Regiment but within a matter of weeks was offered a commission.[117] At the time of his death on 12 October 1914 he was a Second Lieutenant with the 3rd Battalion, Dorset Regiment in training at Wyke Regis. His death would typify

---

[110] *Gloucestershire Chronicle* 10 October 1914

[111] The original family name had been Champain but had changed to Bateman-Champain in 1872; contemporary sources throughout the Great War use both forms but Bateman-Champain will be used throughout this book.

[112] *Gloucestershire Chronicle* 10 October 1914

[113] The 2/5th Gloucesters formed in September 1914 remained in the Gloucester area for a period before moving to Northampton and then to Chelmsford in April 1915 after the 1/5th Battalion had gone to France. The 2/5th Battalion landed in France on 23 May 1916

[114] The ground would again be used on 17 October as the 5th (Reserve) Battalion, Gloucestershire Regiment, wearing the Gloucester Club's Cherry and White jerseys, took on the Reserve Battalion, Royal Gloucestershire Hussars; the former won by 25 points to 4.

[115] *Western Daily Press* 28 October 1914

[116] For the last five years before the war there was a shortfall of between £800 and £1,000 for each season; this would equate to a debt of £4-5,000

[117] *Gloucestershire Chronicle* 17 October 1914

that of many others who had been plucked from the relative comfort and safety of a home environment and thrust into the harsh and demanding one of the British Army as it prepared its young men for what would be the unimaginable rigours and hardships of the battlefield. Within weeks of his arrival at the camp William had contracted and died of meningitis. As a casualty of war the whole of the military establishment at Weymouth followed his coffin draped in the Union Flag and decorated with a full length floral cross to the railway station where a salute was fired over his body. His funeral took place at Arnos Vale Cemetery Bristol in the presence of representatives from various cricket clubs and the military including fellow Gloucestershire cricketers **Alan Imlay** and **Thomas Miller**; full military honours were offered for his funeral by the British Army but were declined by the family who requested a quiet and simple service. A brass plate on the coffin read,

"2nd Lieutenant Wilfred Methuen Brownlee, 3rd Dorset Regiment: died October 12 1914, aged 24".[118]

Photograph 11. Lieutenant William Stanley Yalland (GCCC) (1889-1914): William was photographed amongst the officers of the 1st Battalion, Gloucestershire Regiment at Bordon on 21 March 1914 on the occasion of the 113th Anniversary of Battle of Alexandria. Within seven months of this photograph being taken William would be killed in action at Ypres on 23 October 1914. (*SoGM, GLRRM:04730.1a*)

The first battle fatalities for the cricket club and rugby club came six days apart with both men, Lieutenant **William Yalland** (GCCC) (see Photograph 11) and Corporal **Walter Hancock** (GRFC), serving with the 1/Gloucesters. The complexities and nature of the static trench system had yet to fully mature but on 10 October the Germans attacked the British at Ypres in what would be termed the First Battle of Ypres (10 October – 22 November 1914) (see Map 2). The attacks used superior numbers of artillery and infantry against a still weak BEF, even though a third corps (III Corps) had now joined. The British line came under immense pressure and the entry in the 1/Gloucesters' Battalion War Diary for the 23 October indicated that the battalion, north-west of Langemarck, was

---

[118] *Western Daily Press* 16 October 1914

under attack from a German advance from Koekuit supported by heavy artillery fire. The Coldstream Guards fell back under pressure but platoons from A and D Companies of 1/Gloucesters offered "...*vigorous resistance*..." which averted the development of a critical situation for the 1/Gloucesters and the 2/Welsh, the latter with **Cornelius Carleton** (GRFC) in its ranks. Lieutenant **William Yalland** (GCCC) and his platoon (No. 15, A Company) were ordered to re-take the trenches lost by the Guards, an action which resulted in many casualties. A fellow officer wrote to William's father,

> "*He died very gallantly. The Germans had driven some of the Guards out of their trenches. He was told to take his platoon to a trench and prevent the Germans making further ground. This he did and his platoon at considerable loss drove the Germans back, and the trenches were re-occupied. It saved the situation as the Germans would have undoubtedly broken through the line. He was shot in the head and death was instantaneous*"[119]

As Yalland's platoon had moved forward, D Company under Captain Burns was sent in to support it but was forced to take cover in derelict buildings as the German fire was too intense. After darkness fell the men of D Company moved forward and on reaching Yalland's trench one of the NCOs wrote,

> "*What a sight met my eyes! Outside the trench lay eight dead men, and also poor Lieut Yalland. All these men were killed in holding the trenches against the Germans. I was detailed, with six others, to bury these men - and after two hours hard work our task was finished. But not before I had said a few prayers for our fallen comrades*"[120,121]

Another member of the 1/Gloucesters wrote home,

> "*One of our platoons under the command of Lieutenant Yalland was caught while going across to take up a position by the enemy's cross-fire from machine guns. The officer commanding and a large number of men were killed. Colonel Lovett afterwards told us that this platoon had acted very bravely and was a credit to the regiment.*"[122]

A Grenadier Guardsman, Lance Corporal Davies testifying to the ferocity of the fighting reported that

> "...*at the latter place* [Ypres] *they* [had] *found one of the Gloucesters lying dead. 'We counted 21 wounds on him, all in front!'*..." [123]

It was generally considered that William Yalland's actions had "...*saved the situation*...",[124] although the Battalion War diary simply stated that,

> "*During* [the attack between] *9 a.m. – 1 p.m. Lt. Yalland was killed by a shot thro' the head...*"[125,126]

Although William Yalland was the first GCCC cricketer to die, he was also a very good rugby forward and represented the 1/Leicesters in four Army Cup Rugby Finals between 1908 and 1912 and was on the winning side three times; in the 1908 Final he played alongside **Basil Clarke** (GCCC) who as a Lieutenant Colonel would command the 4/Leicesters during the Great War. In the 1910 Cup Final,

---

[119] *Western Daily Press* 3 November 1914
[120] *Gloucester Journal* 26 December 1914
[121] Although William Yalland's body was buried in a marked grave, the ground was fought over continuously for the next four years and a s a result his grave was lost. William is commemorated amongst the Missing on the Menin Gate Memorial, Ypres (see Photograph 13)
[122] *Western Daily Press* 22 March 1915
[123] *Gloucester Journal* 28 November 1914
[124] *Western Daily Press* 3 November 1914
[125] Battalion War Diary, *1st Battalion Gloucestershire Regiment 23 October 1914*, TNA WO 95/1278
[126] Official Casualty List issued 6 November 1914

the first Army Cup Final to be held at the new Twickenham Stadium, William played against the 2/Gloucesters with the latter winning with the only score of the game, an acrobatic try scored in extra time by Corporal Henry James.[127,128]

The German attacks continued unabated but the 1/Gloucesters were pulled out of the line and moved to trenches near Gheluvelt. In the absence of telephone communications, on the morning of 29 October news came through to 3 Brigade Headquarters from a wounded officer that the enemy had broken through the British line at Gheluvelt between the 1st and 7th Divisions (Battle of Gheluvelt, 29-31 October 1915). Brigadier-General Charles FitzClarence VC immediately ordered the 1/Gloucesters, which included Corporal **Walter Hancock** (GRFC), holding the line a quarter of a mile west of Gheluvelt to advance and check the German assault.[129] In a desperate and chaotic situation Lieutenant-Colonel Alfred C. Lovett (OC, 1/Gloucesters) sent forward three companies independently.[130] One company rallied the survivors of the first onslaught, another company joined the 1/Scots Guards while the third company which had lost its commanders got into the firing line where it could. The fourth company was also soon sent forward but it was soon overwhelmed by sheer weight of numbers. In the midst of the confused fighting Walter was killed. The Battalion War Diary for the 29 October 1914 recorded that,[131]

> "The early fighting took place in thick mist making interconnection difficult. Fighting round the village throughout the day...Bde orders to push forward...impossible owing to enfilade artillery fire from Berclaere." [132]

The British Official History reported that,

> "...when the 1/Gloucestershire was relieved and reassembled at night at its starting place, its casualties were found to be 7 officers (3 killed) and 160 other ranks."

One of the soldiers fighting with Walter Hancock gave a first-hand account of the situation,

> "...we were ordered to hold some trenches near Ypres. We had been in these trenches three or four days when early one morning we received the order to fix bayonets and advance and drive the Germans out of the trenches they held opposite us. This was a terrible business. We reached the trenches only to find that we had been caught in a trap. A murderous fire from machine guns opened on us, it seemed, from all directions. It was a case of every man for himself and we retired as best we could. The casualties in those few minutes were heavy and a number of men were taken prisoners"[133]

With the movement of both armies across the battlefield men became lost in the muddy wasteland of the Ypres Salient and the bodies of **William Yalland** and **Walter Hancock** were never recovered and both men are commemorated amongst the Missing on the Menin Gate Memorial (see Photograph 13).

---

[127] Sergeant Henry James, 1/Gloucesters, was killed in action on 21 December 1914
[128] William Yalland transferred to the Gloucestershire Regiment in December 1912.
[129] James E. Edmonds, *History of the Great War. Military Operations France and Belgium* 1914 *Vol II: Antwerp. La Bassée, Armentières, Messines and Ypres October-November 1914* (London: Macmillan & Co., 1925), pp.266-267
[130] Alfred Crowdy Lovett was a well-known water colourist of military subjects and eighteen of his paintings are on display at the Soldiers of Gloucestershire Museum.
[131] See Appendix B Note 6 'Battalion War Diaries'.
[132] Battalion War Diary, *1st Battalion Gloucestershire Regiment 29 October 1914*, TNA WO 95/1278
[133] *Western Daily Press* 22 March 1915

At the same time the 1/King's Royal Rifle Corps was fighting at the southern end of the Ypres Salient at Messines and news soon reached Bristol that on 21 October Lieutenant **Douglas Robinson** (GCCC) had been wounded and was now in hospital in Cork. As a professional soldier Douglas had experienced his baptism of fire at Mons and had come through unscathed.[134,135] He would not return to his unit until April 1915, after spending some of his time during his convalescence lecturing to the men of the Reserve Company.[136,137] The reports of heavy losses continued to reach Gloucestershire including the news that Lieutenant **James Horlick** (GCCC) was one of only two officers in the 3/Coldstream Guards to have survived unscathed with all the other officers either killed or wounded.[138]

November:

As the Regular British Army dug in across Europe and the volunteers trained in camps across Britain, the Royal Navy, as the *'true defender of Britain'*, engaged the German Kaiserliche Marine across the World's oceans.[139] On 1 November, off the Chilean coast German forces led by Vice Admiral Graf Maximillian von Spee engaged and defeated a Royal Navy squadron commanded by Rear Admiral Sir Christopher Cradock at the Battle of Coronel. The engagement resulted in 1,570 British casualties when the two cruisers HMS *Good Hope* and HMS *Monmouth* were sunk with the loss of all hands. The local newspapers carried incredulous reports regarding the defeat of the *'invincible'* Royal Navy and within days it was reported that the Reverend **Archibald Fargus** (GCCC), the Chaplain on board HMS *Monmouth*, had gone down with the ship.[140,141] HMS *Monmouth* had been engaged by SMS *Scharnhorst* whose guns out-ranged her and she was soon crippled. As *Monmouth* lay helpless in the water she was engaged for a second time by SMS *Nürnberg* which fired seventy-five shells into her at close point-blank range; HMS *Monmouth* keeled over and sank at 9.18 pm on 1 November.

Archibald, a pre-war Royal Navy Chaplain, had served on a number of ships since 1907 but in August 1914 he was posted to HMS *Monmouth*, a ship which along with HMS *Good Hope* had been assigned to the Third Fleet (Reserve Fleet) and mothballed at Chatham (Pembroke Reserve) in January 1914. In August 1914 both ships were re-activated, crewed with inexperienced and partially trained men from the Royal Naval Volunteer Reserve [RNVR] and assigned to Cradock's 4th Cruiser Squadron in the Pacific. Archibald's obituary appeared in the 1914 edition of Wisden and newspapers articles in 1916 still referred to his demise.[142] But Archibald died in 1963.[143] By a quirk of fate in 1914 whilst travelling to join HMS *Monmouth* he missed his train and, as time and tide wait

---

[134] *Western Daily Press* 27 October 1914
[135] Although Douglas had been Regular Soldier (Lieutenant) since 1906 he had remained in Britain during the pre-war period (*Officer's Record of Service Book, King's Own Royal Lancaster Regiment, Army Book 83*: WO 76/123)
[136] *Western Daily Press* 21 December 1914
[137] *Western Daily Press* 7 April 1915
[138] *Gloucestershire Chronicle* 24 October 1914
[139] The Kaiserliche Marine is the Imperial German Navy.
[140] The Royal Navy would exact its revenge a month later at the Battle of the Falkland Islands on 8 December 1914
[141] *Western Daily Press* 6 November 1914
[142] *Western Daily Press* 28 June 1916
[143] Although Archibald Fargus's obituary appeared in the 1914 edition of Wisden, there was no obituary for him in it in 1963 when he actually died.

for no man, the ship had sailed without him; on 29 August Archibald, no doubt after a suitable reprimand, was re-assigned to the cruiser HMS *Europa* and, with postings to other ships, survived the war.

On the home front Henry W. Beloe, Chairman of the Committee of GCCC expressed thanks not only to the *Gloucestershire Chronicle* but also all the contributors to a Shilling Fund organised by the newspaper.[144] Nearly £1,000 had been collected which would form the basis of the fund which would ensure the long-term survival of the Gloucestershire County Cricket Club after the war. Further subscriptions would follow as expenses were kept to a minimum throughout the war.

Photograph 12. Recruitment Poster, November 1914: At the time of the issue of this poster, the majority of the rugby players and cricketers had already enlisted in the British Armed Forces. (*Library of Congress, Washington, USA*)

December:
Overt displays of military service were seen in every facet of life on the home front. On 11 December the Mayor of Cheltenham, Alderman William Skillicorne, extended a special welcome to Councillor **James Winterbotham** (GCCC) who attended the Council meeting on 11 December wearing the khaki uniform of a private in the Public Schools Corps.[145] The latter, part of the wider Officer Training Corps, would train recruits to a sufficient level to be commissioned and in February 1915 James

---

[144] *Gloucestershire Chronicle* 7 November 1914
[145] *Cheltenham Looker On* 12 December 1914

would become a Second Lieutenant with No.7 Platoon, B Company, 5/Gloucesters. Although military connections were promoted by organisations such as the Council and employers in contrast civilian pastimes were promoted as everyday activities by the military. The start of the war had coincided with the kick-off of the British rugby season and the new civilian-soldiers were encouraged to play rugby whilst in training for which the British Army had a long-held tradition. Cricket matches would have to wait until the spring when most of the soldiers would be fighting in various theatres of war. In Gloucester *The Citizen,* its non-reporting ban lifted for military rugby matches, reported on the Gloucester Rugby Club players who continued with *their* seasonal activities but now no longer wearing the Cherry and White jerseys. These civilian-soldiers were introduced to rugby rivalry, not based on Welsh clubs but based on inter-regiment and inter-battalion confrontations with perhaps the most intense of all reserved for inter-company rivalry.[146]

Photograph 13. Ypres (Menin Gate) Memorial to the Missing, Ypres, Belgium: Erected in 1927 it bears the names of over 54,000 British Empire soldiers who lost their lives in the Ypres Salient and who have no known grave. Each night at 8.00 pm the traffic through the Menin Gate is stopped and buglers of the local Fire Brigade sound the Last Post to commemorate the Missing; with the exception of the Second World War this ceremony has continued uninterrupted since 1929. (*Authors*)

---

[146] Each battalion of a regiment was divided into a number of fighting units known as companies. The traditional number had been eight but the British Army was in the process of reorganising into the more battle effective formation of four companies per battalion. However until January 1915 the 5/Gloucesters still retained the old formation of eight companies (A-H)

For the men with the 5/Gloucesters the Battalion Cup was fought between the different company XVs of which, in 1914, there were still eight (A-H) as the reforms and conversion to the more battle-effective four company structure had yet to be implemented.[147] The annual round-robin competition kicked off on Saturday 26 October with A Company defeating B Company by eighteen points to eleven.[148] The scorers were familiar and included Private **Sidney Smart** (back row) and Lance Corporal **Trevor Powell** (wing) for A Company and Private **Harold Deane** (full back) and Corporal **Alfred Speck** (scrum half) for the losers. In the next round, 5 December G Company beat C Company by eleven points to nil with **William Washbourne** (wing), **Sidney Sysum** (centre) and **Lionel Hamblin** (centre) on the score sheet for the victors despite C Company having within its ranks **Charles Cook** (full back), **'Snowy' Wilkes** (stand off), **William Parh**am (back row) and **John Webb** (front row).[149]

Photograph 14: The combined teams from the 5/Gloucesters and the Canadians after the match played at the Queen's Club, London on 12 December 1914; the 5/Gloucesters won by 49 points to nil. The 5/Gloucesters' players were identified as : (1) Joe Harris; (2) Alec Lewis; (3) William Dovey; (4) James Meadows; (5) Tom Lewis; (6) Fred Webb; (7) Lionel Hamblin; (8) Charles Cook; (9) Syd Millard; (10) Albert Cook; (11) Sidney Sysum; (12) Frank Ayliffe; (13) William Washbourne. The officer on the left is Lieutenant Colonel John Henry Collett. (*CCGG*)

Although other battalions of the Gloucestershire Regiments regularly featured in newspaper-reported games, it was the 5th Battalion's reputation which spread throughout the Army and indeed further afield. As the first contingent of the Canadian Forces landed in Britain it immediately issued a challenge to the 5th which was readily accepted by the Officer Commanding, Major John Collett, a dedicated 'rugby man'. The game was played on 12 December in front of 750 servicemen at the prestigious Queen's Club in London with all proceeds from the match donated to the British Red

---

[147] The eight companies were based around different areas of Gloucestershire – A and B (Gloucester), C (Stroud), D (Tewkesbury), E and F (Cheltenham), G (Dursley) and H (Chipping Campden). *Note*: In September 1914 the new recruits were assigned to the various companies to bring them up to strength regardless of geographical location.
[148] *The Citizen* 2 November 1914
[149] *Gloucester Journal* 12 December 1914

Cross Society. The Gloucester newspapers carried a lot of rhetoric and bravado *purported* to have come from the Canadians but the forty-nine points to nil score line favoured the Gloucester boys with the 5/Gloucesters XV closely resembling the Gloucester Rugby Club's First XV as the "...*Gloucester City players* [had joined] *the regiment practically en bloc...*" (see Photograph 14).[150] This game would capture the popular imagination as '*Gloucester defeated Canada*' and would live long in the memory being re-called twenty-five years later in 1939 as another war threatened and the players were again donning khaki uniforms.

On 11 December *The Times* published a list of county cricketers who were serving their country. For Hampshire CCC twenty-four names were listed while for Gloucestershire CCC, there were just three names, **C.O.H Sewell***, **Alf Dipper*** and **George Dennett,*** while the *Manchester Evening News* on the same day listed **C. Sewell***, **M. Green***, **F. Bateman-Champain***, **William Grant***, **Alf Dipper***, **D. Robinson***, **Captain A. White*** and **T. Miller***.[151,152] The following day, 'in response', the *Western Daily Press'* listed eleven names, **Cyril Sewell***, **Claude Mackay***, **William Grant***, **Tom Miller***, **Douglas Robinson***, **Basil Clarke***, **Michael Green***, **Theodore Fowler***, **Francis Bateman-Champain***, **Alfred Dipper*** and **William Brownlee*** (deceased) while the *Manchester Evening News* now included Captain **Alison White***. However to this list can now be added **Charles Barnett***, Claude Bateman-Champain, Hugh Bateman-Champain, Hugo Charteris, Edgar Chester-Master, **Lionel Cranfield***, Eric Crankshaw, **George Dennett***, Arthur Du Boulay, Charles Edwards, **Francis Ellis***, Ernest English, Archibald Fargus, **Thomas Gange***, William Hacker, George Holloway, James Horlick, **Burnet James***, **Gilbert Jessop***, Sidney Kitcat, Solomon Levy, Maurice Mainprice, Herbert Manners, Edmund Marsden, Horace Merrick, Donald Morgan, **John Nason***, Arthur Penduck, George Pepall, Andrew Pope, Gilbert Rattenbury, **Francis Roberts***, **Percy Robinson***, Herbert Timms, Walter Troup, Ronald Turner, Frederic Watts, **Alison White***, Frank Wicks, John Williams, James Winterbotham, Claude Woolley, Oswald Wreford-Brown and **William Yalland**; by December 1914 **William Brownlee** and **William Yalland** were dead and **Archibald Fargus** was presumed dead.

By December 1914 fifty-seven cricketers were with the Colours, of which nineteen played in the 1914 season which is far in excess of the nationally published three. Of the thirty-three players who represented Gloucestershire CCC in the 1914 season, twenty-eight (85%) would fight with the Armed Forces and eight (24%) would pay the ultimate sacrifice.[153]

Despite the best of intentions not all the players were destined to become soldiers. **Herbert Manners** (GCCC) had enlisted on 11 September in the 19th (service) Battalion, Royal Fusiliers but was discharged from the Army within months on 15 December under King's Regulations paragraph 392 (iii) as "*...not likely to become an efficient soldier due to chronic sciatica and lumbago and muscular rheumatism*"; all this despite having been passed fit by Army doctors on 16 September. Similarly **Edwin Wootton** (GRFC) had enlisted on 28 August at Gloucester's Shire Hall in the 7th (Service) Battalion, Gloucestershire Regiment and was passed fit by the Army doctors on 5 September. However, after forty-seven days of service, Edwin was discharged under King's Regulations Paragraph 392 section (iii)c as "*...not likely to become an Efficient Soldier* [and] *recruit within three*

---

[150] *Gloucester Journal* 19 December 1914
[151] *Manchester Evening News* 11 December 1914
[152] The asterisk (*) denotes the men who had played in the 1914 season and hence were current GCCC members.
[153] The identification of the rugby and cricket players is based on information published on two websites - see Appendix B Note 1

months of enlistment considered unfit for service"; the cause of Edwin's problem was officially listed as an "*internal derangement knee joint, some semilunar* [cartilage damage]" However the problem, possibly as a result of a rugby injury, seemed to have miraculously resolved itself as early in 1915 Edwin successfully re-joined the Army this time with the 9/Gloucesters. Edwin's good fortune would desert him in 1917 when he was killed in action whilst, under heavy fire, helping a wounded comrade stranded in No Man's Land by which time he had become an "*…efficient…*" soldier. Inevitably across Britain a large number of men were judged by the Army doctors as "*…not likely to become an efficient soldier…unfit for service…*" and in September, in Bristol, these men joined the Bristol branch of the Voluntary Social Service Bureau which was based at 49 Broad Street. The aim of the bureau was to free-up the War Office to deal with military applications, leaving the bureau to deal with the remainder. By 4 September about one hundred men had volunteered to act as clerks, typists and messengers. Organisations such as the Boy Scouts joined in by offering Scout huts for the Bureau's meetings.[154] The Bureau would assist in the re-homing of the Belgian refugees while **Foster Robinson** (GCCC) would provide stationary and printing facilities to enable the Bureau to conduct its business.

Likewise **Sidney Kitcat** (GCCC) tried to re-join his old unit, the Artists' Rifles which in 1908 had become 28th (County of London) Battalion (Artists' Rifles), London Regiment. Sidney had served with them as a volunteer part-time soldier between 1889 and 1895 and as a consequence his service records showed that he was, at 46 years old, well over-age and was consequently rejected. Desperate to play his part he wrote to a friend, Captain J.H. Levey, for advice on joining the Army, but Levey promptly appointed him as a Sub Lieutenant in the Royal Naval Volunteer Reserve [RNVR] on HMS *Victory VI* (also known as HMS *Crystal Palace*) a shore-based establishment which trained 125,000 Officers, Petty Officers and men throughout the Great War. As Sidney commented "*…I never worked so hard in all my life…*"[155]

As Christmas approached the killing continued in the season of goodwill despite widespread rumours that there had been a 'Christmas Truce' along many parts of the Western Front.[156] **Bernard Roach** (GRFC), a Regular soldier with the 2/Grenadier Guards, had initially remained in Britain to fulfil certain duties one of which was to carry the body of Carl Lody, the ineffectual German spy executed on 6 November by firing squad, out of the Tower of London for burial. On 23 November he travelled across the Channel and joined his battalion at Méteren, eight miles north-west of Armentières, which had been placed under orders to move out at two hours notice. By 22 December it had moved twenty miles south to a bivouac in a field at Essars near Le Touret. The trenches were waist deep in mud and water and although offensives were shut down for the winter the area still remained dangerous.[157] On Christmas Day, rumours of a truce abounded but the 2/Grenadier Guards Battalion War Diary indicated that there was "*…a great deal of shooting all day…*" and the reported casualties amongst the men and NCOs were three killed, nineteen wounded, two missing and one in

---

[154] *Western Daily Press* 4 September 1914
[155] *The Singapore Free Press and Mercantile Advertiser* 7 July 1931
[156] Subsequent research has shown that a 'Christmas Truce' did exist along various sectors of the Western Front when both British and German soldiers got out of their trenches and met in No Man's Land.
[157] The harsh winter conditions on the Continent meant that Armies did not go on the attack during the winter months and settled down to aggressive defence; both sides respected the conditions.

hospital with frostbite.[158] Amongst those killed was Bernard Roach who died in a sector where historians would later determine that the infamous truce had taken place.[159]

By Christmas the country, the people of Gloucestershire and the cricket and rugby players had begun to get a real idea of their *'great adventure'*; already two rugby players, **Walter Hancock** and **Bernard Roach** and one cricketer, **William Yalland**, had been killed in action while **William Brownlee** (GCCC) had died in training. A regular feature in the local newspapers since the beginning of September had been the reporting of the rapidly mounting casualty lists indicating the number of dead and wounded as well as the numbers of British, French and Belgian soldiers currently being treated at the local hospitals although there were issues with the accuracy of the casualty numbers. At the end of November the Prime Minister, Herbert Asquith, had announced that British casualties had reached 57,000 although Lord Newton at a recruitment meeting suggested that the real casualty figures, because of reporting irregularities, could be nearer 80,000.[160,161] The plight of Belgian refugees, together with organisations set up to raise funds for their welfare and find them jobs, were also a new feature in the local newspapers.

By the end of December the ideas of a *'great adventure'* and *'over by Christmas'* had been utterly dispelled and the population of Great Britain, now realised that *this* war was not like the Boer War!

---

[158] Battalion War Diary, *2nd Battalion Grenadier Guards 25 December 1914,* TNA WO 95/1342
[159] Malcolm Brown and Shirley Seaton, *Christmas Truce* (London: Pan Grand Strategy Series, 1999).
[160] *Dean Forest Mercury* 27 November 1914.
[161] Thomas Legh, Lord Newton, was a member of the House of Lords but in 1915 was appointed by the Prime Minister, Hubert Asquith, as the Paymaster General with responsibility for representing the War Office in Parliament in the absence of Lord Kitchener, the Secretary of State for War.

For Club, King and Country

2

1915: TRULY A FIRST WORLD WAR

"He was killed leading and setting a most excellent example to the men in the forefront of the Battalion…."
　　Major General Sir Alexander Godley writing about **John Williams** (GCCC), killed in action 25 April 1915

"…hostile troops facing the Gloucesters did not even take shelter…"
　　Everard Wyrall writing in 1931 about the Battle of Aubers Ridge 9 May 1915

"…this isn't war, not as civilised people understand it. It's simply scientific murder…"
　　Harry Lane DCM (GRFC) in a letter home to his parents, 20 May 1915

The land war in 1914 had been largely confined to France and Belgium (Western Front) although there were engagements in Mesopotamia as Britain secured the Royal Navy's vital oil supply by occupying the oilfields and pipelines near Basra, and in East, West and German South-West Africa. But 1915 would see the global nature of the war emerge and was the start of truly the first world war in history. Turkey had joined the Central Powers (Germany, Austro-Hungary) and declared war on 31 October 1914 and although major engagements continued on the Western Front, the war in Mesopotamia escalated and new fronts opened up in Sinai and Palestine (January), the Gallipoli Peninsula (April), Italy (June) and Salonika (October); all these actions took place against the background of the war at sea (see Map 1 for the location of the relevant theatres of war).

On the Western Front the soldiers of the Regular Army were still actively engaged with the Germans but 1915 would see the British Army fight its first battles, independently of the French Army, at Neuve Chappelle (10-13 March), Aubers Ridge (9-10 May), Festubert (15-27 May) and Loos

(25 September-14 October). Already it had become apparent that the resolution of the trench stalemate on the Western Front would result in high casualty levels and in an attempt to 'unlock the back door' into Germany, Winston Churchill, First Lord of the Admiralty, despite significant military opposition, vigorously canvassed for a campaign in the Dardanelles against the Ottoman Empire (Turkey). Before the end of the year this campaign would also result in a trench stalemate and high casualty levels which would lead in November to Churchill's demotion and resignation from the British Cabinet; for a period he would command the 6/Royal Scots Fusiliers on the Western Front near Ploegsteert Wood.

January:
Private **George Halford** (GRFC), the elected captain of the Gloucester Rugby Club, before the Army had requested his services in France with the 1/Gloucesters, had been regularly sending letters and postcards to friends and relatives in Gloucester and at the Rugby Club assuring them of his well-being. At the end of January his good fortune came to an end when he was hit in his side by a metal fragment of a German bomb whilst making a cup of coffee in the trenches near Cuinchy.[162] George remarked to his friend **Arthur Hudson** (GRFC),

> "…I have been wounded by a piece of a German bomb, but I don't think it is as bad as they said it was. I have got the piece as a curio – from your old pal, Biddy." [163,164]

Despite treatment in France and ultimately in Britain at a Northampton hospital and George's own diagnosis, the severity of the wound resulted in his discharge from the Army as "…*unfit for service.*" Notwithstanding the poor prognosis he would regain a level of fitness over the next few years that would enable him to don the jersey of the Gloucester Football Club for the 1919-20 season and once more serve as Club captain.

Meanwhile the intense training of the 5/Gloucesters which continued unabated was insufficient to dampen the sporting enthusiasm of the men. It was noted that when one of the companies, billeted in Chelmsford, arrived tired and dishevelled after marching seventy miles in five days in full kit, after removing their accoutrements, the first thing they asked for was "…*a football to play with.*"[165] The training now reflected the level of war readiness with route marches and Brigade field exercises prominent. New modern web equipment was issued which made the route marches easier although "…*the large number of buckles that have to be adjusted appear rather complicated at first sight.*"[166] New rifles were issued which, although of the same pattern as the old models, were slightly modified to take the new ammunition which would be used at the front. Perhaps the biggest

---

[162] *Gloucester Journal* 30 January 1915
[163] *Gloucester Journal* 30 January 1915
[164] It was frequently reported that wounded soldiers often saved the shrapnel, shell fragment or bullet as a memento. However the surgeon often tried to claim it as well and a lively debate began, played out in the newspapers, as to who had claim to the metal objects. The newspapers and general public made it clear that the wounded soldier had the best, if not the only, claim.
[165] *Dursley, Berkeley and Sharpness Gazette* 9 January 1915
[166] *Dursley, Berkeley and Sharpness Gazette* 23 January 1915

February:

In the previous November Private **George Cook** (GRFC), 2/Gloucesters, had been reported as missing in action but any 'hope' of a positive outcome disappeared when he had been officially declared 'killed in action' on 11 November 1914.[168] For his parents this was a double tragedy as their eldest daughter, Emily, had died the previous week. However such was the fog of war that on 15 February George's parents received an official postcard stating that he was wounded and a prisoner of war being held at a hospital at Lille. The postcard confirmed information that they had received by a letter a few days earlier from a Scottish soldier who had been at the same hospital in Lille but who had been repatriated to Britain under an exchange scheme due to the severity of his wounds. George's tale of survival was remarkable in that he had received gun shot wounds [GSW] to his back and, unable to move, had lain out in no man's land for thirty-six hours until found by a German patrol. He had first received treatment from a French doctor and nurse, both of whom were prisoners but he would require periodic treatment over the four years at a POW camp in Germany and shortly before the Armistice his final operation was performed to remove a bone fragment from his back. In George's case the period between being declared 'missing' and being declared a 'POW' was relatively short but often this process could take up to a year when it was usual for a 'missing' status to be amended to 'killed in action' which would then enable his widow and dependants to claim a state pension.

March:

Although at Chelmsford the 5/Gloucesters Inter-Company Rugby competition had neared completion, the re-organisation of the Battalion on a four-company structure, in readiness for its entry into a theatre of war, had negated all previous results. The A, B, C and D Companies hastily arranged a new series of round-robin games and on 6 March the final featured C and D Companies as the two most successful company XVs.[169] The strong wind in C Company's favour in the first half, failed to prevent D Company's Private **Harry Pollard** (GRRC) scoring a try which was converted by Private **Sidney Sysum** (GRFC). The second half was dominated by D Company, despite the loss at half time of **Alec Lewis** (GRFC) through injury with tries coming from Lance Corporal **Syd Millard** (GRFC) and Private Alfred White (second row).[170] D Company which won by eleven points to nil, boasted twelve Gloucester Rugby Club players - Privates **Hubert Smith** (full back), (**Alec Lewis**, centre, retired), **Harry Pollard** (centre), **Sidney Sysum** (centre), **William Washbourne** (wing), **Ernest Cummings** (stand off), **William Egerton** (scrum half), **Joe Harris** (front row), Lance-Corporal **Syd Millard** (second row), Privates **George Lane** (back row) and **William Dovey** (back row) (see Photograph 15). C Company was supported by the Gloucester players, Privates **Tom Lewis** (stand

---

[167] The two Gloucester Companies, A and B, formed the new A Company, the C (Stroud) and D (Tewkesbury) Companies became B Company, the E and F Companies (Cheltenham) became C Company and the G (Dursley) and H (Campden) Companies became D Company.
[168] *Gloucester Journal* 20 January 1915
[169] *Gloucester Journal* 13 March 1915
[170] Personal Communication: Roger Hiam, great nephew of Alfred White. Alfred James White born in 1883 was a St Mark's rugby player; he was killed in action with the 5/Gloucesters on 16 August 1917

off), his brother, **Melville Lewis** (back row) and **Fred Webb** (wing) while the game was refereed by Captain **Gilbert Collett** (centre) (GRFC and GCCC) who also donated the Inter-Companies Cup.

Photograph 15: D Company Rugby XV, winners of the 1/5th Battalion, Gloucestershire Regiment Inter Company Rugby Competition, 6 March 1915. The photograph shows the Gloucester Rugby Club players: (1) Hubert Smith; (2) Syd Millard; (3) Joe Harris; (4) William Dovey; (5) William Washbourne; (6) Sydney Sysum; (7) Bill Egerton; (8) Alec Lewis and (9) Ernest Cummings. Also in the photograph but not identified are George Lane and Harry Pollard. The player standing fourth from left is Alfred White (St Marks) one of the try scorers. (*SoGM, GLRRM: 04926.2*)

On 19 March the 5/Gloucesters, with its rugby players now *fully* trained British soldiers, was ordered to prepare for foreign service and the men warned that they should expect to be in France by the end of the month (see Photographs 16 and 17).[171] Inventories of the kit and equipment were established and lists of deficiencies were sent to the Director of Overseas Operations [DOO] for rectification. All deficiencies were made good including the issue of New Army Pattern boots and by 26 March the Battalion was ready for war. Two days later an advance party landed at Le Havre at 3.30 pm with the main body of troops setting foot on French soil at Boulogne at 11.00 pm on 29 March before marching for 2.5 miles to a rest camp.[172] By 9.00 am the following morning the men had moved a further three miles to Pont de Brique before entraining in cattle trucks for Cassel and a five mile march to Steenvorde on the Belgian border. It was here that the former rugby players began their battle training and acclimatisation to conditions on the Western Front. Through a series

---
[171] *Dursley, Berkeley and Sharpness Gazette* 20 March 1915
[172] Le Havre and Boulogne were the main entry ports for the British Army into France and which port was chosen was determined by the activity at the ports and the availability of berths for the ships.

of billets they moved closer to the front line, taking over trenches for the first time at 5.00 pm on 8 April in Ploegsteert Wood which at that time was a quiet section of the Western Front although there was the ever present danger from German snipers who were between seventy and two hundred yards away depending on the section of trench.[173]

Photograph 16. Muster Parade at Chelmsford: The 1/5th Battalion Gloucestershire Regiment on muster parade at Chelmsford training camp *circa* January-March 1915. The men would have been assembled for inspection which would have been a frequent occurrence during their Army life. (*SoGM, GLRRM:01802.6*)

April:
Elsewhere Churchill's Dardanelles campaign had reached a crisis point. Between 9 February and 18 March the Royal Navy had failed to force the Dardanelles Straits and in an attempt to alleviate the situation it was decided to land troops on the Gallipoli peninsula. Although much importance has been given to the presence of ANZAC forces, there were more British and French forces involved in the campaign, including several rugby players and cricketers.[174] The first British landings took place on 25 April near Gaba Tepe (now known as Anzac Cove) and at Cape Helles, on the western and southern tips of the peninsula respectively, supported by a French Army landing on the Turkish mainland; those on the Gallipoli peninsula met with fierce resistance and high casualties.

---

[173] Battalion War Diary, *5th Battalion Gloucestershire Regiment 8 April 1915*, TNA WO 95/2763
[174] ANZAC is acronym for Australia and New Zealand Army Corps.

Photograph 17. On Parade at Chelmsford: The 1/5th Battalion Gloucestershire Regiment on parade at it Chelmsford training camp *circa* March 1915. The officer in the centre on horseback is the Commanding Officer, Lieutenant Colonel John H. Collett. The eighteen arch viaduct in the back ground which brings the railway line to the main station is still in existence and the parade ground is now Chelmsford Central Park. (*SoGM, GLRRM:04740.2*)

Landing at Anzac Cove with the 6th (Hauraki) Company, Auckland Regiment was Private **John Williams** (GCCC). John, the son of Colonel Sir Robert Williams MP, had been a Captain in the 4/Dorsets (TF) before the war but had moved to New Zealand in 1910 to work for the Waihi Gold Mining Company. On the declaration of war he had enlisted as a Private in the New Zealand Expeditionary Force although with his previous military experience it had been decided to give him a commission after the landings had been completed. Under the cover of darkness the New Zealanders, supported by warships firing broadsides into the Turkish positions, were off-loaded into barges which were towed into the shallower waters near the beach. There they were greeted by small arms fire from the Turkish trenches and shrapnel from the Turkish artillery further inland. The 6th Company was on the left of the landing but in the ensuing chaos the New Zealand and Australian companies became mixed and command disjointed as the,

"...officers went down fast...and everywhere the born leaders and the fine fighting men were coming to the front"[175]

Amongst them was John Williams a Private by rank but a Captain by military training and it was the latter rank which came to the fore. Tragically John was killed during the landings and afterwards Major General Sir Alexander Godley, Commanding New Zealand Forces wrote,

---

[175] O.E.Burton, *The Auckland Regiment* (Auckland: Whitcombe and Tombs Ltd, 1922) pp.25-32 (available from New Zealand Electronic Text Collection (NZETC), Victoria University of Wellington Library)

> "He was killed leading and setting a most excellent example to the men in the forefront of the Battalion...and had he not fallen he would have been given a commission in this force immediately after the first action. I believe the example which he set in enlisting and dying as he did in the ranks has done more for this force and perhaps for the Empire than he would have done as a commissioned officer"[176]

Under the cover of darkness the Auckland Regiment buried its dead in No Man's Land but sadly John's body was never recovered and identified and he is listed amongst the 4,932 Missing on the Lone Pine Memorial. His qualities as a potential officer became known to the authorities after the Auckland Regiment which had left New Zealand in October 1914, had repulsed a Turkish attack in February 1915 whilst defending the Suez Canal in Egypt; it is probable that John's training as an officer with the 4/Dorsets had instilled in him a military discipline which did not abandon him in the heat of a battle.

Once ashore the Allied troops on the Gallipoli peninsula suffered from a situation reminiscent of that on the Western Front, as a trench stalemate rapidly became the norm after the landings with the Turks commanding and dominating the high ground. With high casualty rates and the harsh disease-ridden environment life was miserable for the troops; reinforcements were always desperately needed. An Army Veterinary Corps officer, considering existence on the peninsula, explained that,

> "France and Belgium were a pleasure trip to this life! ...Shells are our chief 'delight' – especially the dodging of them!"[177]

On 11 July at 10.30 pm the troops at Cape Helles were reinforced by the 39th (Western) Division, including the 7/Gloucesters (39 Brigade), which landed at Y Beach. Amongst the latter were Privates **James Westbury** (GRFC) and **James Hamblin** (GRFC) and Sergeant **Frank Smith** (GRFC). Privates Westbury and Hamblin were Kitchener's Men but Frank Smith was a reservist who had been re-called to the Colours in August 1914. Frank had fought with the 1/Gloucesters at the Battle of Mons and was wounded twice but on recovery was transferred to the 7/Gloucesters which was in need of experienced NCOs. Frank Smith would survive the Gallipoli Campaign but would be killed in action in Mesopotamia in 1916. On 13 August James Westbury was wounded whilst in the trenches which were under constant sniper fire on a day which resulted in seven dead and fourteen wounded. On 25 September James Hamblin suffered the same fate. Both men were evacuated to Egypt and subsequently transferred to the Western Front, James Westbury to the Labour Corps and James Hamblin to the 13/Gloucesters (Pioneers).[178,179]

Meanwhile on the Western Front the acclimatisation of the men of the 5/Gloucesters continued. Second Lieutenant **James Winterbotham** (GCCC) who had obtained a commission in February was attached to B Company which included the rugby players, brothers **Charles** and **Harry Cook**, **Hugh Thomas**, **John Webb** and **William Wilkes**. James commanded No.7 platoon and along with **Gilbert Collett** were the only county cricketers with the 5/Gloucesters although **Thomas Miller** would join the 2/5th Battalion in April 1918 and **Charles Barnett** the 1/5th Battalion in November 1918. Gilbert

---

[176] *De Ruvigny's Roll of Honour* Volume 1 (1922) p.380
[177] *Cheltenham Chronicle and Gloucestershire Graphic* 4 September 1915
[178] The 13th (Service) Battalion (Forest of Dean) (Pioneers), Gloucestershire Regiment was a pioneer battalion raised in 1915 by Lieutenant Colonel Henry Webb, MP and based on men local to the Forest of Dean.
[179] In September 1916 **James Westbury** (GRFC) would be wounded for the second time whilst serving on the Western Front.

Collett, both a rugby player, cricketer and pre-war Territorial, went with A Company to France in 1915 and would spend a period commanding both the 1/5th (April-June 1916 and September-November 1916) and 2/5th (April 1917-March 1918).[180] James Winterbotham would get to know the rugby players and would play cricket with them behind the lines throughout the war.

The 5/Gloucesters had been in their 'quiet' sector for less than three weeks but already the German snipers had accounted for two dead and eight wounded. On 11 April the Battalion came out the line and the following morning marched to billets at Steenwerck. Two days later on Friday 13 April ten of the Gloucester rugby players represented to 48th (South Midland) Division in a match against the 4th Division at Pont de Nieppe.[181] The 48th Division XV, which included Lance Corporals **Alec Lewis** and **Sydney Millard** and Privates **Charles Cook**, **Fred Webb**, **William Washbourne**, **Lionel Hamblin**, **Sidney Sysum**, **Sid Smart**, **Joe Harris** and **Albert Cook**, won by seventeen points to nil; the team was captained by Lieutenant Ronald Poulton-Palmer (Royal Berkshire Regiment), the England International who would be killed within three weeks by a sniper's bullet.[182] Once more the team with the Gloucester players swept all before it despite the presence of English, Irish and Scottish Internationals in the opposition. The Gloucesters sojourn at Steenwerck was short-lived and by 15 April the men were again facing the German snipers who continued to exact their toll. On 26 April it included Private **Ernest Cummings** (GRFC) who was shot in the head and died after several hours at 8.30 pm without regaining consciousness; he became the first of the volunteers from either the rugby or cricket clubs to die in the Great War (see Photograph 18).[183] Ernest and his father, Private **Albert 'Car' Cummings** (GRFC) had enlisted together in September 1914 and whereas Ernest opted for a Territorial unit, Albert joined one of Kitchener's New Army battalions, the 10/Gloucesters. Albert was an old soldier and was soon transferred to the 1/Gloucesters, although it emerged that he had lied about his age claiming on his Attestation papers that he was 41 years old despite being born 45 years previously; he was however still sufficiently fit to pass the medical examination and a fitness test which involved a ten mile march carrying a rifle and 150 rounds of small arms ammunition [SAA]. With the news of his son's death Albert was distraught and his friend, **Fred Goulding** (GRFC) wrote that,

> "...Car Cummings is gone home. I was along with him when we heard the sad news of his son. I think it broke him up. "[184]

Albert would return to Gloucester and join the 3rd (Reserve) Battalion at the Deport but was transferred to civilian employment on 28 January 1916 to use his skills as a Blacksmith in the vital National Steel Factory at Lancaster.[185]

---

[180] **Cyril Sewell** (GCCC) had been a pre-war Territorial with the 5/Gloucesters but by October 1914 had been promoted to Captain and transferred to the Oxfordshire and Buckinghamshire Light Infantry.

[181] Personal Communication: James Corsan. It is probable that this match actually took place on 14 March.

[182] Despite independent research by several individuals it has proved so far impossible to name all fifteen players from the 48th (South Midland) Division XV. Within six weeks of the game, Gilbert Collett wrote to Basil MacLear's father after he had been killed in action in a letter which named the team but provided only fourteen names. Further in 1919 Ronald Poulton-Palmer's father wrote a book which again listed only fourteen names in that final XV (Edward Bagnall Poulton, *The Life of Ronald Poulton* (London: Sedgwick and Jackson, 1919)

[183] Ernest Cummings was buried in what is now Ploegsteert Wood Military Cemetery and in April 1917 a soldier writing home to Gloucester mentioned that his grave was well tended. It was not unknown for women volunteers to travel to France to tend the soldiers' graves.

[184] **Fred Goulding** (GRFC) quoted in *The Citizen* 17 May 1915. Fred and Albert played together 28 times in the 1897-98 season.

Photograph 18. Ernest Cummings (1892-1915) (GRFC): Private, 2647, Ernest Cummings, D Company, 1/5th Battalion, Gloucestershire Regiment, killed by a sniper in Ploegsteert Wood, 26 April 1915, 23 years. The photograph was taken between September 1914 and March 1915. Ernest was the first of the volunteers from the Gloucester Rugby Club to be killed in action. (*CCGG*)

With mounting casualties, the recruitment drives continued unabated across the country with regiments utilising all means possible to entice young men to join their ranks voluntarily. Sporting celebrities such as **Gilbert Jessop** (GCCC), 14/Manchesters were used to bring in the recruits – at one meeting on 20 April in Manchester the recruiting party with Gilbert as its focus and having marched from the railway station to Albert Square proceeded by forty drummers, enlisted 189 new recruits.[186]

May:

In March at the Battle of Neuve Chapelle the British Army had taken its first tentative steps in its transformation from a 'colonial' army into an 'industrial' army capable of waging modern warfare against equally industrialised nations. The next step along this learning curve was the Battle of Aubers Ridge (9-10 May 1915) which would etch itself into the minds of the people of Gloucester following the death of one of its more celebrated rugby players, **Harry Berry**, a veteran of 144 games for Gloucester and an England International player (see Photograph 19). Harry, an Army Reservist, having fought in the Boer War (1899-1902), had joined the Gloucester Football Club in 1907 but on the declaration he had been recalled to the Colours although he did not land in France until 2 February 1915. At 7.00 pm on 7 May, Harry with the 1/Gloucesters marched to the assembly trenches ready for the attack early the following morning, but the sense of dread had only been heightened when the attack was postponed for twenty-four hours. After spending the day in billets at Lannoy the Gloucesters marched to Windy Corner and by 11.30 pm occupied the trenches at Rue de Bois where the night was spend issuing bombs, respirators, rations and additional ammunition and no doubt in thought for the forthcoming attack (see Map 2).[187] Harry however was amongst

---

[185] Although Albert was transferred to war work in Britain it was not before he participated in the Battle of Aubers Ridge on 9 May 1915.
[186] *Manchester Courier* 21 April 1915
[187] Battalion War Diary, *1st Battalion Gloucestershire Regiment 8 May 1915*, TNA WO/95/1278

friends including fellow Gloucester players Private **Albert Cummings** (stand off), Private **Charles Rose** (front row), Lance Corporal **Fred Goulding** (front row/second row), Private **Harry Barnes** (centre) and Lance Sergeant **John Robinson** (centre).

The 1/Gloucesters and the 1/South Wales Borderers were in the reserve line at 5.30 am on 9 May when the front-line battalions went 'over the top' only to be met with a terrific machine gun and rifle barrage. As the attacking battalions moved across No Man's Land, the 1/Gloucesters now had to move above ground the 150 yards to the front-line trenches, which by now were full of dead and wounded men. A second artillery bombardment followed and at 7.00 am as it died away C and B Companies of the 1/Gloucesters went over the top. The British Official History [BOH] recorded that,

"...On the front of the 3rd Brigade German observers were seen looking over the parapet, and as soon as the assaulting lines of the 1/Gloucestershire and 1/South Wales Borderers crossed the British breastwork the machine guns opened a heavy fire. The leading companies advanced eighty to a hundred yards in face of a hail of bullets, but were unable to go further and lay down in No Man's Land, taking what cover they could..." [188]

Another attack went in at 4.00 pm but this time the,

"...hostile troops facing the Gloucesters did not even take shelter, but lined the parapet and greeted the new attack with intense small-arm and machine-gun fire..." [189]

This hail of flying metal which greeted the Gloucesters was captured in a letter sent home by Sergeant Wadley to his mother in Parliament Square, Gloucester,

"...I had a near one. A bullet just knocked the skin off my eyebrow [then there was a shrapnel burst with] *one piece knocking me to the ground for a few minutes, another cutting my chin strap through and a third cutting my back badge clean in half. I have been hit five times in all..."* [190]

Of the men still alive a few managed to crawl back to their trenches with the majority having to wait for darkness. That day three hundred and fifty-two men of the Gloucesters never returned from No Man's Land.

The first indication that Harry Berry had been killed appeared in a letter from Private George Young to his brother living in Norfolk Street in Gloucester. He wrote,

"...I have been in the thick of a big fight and pulled through safe - I must not describe the fight as the censor says we are not to do so until the battle is over. Harry Berry, the Gloucester and International footballer, was killed and several other local men were killed and wounded. Our casualties are rather heavy." [191,192]

The news was confirmed when fellow player **Fred Goulding** (GRFC) wrote to his wife, Florence,[193] who in a subsequent letter added,

"...I shall never forget last Sunday as long as I live. Our chaps call it 'Bloody Sunday'. Our Division bore the brunt of the attacks on German trenches. [Despite the massive British bombardment which] *was like hell on earth* [as] *they shelled the German trenches for about 40 minutes,* [when] *our troops got out of their trenches and went for the enemy...I*

---

[188] J.E. Edmonds, *History of the Great War. Military Operations France and Belgium, 1915. Vol II* , p.28
[189] Wyrall, *The Gloucestershire Regiment in the War 1914-1918,* p.117
[190] *Gloucester Journal* 22 May 1915
[191] *The Citizen* 15 May 1915
[192] *Gloucester Journal* 22 May 1915
[193] *The Citizen* 17 May 1915

am sorry to say they got mowed down and had to retire.. It was murder. I never seen such sights in my life; some men had their arms and legs off, and the moans were pitiful to hear..." [194]

Fred himself was wounded in June 1915 fighting with the Gloucesters near Ypres, after gaining his Lance-Corporal's stripe. On recovery he was transferred to a munitions factory in Northwich, Cheshire where he spent the war and the rest of his life although sadly his wife and two children died of pneumonia during the Spanish Flu pandemic in December 1918 (see Photograph 19).

Photograph 19. Corporal Harry Berry (GRFC) and Lance Corporal Fred Goulding (GRFC): Both men fought with the 1/Gloucesters at the Battle of Aubers Ridge, 9 May 1915. Harry was killed in the battle while Fred survived and would have letters published in the local newspapers which told of the experiences of the men of the 1/Gloucesters during the battle. (*CCGG*)

Gradually other chilling accounts of the battle emerged. Private E. Herbert, D Company, 1/Gloucesters exploded the myth that all men died 'instantly'. He thought that the Germans,

"...let us advance 200 yards, then we dropped on the ground, for it was too far to advance all at once. Then they picked us off. All the four officers of our company were shot. I saw three of them drop myself. There were about eight of us in a bunch and after we dropped on the ground I spoke to them and there was only one answer. All the other six were shot. The one that answered me was brought in to be buried after dark. I had to wriggle back on my stomach about 200 yards like a snake; then I took a short run and jumped over the parapet. Our men were ready waiting for the stragglers and they kept a clear space so that you could jump into the trench. It was horrible lying out there for hours amongst the

---

[194] *Gloucester Journal* 22 May 1915

dead and wounded. One boy, for he was nothing else, lying not far from me had five bullet wounds in the leg and shrapnel in the shoulder. He looked at me piteously but I could do nothing; it was instant death to lift your head...I hope I shall never experience anything like what I saw on May 9 1915 – and the attack failed." [195]

Private T. Priday who also took part in the attack wrote to his wife in Granville Street making specific reference to Harry Berry. Just before zero hour he wrote that,

"We shook hands with one another. When we returned the next time, my mate, poor Mr Berry was missing. When it was dark I went out to try and find him but was not successful. I am downright sorry for him and his wife and two dear little ones. We kissed the photos of our wives and children before we made the charge. There were twelve of us in our section, and only seven returned. Most of them were wounded, all but Mr Berry." [196]

Private **Harry Barnes** (GRFC), a Reservist, was also lost in the battle and his mother received a letter from Captain A.W. Pagan, dated 7 June which stated that he,

"...died at once suffering no pain. He was buried where he fell along with two other men from his company." [197]

Neither Harry Barnes' or Harry Berry's bodies were found and identified after the war thus becoming two of the 526,816 British and Commonwealth missing servicemen of the First World War. Both men are commemorated amongst the 13,394 Missing on the impressive Le Touret Memorial, near Richebourg L'Avoué (see Photograph 20).

Sergeant **John Robinson** (GRFC), a former Gloucester player who had joined the Northern Union club Rochdale Hornets and had been on tour in Australia and New Zealand when war had been declared, was wounded in the attack and transferred to a Base Hospital in France for treatment; he would recover and survive the war.[198]

However enemy fire was not the only danger that infantrymen faced in the trenches as many of the new weapons developed as well as improvised devices could be temperamental. After being at the front for less than two months Private **Walter Cromwell** (GRFC), 5/Gloucesters, was injured by the accidental explosion of a hand grenade that was so severe that Walter was invalided out of the Army and awarded a Silver War Badge (76091).[199,200] The Battalion War Diary recorded that on 6 May at 5.30pm:

"Lieut H.G.C. Guise while instructing his platoon Grenadiers, accidently exploded a Jamtin Grenade which killed himself and Pte Bates and wounded 6 others seriously." [201,202]

---

[195] *Gloucestershire Chronicle* 22 May 1915
[196] *Gloucestershire Chronicle* 22 May 1915
[197] *Gloucester Journal* 19 June 1915
[198] *Gloucester Journal* 15 May 1915
[199] *Cheltenham Chronicle and Gloucestershire Graphic* 22 May 1915
[200] Silver War Badges [SWB], mistakenly referred to as Silver Wound Badges, were awarded to servicemen invalided out of the Armed Forces and were intended as recognition of the fact that they had served their country and had suffered as a consequence. The badge also gave some protection from the public who would sometimes verbally abuse seemingly eligible men in civilian clothes; after January 1916 with the introduction of conscription this ceased to be an issue although the SWBs were still issued until 1922. Men and women engaged on vital war work (starred occupations) were also awarded specific 'on war work' badges in recognition of this fact.
[201] *Battalion War Diary, 1/5th Battalion Gloucestershire Regiment 6 May 1915*, TNA WO 95/2763
[202] Jamtin Grenade – this was exactly what the name implies. Old jam tins were improvised in the absence of hand grenades by filling them with explosive and metal debris and inserting a fuse – by their very nature they

Photograph 20. Le Touret Memorial: The Le Touret Memorial, Richebourg-l'Avoue commemorates 13,394 soldiers killed in this sector, from October 1914 until September 1915, who have no known grave. Amongst those commemorated are Corporal **Harry Berry** (GRFC) and Private **Harry Barnes** (GRFC), both of the 1/Gloucesters. (*Authors*)

The 'romantic' notions of the nature of the fighting on the Western Front and of a 'great adventure' initially held by the citizens of Gloucester and Bristol had long been dispelled by tales from soldiers on leave and by soldier's letters published in the local newspapers. Guardsman **Harry Lane** (GRFC), 1/Grenadier Guards, in a letter to his parents stated that the Germans had been driven back and that those found in the captured trenches,

> "...beg for mercy when the boys charge, but you can't trust them, not even after they are wounded. Some of them fight like tigers right to the last, but I am sure they don't know they are fighting a losing game. They are still told they are winning..."

He added after searching a German dugout that it was like a,

> "...butcher's shop! There were five of them – three dead and two badly wounded. One of them told us they knew nothing about the Lusitania...this fellow had worked in Russell

---

were temperamental and could be lethal to friend and foe alike. The first specifically-developed widely-available effective hand grenade, the Mills Bomb, gradually came into service from May 1915 onwards.

Square, London for ten months prior to the war...but this isn't war, not as civilised people understand it. It's simply scientific murder...."[203],[204]

On 12 May reports reached Gloucester that the RGHY was engaged in its own hard battle against the Warwickshire Yeomanry in a cricket match at a location described only as '*somewhere in Egypt*'.[205] Set a target of 190 by the Warwicks, the Gloucester yeomen failed by twenty-nine runs at the close of play and a draw was declared. **Hugo Charteris (Lord Elcho)** (GCCC) took four wickets and emerged as the second highest scorer with thirty-six runs; the newspaper lamented the fact that **Alf Dipper** (GCCC) had been unavailable for the Hussars. Interestingly although the *Gloucestershire Chronicle* censored the location of the match, *The Dursley, Berkeley and Sharpness Gazette* announced it as Alexandria in Egypt.[206] On 11 August A and B Squadrons of the RGH would be ordered to Gallipoli as dismounted infantry, leaving their horses behind in Egypt with four officers and one hundred yeomen.[207] Hugo Charteris was one of the officers who would remain in Egypt for the next five months, playing chess with his friend Major Henry Clifford, both wishing that they were in the Dardanelles.[208]

The battles of 1914 and the first half of 1915 had been fought by regular troops and reservists and included many soldiers pulled out of garrison duty across the British Empire to be replaced by older men; garrison duties were considered to be less exacting than duty on the Western Front and other theatres although this was not always the case. On 26 May 1915 Captain **Edmund Marsden** (GCCC) who had been on the Indian Army Reserve of Officers, died of malaria after a five month illness whilst constructing a military road in Burma, having previously distinguished himself in action as part of the Burma Division at Wawang on 28 January 1915 following the Kachin tribal uprising.[209]

During a break from training Second Lieutenant **Frank Cowlin Wicks** (GCCC), 22/Manchesters, presided over a meeting at the County Ground Hotel which affiliated the Bristol Rugby Training Corps with the Athletes Volunteer Training Corps to standardise the training of potential officer recruits, especially has it had become apparent that there was a high level of attrition amongst officers at the front.[210] Further Lieutenant **Arthur Pickering** (GCCC) with the Merchant Venturers Cadet Corps performed drills at Golden Hill before marching back to Headquarters through Henleaze, Westbury Road, White Ladies Road and Park Street. The drills and the march were designed to attract the attention of young under-age men to join the Corps and receive basic

---

[203] *Gloucestershire Chronicle* 29 May 1915

[204] The *Lusitania* was a passenger liner sailing between America and Britain when it was torpedoed off the coast of Ireland by U-boat U-20 on 7 May 1915 with the loss of 1,198 lives including 128 Americans. This was one of the acts which provoked the United States of America into entering the war.

[205] *Gloucestershire Chronicle* 5 June 1915

[206] *The Dursley, Berkeley and Sharpness Gazette* 5 June 1915

[207] John Lewis, *Yeoman Soldiers. The Royal Gloucestershire Hussars 1785-1920* (Victoria BC: Trafford Publishing, 2008) p.58

[208] Personal Communication: Lieutenant Colonel Rollo Clifford former Commanding Officer Royal Wessex Yeomanry (1987-1989) and author of '*The Royal Gloucestershire Hussars*' (Stroud: Alan Sutton Publishing Inc., 1991). Major Henry Francis Clifford, B Squadron, Royal Gloucestershire Hussars, would be killed in action near Kantara on 9 January 1917.

[209] Edmund Marsden's name was not originally included in the CWGC Debt of Honour Register which was amended in 2006 following submissions from '*Leaving Cheltenham...and all that was dear*' (ww.remembering.org.uk)

[210] *Western Daily Press* 11 May 1915

military training in readiness for their enlistment into the British Army proper when they became eligible.[211]

June:

At the Annual General Meeting of the Gloucestershire County Ground Company the Directors, similar to those of the Gloucester Football and Athletic Ground Company Limited a year previous, decided not to pay any dividends for 1914-15 as there had been no income from cricket or football matches with the only income generated coming from leasing the ground to the War Office for the training of the various battalions stationed in Bristol and agreements reached with the cricket and football clubs for nominal sums in lieu of rent.[212] The net profit of £94 from the year 1914-15 was retained to cover a forecasted even tougher year ahead.[213]

At the start of the war Second Lieutenant **Claude Mackay** (GCCC) had been a Lance Corporal at Clifton College OTC but on 11 August he applied for a commission with the "*3rd Gloucesters or any other Regt in which vacancy may occur*", although as a 20 year old his mother, Mrs E.V. 'Jane' Mackay had to grant approval for the request and supply his Baptism certificate as proof of age.[214] He was awarded a commission as a Second Lieutenant with the 3/Gloucesters on 12 August but when he entered France on 7 November 1914 he was with 2/Worcesters having previously been transferred from the regiment's 5th (Reserve) Battalion. In March he was admitted to hospital suffering from influenza and his mother, Jane Mackay, listed as his next-of-kin, received two telegrams,

> To: Mrs Mackay, 10 College Road Clifton [1 March 1915]
> "*Beg to inform you that 2nd Lieut C.L. Mackay Worcester Regt was admitted to British Red Cross Hospital Rouen with influenza on Feb 22nd*"
> From: Secretary, War Office

> To: Mrs E.V. Mackay 10 College Road, Clifton [16 March 1915]
> "*2nd Lieut C.L. Mackay Worcester Regt was discharged to duty March 12th*"
> From: Secretary, War Office

Following his discharge he did not return to the Worcesters but was attached to and fought with the 2/Manchesters (14 Brigade, 5th Division). The 5th Division held the sector south of Ypres including The Dump and opposite Hill 60 which was attacked variously between 10 April and 5 May. Between 22 April and 31 May the 5th Division had suffered 7,994 casualties including 71 Officers killed and 209 wounded. Claude was amongst the casualties, wounded on 20 May and transferred to the base

---

[211] *Western Daily Press* 11 May 1915
[212] The County Ground covered a considerably larger area than today and hosted cricket, football, hockey and rugby; Bristol RFC regularly played at the ground.
[213] *Western Daily Press* 1 June 1915
[214] Second Lieutenant **Claude Mackay**, 2/Manchesters, Service Record TNA WO 339/17082-C569238

hospital at Boulogne. Throughout May and June telegrams regarding Claude would be sent from France to the War Office (addressed to *'Troopers, London'*) and thence to his mother,[215]

> To: Mrs E.V. Mackay 10 College Road, Clifton [21 May 1915]
> *"Regret to inform you that 2/Lieut C.L. Mackay Worcester Regiment admitted 7 Stationary Hospital Boulogne gunshot wound head dangerously ill"*
> From: Secretary, War Office

> To: Troopers, London [29 May 1915]
> *"Lt. C.L. Mckay, Worc. Regt. Attd 2nd Manchr Regt GSW head is dangerously ill"*
> From: Medical Officer, 7 Stationary Hospital, Boulogne

> To: Mrs E.V. Mackay 10 College Road, Clifton [2 June 1915]
> *"7 Stationary Hospital Boulogne reports 2/Lt C.L. Mackay Worcester Regiment seriously ill, progressing favourably 30th May"*
> From: Secretary, War Office

The 2 June telegram which toned down the language used in the telegram to the War Office, offered some hope for his mother that her son was on the way to recovery but,

> To: Troopers, London [7 June 1915]
> *"2 Lt C.L. Mckay Worcester Regt attd 2 Manch Regt died 7th June GSW head"*
> From: Medical Officer, 7 Stationary Hospital, Boulogne

The same day that the news of his death was notified to London, the War Office sent a final telegram to his mother

> To: Mrs E.V. Mackay, 10 College Road, Clifton [7 June 1915]
> *"Deeply regret to inform you that 2/Lieut C.L. Mackay Worcester Regt attached to 2 Manchester Regt of Stationary Hospital Boulogne died of wounds today. Lord Kitchener expresses his sympathy"*
> From: Secretary, War Office

---

[215] The address "Troopers, London" was the telegraphic address of the War Office and therefore all the telegrams contained within the service record have the War Office and date received stamps on them.

The knock on the door for the delivery of a War Office telegram would become a dreaded event for many households across Britain over the four years of the war. For the close knit communities in towns and villages alike the arrival of the Telegram Boy would not go unnoticed by neighbours who came to understand the serious sad significance of his appearance.[216] Claude at 20 years was the youngest of the cricketers to die during the war. In August 1915 Mrs Jane Mackay would receive a letter,

> "The Military Secretary presents his compliments to Mrs E.V. Mackay, and begs to inform her that a report has just been received from Army Head quarters in the Field which states that the late Second Lieutenant C.L. Mackay, Worcester Regiment, was buried in Boulogne Cemetery and the grave is numbered 2393..." From: The Military Secretary.[217]

Horace Merrick (GCCC) had enlisted as a private on the outbreak of war in the 4th (City of Bristol) Battalion (TF), the Gloucestershire Regiment but had subsequently gained a commission, as a Second-Lieutenant in January 1915. The Battalion landed in France two months later but in June he was shot through the mouth and invalided back to Britain. After almost five months in hospital he was granted leave a period of leave in Bristol before re-joining his battalion.[218] As a great deal of time had been invested in the training of officers, there was a constant drive to return the recovered men back to their units as fast as possible regardless of the severity of the wounding and regardless of the notion that *'he had done his duty'*. Fortunately Horace would do his duty and go on to win the Military Cross for bravery (June 1917) and would survive the war.

With the rugby season over the men of the 5/Gloucesters now turned their hand to cricket behind the lines and in a game between A and D Companies the Rugby Club was well represented by **Gilbert Collett** (also a GCCC player), **Sidney Sysum**, **Lionel Hamblin**, **Harry Pollard**, **Bill Egerton** and **Joe Harris**; A Company won by twenty runs. The match was described as,

> "...rather a novel game for in the next field was a battery of artillery blazing away and the game had just been in progress about ten minutes before the Germans were shelling a small village not a quarter of a mile away. Yet the game was proceeded with as if it was being played on the Spa at home..."[219]

The games were not always completed as the Medical Officer of the 2/Royal Welsh Fusiliers commented that their games of rugby had been frequently interrupted by German shells landing "*...on the field of play.*"[220] It is interesting to note how soldiers who were civilians ten months earlier rapidly adapted to life on the Western Front and how sights, sounds, smells and fears which would have caused distress on the streets of Bristol and Gloucester were now ignored and accepted as part of everyday life. Further evidence that the soldiers in the fighting line had become distant from the Home Front and their attitudes to the civilians back home was expressed in letters including one from **Lionel Hamblin** (GRFC) how wrote,

---

[216] In general telegrams were reserved for officer casualties and War Office letters for Other Ranks.
[217] Today Claude Mackay lies in the Boulogne Eastern Cemetery, a CWGC cemetery, and the grave reference is II.A.31
[218] *Cheltenham Chronicle and Gloucestershire Graphic* 9 October 1915
[219] *Gloucester Journal* 25 June 1915
[220] James Churchill Dunn, Captain, DSO, MC and Bar, DCM, *The War the Infantry Knew* (P.S. King Ltd, 1938) p.133

"It is a little annoying to read of strikes in England, but I wonder how they would manage if we were to strike – we, the big waged infantrymen who are bearing the brunt of the world's greatest war. They should all be 'welcomed at dawn' the same as we should be if we struck for a war bonus. That is the opinion of the boys out here." [221,222]

Photograph 21. Leaving Bristol: The men of E and F (Depot) Companies, 12th (Service) Battalion (Bristol's Own), Gloucestershire Regiment leave Bristol on 25 June 1915 to continue their training in Birmingham. (*SoGM, GLRRM:02557.46*)

July:

In Britain the first season cricket season of the war saw scratch games organised between college and representative sides which would include servicemen home on leave and older players. **Jack Board** (GCCC) at the age of 48 years still proved a draw having played 430 matches for the County between 1891 and 1914. Another active player, Captain **Gilbert Jessop** (GCCC), 14/Manchesters, organised games which were overtly part of the recruitment drive of which he was involved particularly in the summer of 1915 as the enlistment rates began to fall (see Photograph 22).[223] The

---
[221] *Gloucester Journal* 19 June 1915 published a letter from Private **Lionel Hamblin** (GRFC), 5/Gloucesters.
[222] It was not uncommon for the various industries particularly the miners and the dockyard workers to take industrial action for wage increases which they argued were needed to cover the rise in the cost of living which they blamed directly on the Government (*Dean Forest Mercury* 28 May 1915). However throughout the war the miners often raised considerable sums of money for local charities.
[223] *Tamworth Herald* 14 August 1915

proceeds from the cricket matches were given to charity usually the British Red Cross and Gilbert organised a number of games at the Fazeley CC ground which became so useful that it was subsequently leased to him and the other officers of the 14/Manchesters from June until September.²²⁴ On 1 September the match between Sir John Peel's XI and Captain **Gilbert Jessop**'s Brigade XI raised funds for the British Red Cross. The team lists always listed eligible men with their Army or Navy rank which avoided any repercussions particularly from members of the Suffragette Movement.

Photograph 22. Gilbert Jessop (GCCC): Captain Gilbert Jessop, 14/Manchesters, at a recruitment rally in 1915. (*Roger Gibbons*)

The Government's response to the decline in the enlistment rate was the introduction of the National Registration Scheme on 15 July 1915, designed to identify all men <u>and</u> women between the ages of 15 and 65 years; this list would enable the Recruiting Officers to target those men who were deemed eligible for enlistment and were morally seen as not 'doing their duty'.²²⁵ The Government however did understand some of the reticence and Lord Derby, the Director General of Recruiting, introduced the Derby Scheme (Group Scheme) on 11 October which was specifically designed to allow enlisted men to settle their home affairs before actually being called up. The 'Derby men' were

---
²²⁴ *Tamworth Herald* 19 June 1915
²²⁵ The information generated by the National Registration Scheme was unfortunately destroyed shortly after the war.

classified into forty-six groups on the basis of marital status and age which were gradually called up over the coming months beginning with Group 1, youngest single men, through to Group 46, the oldest married men.[226]

The cricket season was also progressing well on the Western Front and the 5/Gloucesters matches were reported in the *Fifth Gloucester Gazette*, extracts of which were published regularly in the *Gloucestershire Chronicle* (see Photograph 23).[227,228,229]

Photograph 23. Fifth Gloucester Gazette: Front cover of the Fifth Gloucester Gazette, August 1915. This magazine written by various members of the 5/Gloucesters was the first of the trench magazines. (*Authors*)

The pursuance of these matches had been made possible by a number of '*Gloucester Sports*' who had clubbed together and provided sufficient kit for the use of the whole Battalion. To commemorate the receipt of the equipment a Gloucester Men's XI played a Rest of the Battalion XI on "*...D Company's field in which a very carefully selected pitch was preserved with matting which somewhat unsettled some of the 'cracks'...*" to create some sort of semblance of an even surface.

---

[226] The Derby Scheme did not solve the recruitment problem and in January 1916 the Government introduced conscription (compulsory enlistment).
[227] *Fifth Gloucester Gazette* 12 July 1915
[228] The *Fifth Gloucester Gazette* was the first of a growing number of trench newspapers. It was written by various 5/Gloucesters' soldiers, particularly F.W. Harvey, the Gloucestershire poet, and produced periodically throughout the war – it often poked fun at the officers and the Army. Twenty-five editions were produced between April 1915 and January 1919. The *Fifth Gloucester Gazette* was revived during the Second World War.
[229] *Gloucestershire Chronicle* 21 August 1915

Cricket pitches and rugby fields even some distance behind the front line suffered the same problems – usually created by the German artillery – and the expertise of the Royal Engineers and the Labour Corps was frequently called upon to alleviate the problem; even so massive shell craters often dictated the size of the field of play. The games were played with an awareness of shells passing overhead and like all experienced soldiers they came to instinctively known how close shells were likely to land although howitzer shells with their almost vertical trajectory proved a lot more problematic. The mix of players for the inaugural game was interesting. In the ranks of the Gloucester XI were Privates **Lionel Hamblin** (GRFC), Will Harvey, **Harry Pollard** (GRFC), **Sidney Sysum** (GRFC), **Bill Egerton** (GRFC), **Frank Mansell** (GRFC**), Fred Webb** (GRFC) and Lieutenant Lionel R.C. Sumner,[230] while the Rest XI contained Lance Corporal **Syd Millard** (GRFC) and Lieutenant **James Winterbotham** (GCCC); the Gloucester Men's XI won by twenty-two runs. Throughout that summer eight other matches were reported in the *Fifth Gloucester Gazette* with **James Winterbotham** (GCCC) and **Gilbert Collett** (GRFC and GCCC) included in the Officers' side. Other Gloucester battalion's cricket matches were frequently reported by the local newspapers particularly that of the 9th Battalion which was captained by Private **Edwin Wootton** (GRFC) although most of its matches were played whilst in training as the Battalion spent only two months on the Western Front before it was transferred to Salonika. **Fred Webb** (GRFC) who had played for the Gloucester XI was soon incapacitated after the accidental explosion of a British bomb which wounded him the face and ear which required hospitalisation.[231]

August:

With the Army established on the Gallipoli peninsula at Anzac Cove and Cape Helles, the front had rapidly deteriorated into a Western Front type stalemate and as a consequence it was decided to force another landing, further north, at Suvla Bay early in August. Supported by a complex deception plan these landings were a success but through a lack of communication and initiative, advantage was not taken of the situation and stalemate rapidly set in there as well.[232] The landings at Suvla Bay took from 10 to 15 August to get all the troops ashore including the 5/Essex (161 (Essex) Brigade, 54th (East Anglia) Division) with Second Lieutenant **Ronald Turner** (GCCC). Ronald had enlisted in the 28/London (Artist's Rifles) and went to France on 22 January 1915 as a Private but rapidly gained a commission and joined 5/Essex on 18 May 1915. By the end of August however Ronald was reported as missing after the recent operations to secure the beachhead and, [233] as his status as a prisoner of war could not be confirmed, in May 1916 he was officially declared as having been 'killed in action' at Suvla Bay on 15 August 1915; his body was never found and he is commemorated amongst the Missing on the Helles Memorial.

---

[230] Will Harvey was the famous Gloucestershire poet and one of the originators of the *Fifth Gloucester Gazette*. For a summary of Will Harvey's military career see Teresa Davies' article *'Frederick William (Will) Harvey – Soldier Poet'* published in the Newsletter of the Friends of the Soldiers of Gloucestershire Museum, Autumn 2013.
[231] *Gloucester Journal* 24 July 1915
[232] Martin Davies, *Conceal, Create, Confuse. Deception as a British Battlefield Tactic in the First World War* (Stroud: Spelmount, 2009), pp.191-95. The deception plan is described in detail.
[233] *Cheltenham Chronicle and Gloucestershire Graphic* 4 September 1915

1915 had not been a good year for Corporal **Theodore Fowler** (GCCC), C Company, 1/Honourable Artillery Company [HAC].[234] On the outbreak of war he had initially enlisted in the University and Public Schools Corps at Epsom but subsequently joined the HAC on 3 October 1915, completed his training on 18 December and landed in France on 29 December, joining C Company in the field on 13 January 1915 at Givenchy-lès-la Bassée where he took part in his first attack on 25 January (see Map 2).[235] He was wounded on 12 March but soon returned to duty. On 17 April at Dickebusch, the HAC having moved north to just south of Ypres, he suffered a gun shot wound to the face and went initially to No.14 General Hospital at Boulogne and subsequently the No.9 General Hospital at Rouen before returning to his unit after only nine days on 26 April. During the attack at Hooge, east of Ypres on 16 June Theodore was found to be suffering from shell shock and thirteen days later from a hernia. He was moved to No.5 CCS at Hazebrouck and subsequently evacuated to the County of London War Hospital where he died of pyrexia (fever) possibly as a result of an infection on 17 August following an operation for his hernia. In his will published in August he left some money to **Cyril Sewell** (GCCC) in "...*recognition of many good times together*..." and to H.C. Stephens, an HAC comrade, "...*in memory...of the arduous times we have had together in the war*"[236]

September:

At 6.30 am on 25 September the I and IV Corps of the British First Army attacked the coal fields north of Lens (Battle of Loos, 25 September-8 October) but in order to prevent the German Army transferring reserves to the main battle sector the British launched a series of timed coordinated diversionary attacks.[237] As part of the latter, thirteen miles from the main battle zone near Armentières, the 20th (Light) Division (III Corps) targeted Bois Grenier at 4.30 am. Amongst the attacking units of the 59 Brigade was the 10/King's Royal Rifle Corps [KRRC] with Rifleman **Tom West** (GRFC) in its ranks. The Division suffered a total of 561 casualties including Tom who was killed when a "...*a bullet passed through the side of his face [and] he died immediately without saying a word...*" in action on 29 September having been at the front for only ten weeks.[238,239] Amongst Tom's effects was an un-posted letter to his mother in which he stated that she "...*must not worry if you don't hear from me. I shall be quite all right...*"[240,241]

Second Lieutenant **Burnet James** (GCCC), 7th Squadron, Royal Flying Corps [RFC], was a pre-war Territorial from 1907 to 1912 with the 1st Gloucestershire Royal Garrison Artillery (Volunteers). On the outbreak of war he re-joined his old unit, now designated CCXL (I South Midland) Brigade, Royal Field Artillery which was part of the Divisional Artillery for the 48th (South Midland) Division. At the end of March the Division had moved to France where the Divisional Artillery supported the infantry

---

[234] The Honourable Artillery Company [HAC] was a gun battery of the Territorial Royal Horse Artillery which also provided infantry units.
[235] Theodore Fowler twice declined a commission (Wisden Obituary)
[236] *Cheltenham Chronicle and Gloucestershire Graphic* 20 October 1915
[237] Davies, *Conceal, Create, Confuse*, pp.87-93. The timed coordinated diversionary attacks are described in detail.
[238] *Gloucester Journal* 9 October 1915
[239] *Bath Chronicle* 16 October 1915
[240] *Bath Chronicle* 9 October 1915
[241] **Tom West** had originally played for Bath RFC and fellow wing at the Club, Bert Lewis was by his side when he was killed; Bert wrote to Tom's parents informing them of his death.

which included the 5/Gloucesters and the majority of the Gloucester rugby players. However Burnet joined the Royal Flying Corps [RFC] in July 1915 and became an observer in a French-designed two-seater *Voisin LA* aircraft used as a bomber or in a ground attack role. By September Burnet and his pilot Second Lieutenant Louis Yule were flying a *BE 2c*, a British designed two-seater biplane used primarily for reconnaissance, artillery observation and aerial photography.[242] On 26 September whilst on a reconnaissance mission over the on-going battle at Loos, the aircraft was damaged by enemy fire which forced Yule to try and land the aircraft but the damage was so great that the aeroplane crashed near Helvele killing both Yule and Burnet James. Both men were buried at Cement House Cemetery near Langemarck.[243] Burnet was initially reported as missing and was not confirmed as dead in Gloucester until February 1916 after extensive searches by the British Red Cross had failed to verify that he was a prisoner of war.[244,245,246]

October:

Despite the deprivations of 'total' war, there were still aspects of life on the home front which carried on regardless. Whilst on leave from the 5/Royal Fusiliers, Lieutenant **Edgar Chester-Master** (GCCC) married Sylvia Butler at Henbury Parish Church although as a reflection of the privations of the war, the ceremony was a small affair with only close relatives invited.[247]

On the Western Front Lieutenant **James Winterbotham** (GCCC), 5/Gloucesters, became the latest player to qualify as a Grenadier from the Brigade Grenade School and joined the already qualified men from the rugby club including **Hubert Barnes, Charles Cook, Lionel Hamblin, Alec Lewis, Syd Millard, William Parham, Percy Simmons, Sid Smart** and **William Washbourne** as Battalion Grenadiers. Only the most athletic and bravest men were chosen to attend the course at the Grenade School to qualify for this dangerous role, the hazardous nature of which was even apparent in training as both **Fred Webb** (GRFC) and **Walter Cromwell** (GRFC) were wounded following accidental explosions.

November:

Throughout **Gilbert Jessop**'s training it had been noticed that his ability as a cricketer had been transferred across to his military role as he could throw the a Mill's Bomb (hand grenade) considerably further and more accurately than any of his comrades and that with his 'flicking' wrist action he was able to throw them without exposing himself above the trench parapet unlike his

---

[242] The French Voison LA or Type III aircraft was essentially a bi-plane bomber but was much was used for reconnaissance. The British BE 2c bi-plane was specifically designed for reconnaissance missions and provided a stable platform to enable the crew to concentrate on objectives and obtain clearer photographs.

[243] David O'Mara, Article September 2012: *26 September 1915 Lieut Burnet George James,* www.westernfrontassociation.com,

[244] *Flight* 8 October 1915

[245] *Flight* 10 December 1915

[246] *Cheltenham Chronicle and Gloucestershire Graphic* 19 February 1916. This article also reported the death of **Francis Roberts** (GCCC) – see Chapter 3 for details.

[247] *Gloucestershire Chronicle* 9 October 1915

fellow throwers.[248,249] However circumstances would conspire against him in June 1916 and he would never go to an active theatre of war.

December 1915-January 1916:

By the autumn it was apparent that the Allied position on the Gallipoli peninsula was now untenable and after an inspection by Kitchener who personally reviewed the situation, the order to evacuate the peninsula was given. The evacuation would pose of major problem with the potential to incur significant numbers of casualties as the Turkish forces dominated the high ground and were easily able to observe any Allied activity and direct their artillery fire accordingly. As the troops had to be evacuated by sea the Turkish artillery would be able to bombard the defenceless troops on beaches totally devoid of any cover! However the British devised an evacuation plan based on deception which convinced the Turks that the British presence on the peninsula was increasing and not decreasing. In December 1915 83,000 men together with animals and equipment were evacuated from the Suvla Bay-Anzac Cove region and even more amazing the deception was repeated for a second time in January 1916 as 36,000 men were evacuated from Cape Helles. The deception plan was so complex and complete that not a single life was lost despite the Allies being in full view of the Turkish positions at all times.[250] Initially the wounded together with equipment, ammunition, stores and animals had been evacuated at night whilst pretending during daylight hours to do the exact opposite.

On the night of 17 December the majority of the 7/Gloucesters consisting of thirteen Officers and 396 Other Ranks and including Lance Corporal **Frank Smith** (GRFC) were evacuated from Suvla Bay to the Island of Mudros, to be joined six days later by the Rear-Guard of two Officers and forty-eight Other Ranks which had been left behind to aid with the deception plan.[251] With only a few days rest the Battalion was on the move again back to the peninsula, landing at V Beach, Cape Helles, at 6.30 pm on 27 December.[252] The Turks had by now discovered that the British troops had 'disappeared' from the Suvla Bay area and were determined that at Cape Helles they were not going to be fooled for a second time. On 7 January 1916 they subjected the British to a six hour artillery bombardment followed by a shrapnel and machine gun barrage but the attendant infantry attack was met with such a ferocious British defence, now bolstered by the 7/Gloucesters, that many of the Turkish infantrymen refused to leave their trenches. The strong defence convinced the Turks that the British Army would remain on the peninsula which helped the British to enact their deception plan for the second time. On 8 January the Turks used "...*a great quantity of Bombs and 'Wiss Bangs'* [sic]..." but failed to prevent the British slipping away; at 9.15 pm in darkness the 7/Gloucesters embarked on SS *Ermine* from W Beach arriving at Mudros early in the morning. For the second time within a month the Turkish forces had been duped without inflicting serious casualties on their enemies and after a

---

[248] Brodribb, *The Croucher,* p.180
[249] The distance that **Gilbert Jessop** (GRCC) could throw the hand grenade was not recorded but twenty yards was the average so presumably Gilbert's was considerably further.
[250] Davies, *Conceal, Create, Confuse*, pp.195-200. Full details of the British deception plan which completely concealed the evacuation of the Gallipoli peninsula.
[251] This Rear-Guard would spend a lot of time running around and firing rifles pretending that they were in fact fifteen officers and 444 ORs rather than simple two officers and forty-eight ORs
[252] Battalion War Diary, *7th Battalion, Gloucestershire Regiment 18-27 December 1915* TNA WO 95/4302

brief stay at Mudros the 7/Gloucesters sailed for Alexandria in Egypt for a month of rest and training before joining the North Persian Force in Mesopotamia (modern day Iraq).

Throughout 1914 and 1915 the local British newspapers published detailed reports of soldiers and their units, and sometimes even their marital status, home addresses and employers, which could be used by the enemy whilst interrogating British prisoners of war [POWs] to portray themselves as more knowledgeable of British units than they actually were which could trick the POWs into revealing sensitive military details. In early December the Government used the Defence of the Realm Act [DORA] to ban the publication of recruit details and the movement of British Army units.[253] The ban came into immediate effect although some local newspapers, the *Dursley, Berkeley and Sharpness Gazette* for example continued to publish this type of information for a few more months.

---

[253] *Dean Forest Mercury* 10 December 1915

For Club, King and Country

3

1916: INDUSTRIALISED MODERN WARFARE. THE REAL COST

"...kept on firing until they were on and each man was surrounded by three or four Turks."
Lieutenant A.W. Strickland on the Battle of Katia, 23 April 1916

"...died like all True British Blood Heros [sic]..."
Extract from a letter by Private James Skidmore, dated 6 July 1916, on the death of John Price (GRFC).

"...German machine guns for the most part unharmed by the British bombardment – opened with deadly effect".
Extract from the British Official History on the Battle of Pozières Ridge.

The main focus for the British Army in 1916 would be the 142 days of the Somme Offensive which began on 1 July, a day which became synonymous with the Great War as a whole. The British attack across the River Ancre in the Department of the Somme advanced the front line about five miles and resulted in 419,654 casualties (95,675 killed), of which 57,470 (19,240 killed) were on the first day alone. In the history of the Great War this offensive was characterised by the test of blood and steel for Kitchener's New Army - raised from August 1914 onwards, the men were trained, equipped and ready for their first battle and amongst these men were volunteers from the Gloucester Rugby Club and the Gloucestershire County Cricket Club.[254] However the Somme Offensive was only one of a

---

[254] The Somme Offensive was not the first battle deployment of Kitchener New Army units as some had been deployed at the Battle of Loos in September 1915 but it was the first mass deployment and was very much a 'Kitchener's New Army battle'.

number of actions across the globe which would not go according to plan for the Allies. For the British and French the withdrawal from Gallipoli, however successful, had been a blow to their prestige and a boost to the morale of the Turkish and German forces.[255] In April in Mesopotamia the British would surrender at Kut following a 147 day long siege by Turkish forces after all attempts to relieve the city had failed. In Egypt and Palestine the British were engaged by Turkish forces intent on seizing the strategically important Suez Canal while in Salonika British and French Army units found themselves up against a well organised Bulgarian Army which had significantly strengthened its defensive positions before aligning itself to the Central Powers. In Italy the Italian Army struggled in the fifth, sixth, seventh, eighth and ninth Battles of the Isonzo against the Austro-Hungarian Army.

January:
Young men between seventeen and nineteen years of age were still eager to join up as officers. Basic military education for these under-aged men was provided at the Bristol Officer Training Corps [OTC] with the result that to-date 356 of the OTC Cadets had gained commissions with British Army units although it was noted that there was a "…*pronounced*…" difference between these 'short-trained' men and peace-trained officers. There were still a further one hundred Cadets in training and, to provide experienced instructors, the local OTCs in Bristol exchanged '*distinguished*' visitors to supplement the training. Notably Lieutenant Ridley and Second Lieutenant **Alan Imlay** (GCCC) from the Clifton College OTC supported the Bristol University Contingent during the school vacation with informal talks and lectures.[256]

February:
Not all of the deaths in the Army would be as a direct result of enemy action as the harsh environment experienced by the recruits both in training and in action made deaths inevitable. Lance-Corporal **Trevor Powell** (GRFC), 5/Gloucesters, "…*one of the most promising footballers in the City* [and] *a great favourite with his playing colleagues*…", a part-time, peace-time Territorial soldier, had, during the period of intensive training at Chelmsford, developed a serious illness which affected his effectiveness as an NCO and prevented him from going with his battalion to France in March 1915.[257] After recovering in a sanatorium, he was assigned to work in a munitions factory, but the illness returned and in January he was admitted to the First Eastern General Hospital in Cambridge, a hospital established in 1908 by the Royal Army Medical Corps [RAMC] for the treatment of both officers and men. However Trevor's condition deteriorated and he died on 3 February and was buried in a military grave in Gloucester Old Cemetery. He was commemorated on the Gloucester War Memorial and by the CWGC despite never having seen action. It is often thought that war memorials commemorate only those who were killed in action or died of wounds received in action, but a significant proportion of men died from illnesses contracted during military service. Some of these illnesses were attributable to the campaign theatre – for instance men of the Mediterranean Expeditionary Force who fought on the Gallipoli peninsula were exposed to 'exotic' diseases which life in Britain had not prepared them for and for which vaccines were ineffective or non-existent.

---

[255] The French forces had withdrawn from the Gallipoli peninsula by 24 December before the British Army had enacted the deception plan and withdrawn its forces.
[256] *Western Daily Press* 10 January 1916
[257] *Gloucester Journal* 5 February 1916

Others became susceptible to other illnesses, due to the harsh regime and extreme conditions of training and active service. Hence men could become casualties of war without ever being exposed to enemy fire - clearly such men deserve their places on the Rolls of Honour and War Memorials.

Although there were no major offensives in the Ypres Salient throughout 1916 the Germans, early in the year, launched a number of attacks designed to distract the Allies from the build-up of their forces in front of Verdun where the Germans would launch their attack on 27 February in an offensive aimed at *'bleeding France white'*.[258] In the northern sector of the Ypres Salient Captain **Francis Roberts** (GCCC), 9/Rifle Brigade, was killed in action at St Julien on 8 February 1916 during the build-up of German forces for a 'distraction' attack at Pilckem on 12 February. Francis had played sixty-seven cricket matches for Gloucestershire between 1906 and 1914 and would have gone on to play many more had the war not cut short his career.[259] He was a Tutor of the Beresford Dormitory at Wellington College and had temporarily left his position to take up a commission in the Army in December 1914.

March:

Despite the war both the rugby and cricket clubs on the Home Front were still accumulating expenses which for the cricket club related mainly to servicing of their existing debt. The Chairman, Henry Beloe, appealing for donations, indicated that over fifty Club members had already paid their annual subscriptions despite the absence of any cricket.[260] Between July 1914 and July 1916 the club collected over £600 in subscriptions and raised the expectation that it could resume debt free after the war; there is no doubt that bizarrely the Great War actually contributed to the survival of the cricket club which undoubtedly would have ceased to exist due to its accumulating debt.[261]

The brothers **Frank Stout** (GRFC) and **Percy Stout** (GRFC) had been working together in Cairo since 1900 but in keeping with their philosophy *"...of going through life side by side* [they had both] *given up their civilian work in Egypt for the King* [of Egypt]..." and had returned to Britain to serve their country. Although Frank had briefly been a Private in the Artists Rifle Corps, both men attended an officer's training course at Colchester and obtained commissions as Second Lieutenants in the cavalry unit, the 20th Hussars.[262] On 15 March Second Lieutenant Frank Stout working as the Machine Gun officer in a 'quiet' sector north of the Somme was awarded the Military Cross [MC],[263]

> "...For conspicuous gallantry and resource. When he heard of an enemy working party in the vicinity [of the British wire], *he took a corporal* [George Tester, later Sergeant] *and a light machine gun down a sap, mounted the corporal on his back to enable the latter to fire over the parapet, and opened fire. Later, mounted on the Corporal's back, Lieut Stout opened fire, although by this time they had been discovered. Next morning fourteen dead enemy were counted, and more must have been wounded."* [264,265]

[258] Davies, *Conceal, Create, Confuse*, p.98-100. This account details the German Army's 'distraction' strategy.
[259] *Cheltenham Chronicle and Gloucestershire Graphic* 19 February 1916. This same article confirmed the death of **Burnet James**, previously reported as missing.
[260] *Western Daily Press* 24 March 1916
[261] *Western Daily Press* 31 July 1916
[262] *The Citizen* 11 September 1914
[263] Pre-war the machine gun was initially a cavalry weapon which was subsequently incorporated into infantry units
[264] *London Gazette* 16 March 1916

The citation for Corporal George Tester, who was awarded the Distinguished Conduct Medal [DCM], stated that he fired at least 150 rounds at the enemy who were thirty to forty yards away before Frank took over and that throughout they were under heavy enemy fire.[266] Frank was an England International with fourteen caps as well as seven caps for the British Isles (*aka* British Lions) on tours to Australia and South Africa. To keep up the family tradition, his brother Percy, another England Rugby International, would win the Distinguished Service Order [DSO] for gallantry in 1917.[267]

April:

After recovering from its experiences in Gallipoli, the 7/Gloucesters (39 Brigade, 13th (Western) Division) had been transferred to Mesopotamia in February 1916 to assist in a conflict which had been on-going since 1914. The country had proved particularly challenging for the British military with its hostile climate and lack of a suitable road and rail infrastructure, with the only feasible means of travel being along the Tigris and Euphrates rivers. Since 7 December 1915 the major British garrison at Kut, about one hundred miles south of Baghdad, had been under siege despite several British attempts to relieve it at a cost of 30,000 casualties. In April another relief force, led by the 13th (Western) Division fought its way along the Tigris capturing Bait Aisa north east of Kut on 17 April. The next obstacle, Sannaiyat, was attacked on 22 April but failed to relief Kut and resulted in significant numbers of casualties; the 13,000 strong British garrison subsequently surrendered to the Turkish forces on 29 April 1916.[268] Sadly the battle for Kut cost the life of Lance Corporal **Frank Smith** (GRFC) who was reported missing on 21 April 1916 and whose death was officially acknowledged two months later after it was established that he had not been taken prisoner.

Besides Mesopotamia the British Army were also up against Ottoman Empire forces in Egypt and although it was considered as a safe staging post for men returning from Gallipoli, the country and particularly the vital link of the Suez Canal were under constant threat from attacks from the east. From the wastelands of the Sinai Desert the routes of attack were dictated by the water supplies and although the wells and oases were well known the vast distances involved made the defence of the canal difficult.

The men of the RGH now re-united with their horses after their Gallipoli adventures, were fanned out across the desert in a defensive shield with effectively their backs to the Suez Canal. The British, accustomed to desert warfare having spent large periods of the nineteenth century in just such environments, established the advanced headquarters of the No.3 (Northern) Sector at Kantara (Qantara) to control the defensive network at the northern end of the Suez Canal. In January 1916 construction began on a new rail link and water pipeline from Kantara across the desert towards Rumani (Romani) pushing the effective British operational base towards Sinai and Palestine. This

---

[265] *Gloucester Journal* 11 March 1916
[266] Corporal, later Sergeant, George Tester was a professional soldier who had joined the Hussars in 1910. He survived the war and retired from the Army in 1920 and died in 1974 (*Information supplied by* Helen Mary Smith (née Tester), granddaughter of George Tester).
[267] See www.gloucesterrugbyheritage.org.uk for profiles of **Frank** and **Percy Stout** by Malc King
[268] The British tried to broker a deal with the Turks for the release of the garrison in return for £2 million pounds and an assurance that they would not fight the Turks again but the offer was rejected which turned out to be a costly mistake. New British commanders were appointed and through the employment of new methods a decisive victory was achieved in February 1917 which contributed, along with victories in Palestine, to the armistice signed by the Ottoman Empire on 1 October 1918

would create a viable route into Palestine following a series of oases but equally it would be attractive to the Turkish forces moving in a westward direction, enabling them to launch attacks against the Canal. The developing infrastructure was protected by the British 5 Mounted Brigade (OC, Brigadier General Edgar Askin Wiggin) consisting of the Warwickshire Yeomanry, the Queen's Own Worcestershire Hussars and the RGH including Captain **Hugo Charteris, Lord Elcho** (GCCC) (A Squadron) (see Photograph 24) and **Alfred Dipper** (GCCC) (D Squadron). In April the Brigade was scattered over twenty miles across a large tract of open desert from Oghratina in the north-west to Dueider in the south-east; A Squadron together with the machine gun section was stationed at Katia (Qatia) with orders to hold its position in the event of a Turkish attack.

Photograph 24. Hugo Charteris, Lord Elcho (1884-1916): Hugo Charteris, A Squadron, Royal Gloucestershire Hussars, was killed at the Battle of Katia, 23 April 1916 (*CCGG*)

On 23 April (Easter Sunday) the Ottoman Forces advanced early in the morning at Oghratina, Katia and Dueider in a series of co-ordinated attacks. At 5.30 am amidst thick fog the men of A Squadron could see discernible shapes moving about and as there was no reply to a challenge, **Hugo Charteris** ordered his men to open fire forcing the enemy troops to retire. The British troops had been ordered by Captain Michael Lloyd-Baker (OC, A Squadron) to spread out to create the illusion that they were a much bigger force although this would also have created a defensive weakness. At about 9.15 am long range Turkish rifle fire commenced as they organised for a frontal attack supported by their artillery whose shrapnel rounds caused many casualties amongst the British troops and in the horse lines in the rear. The Turkish troops began to outflank the British positions, which made it impossible to cover the whole of the attack with the single available machine gun and at 500 yards the Turks mounted a bayonet charge. The British,

> "...kept on firing until they were on and each man was surrounded by three or four Turks."[269]

By 3.00 pm the camp at Katia had been overrun by 3,000 Turkish troops with the British casualties eventually listed as four officers killed, two wounded and taken prisoner while sixteen yeomen were killed, fifteen wounded, fifty-one taken prisoners and ten wounded and taken prisoner.[270,271] One of the prisoners was Corporal Hugh Walwin, brother of **Oscar Walwin** (GRFC) a former RGH trooper now attached to the 2/Worcesters, who wrote about his experience as a prisoner of war,

> "Several weeks had now passed. Insufficient food and water, a relentless sun produced a callous feeling of Why was I not shot at Katia?"[272]

On 29 April it was reported in Gloucester that Hugo Charteris had been wounded and taken prisoner.[273] Further information followed when the British Red Cross received information from the Ottoman Red Crescent that Hugo had indeed been wounded and was now a prisoner in Damascus.[274,275] However within three weeks it was announced that despite the previous reports Hugo had been killed in action at Katia on 23 April.[276] Apparently he had been wounded twice and after having his wounds dressed each time had insisted on going back to the front line where he was subsequently killed. His body was never recovered and identified after the battle and he is commemorated on the Jerusalem Memorial to the Missing killed in Egypt and Palestine. A memorial service for Hugo was held in Stanway Church on 16 July attended by family, friends and members of the Royal Gloucestershire Hussars Yeomanry; on the altar steps were his busby, sword and stirrups.[277]

---

[269] Lieutenant A.W. Strickland quoted from exhibition on the Battle of Katia at the *Soldiers of Gloucestershire Museum*. Lieutenant Strickland was captured as a Prisoner of War at the battle
[270] Statistics taken from the exhibition on the Battle of Katia at the *Soldiers of Gloucestershire Museum*
[271] As only nine men escaped unharmed this would represent a 92% casualty rate among A Squadron, RGH, at Katia (Statistics from SoGM Exhibition and Rollo Clifford, *The Royal Gloucestershire Hussars* (Stroud: Alan Sutton Publishing Inc., 1991), p.9)
[272] Corporal Hugh Walwin, quoted from exhibition on the Battle of Katia at the *Soldiers of Gloucestershire Museum*
[273] *Gloucestershire Chronicle* 29 April 1916
[274] *Gloucestershire Chronicle* 17 June 1916
[275] The International Red Cross based in Switzerland co-ordinated activities between the national organisations. As a result all belligerents including the British, Germans and Turks (Red Crescent), would determine whether soldiers posted as missing were in fact prisoners of war and on a regular basis lists would be exchanged. Hence the Ottoman Red Crescent informed the British Red Cross via the neutral international organisation in Switzerland regarding the status of **Hugo Charteris** (GCCC).
[276] *Gloucestershire Chronicle* 8 July 1916
[277] *Cheltenham Chronicle and Gloucestershire Graphic* 22 July 1916

On 23 April 1919 the surviving members of A Squadron, RGH, who had been repatriated after imprisonment in Turkey, met at the Saracen's Head Hotel, Eastgate Street, Gloucester, for an anniversary dinner to commemorate the Battle of Katia. The perennial question arose again about the orders sent or not sent to Captain Michael Lloyd-Baker, Officer Commanding A Squadron, regarding holding its position and why only nine men of A Squadron had managed to escape. There was a consensus that,

> "...so far as A Squadron was concerned, they obeyed orders and could not have done more. There was some doubt as to orders, but orders did actually arrive during the day telling them to hold on. After that no further orders came through."[278,279]

The situation that the RGH found itself in regarding orders had arisen due to various circumstances. Brigadier General Edgar Askin Wiggin, Officer Commanding, 5th Mounted Brigade, based on intelligence, had gone to raid a Turkish camp at Bir el Mageibra but finding it empty returned to Hamisah where he now learnt of the serious situation that had developed at Katia in his absence.[280] After watering the horses he set out for Katia with several squadrons from the Worcester Yeomanry but met considerable Turkish opposition and observing that the Gloucesters' camp was in flames, retired to Romani.[281] The last orders that the Gloucesters had received was to hold their position which they did as disaster overtook the defenders.[282]

In Gloucester on a lighter note, the recovering wounded soldiers from the VA Hospitals including **George Halford** (GRFC) beat their orderlies in a game of rugby on Easter Saturday at the Kingsholm Athletic Ground in a match which was kicked off by the Mayor, Sir James Bruton. A return match was organised for early October. The staff at the Great Western and the Palace VA Hospitals encouraged the recuperating soldiers to engage in sporting activities as an aid to recovery.

May:

With the introduction of conscription in January more men entered the Armed Forces, in a controlled manner, to fill up the vast training camps, particularly across Salisbury Plain. With the summer upon them requests were made, similar to those made in spring of 1915, for cricket clubs and old cricketers to hand over any equipment they did not need as large amounts were needed to meet the demands in the camps.[283] The requests, made through the pages of the *Western Daily Press* in Bristol, were answered with generous contributions with the result that Captain A.J. Garner, 4/Gloucesters, stated that games were now taking place most evenings. Further kit was also sent to the recovering soldiers at Southmead Hospital (Southmead Section, 2nd Southern General Hospital) which no doubt aided in their recuperation.[284] The Great Western VA Hospital in Gloucester continued with its games and the 'boys', this time ably supported by their orderlies played two

---

[278] *Gloucestershire Chronicle* 26 April 1919
[279] Captain Michael Lloyd-Baker was killed at Katia on 23 July 1916 and hence after the war could not explain the situation regarding the orders.
[280] Edgar Wiggin was a cricketer who played for Edgbaston CC (www.cricketarchive.com)
[281] John Robertson, *With the Cameliers in Palestine* (Dunedin: Reed Publising (NZ) Ltd, 1938), pp.59-62 (available from New Zealand Electronic Collection (NWETC), Victoria University of Wellington Library)
[282] The men who died at Katia are commemorated amongst the 225 names on the Royal Gloucestershire Hussars Memorial on College Green, Gloucester, which was unveiled in 1922.
[283] *Western Daily Press* 16 May 1916
[284] *Western Daily Press* 3 July 1916

games early in June against Leckhampton with the honours being shared; the Great Western home game was played at the King's School ground.[285]

June:
Gilbert Jessop (GCCC), suffering from ruptured muscles and severe lumbago, a condition aggravated by trench digging, was now medically classified as "...*lame*..." and was prescribed a course of radiant heat treatment at Bath; the Medical Officer was confident that this would cure Gilbert's condition and that he would be unfit for only "...*1 month*..."[286,287] The course involved total immersion in steam between 100-150°C for up to thirty minutes but following a malfunction of the equipment, during the absence of the attendant, which prevented Gilbert's escape from the contraption, his heart was seriously damaged.[288] The incident would subsequently prevent Gilbert entering a theatre of war.[289] By November 1917 after two years and eleven months of service he was described by the Army doctors as "...*permanently unfit* [and that] *his condition* [was] *unlikely to improve*." His 'celebrity' status however was put to good use and on 15 November 1917 he was appointed as a Second Grade Recruiting Officer within the Ministry of National Service based at Stafford, responsible directly to the Director of Recruiting for the West Midlands Region at Queen's College, Birmingham. Gilbert relinquished his commission on 28 August 1918.[290]

July:
With the fight for Verdun (Battle of Verdun, 21 February-18 December 1916) raging on the Western Front, the Allies main offensive now aimed to tie down as many German troops as possible to prevent their transfer to the Verdun sector. However as circumstances changed the offensive initially planned as an Anglo-French venture became a predominantly British affair although a considerable number of French forces were involved in the southernmost sectors.

The biggest challenge for the British Army as a Continental Army was now imminent as the majority of the civilian-soldiers of Kitchener's New Army faced their first battle - the months of training and skill acquisition would now be tested far from the tranquil training grounds of Britain and the 'quiet' sectors of the Western Front. The real cost of industrialised warfare was about to become all too apparent to these men and to the Home Front population. For the former the reality would come within seconds of 'going over the top' while for the latter the truth would emerge throughout August as the column inches dedicated to the casualty lists in the local newspapers markedly increased; the positive statements issued by Government and General Headquarters throughout August and September regarding progress were challenged by these 'column inches'.

---

[285] The Citizen 16 June 1916
[286] *Bath Chronicle and Weekly Gazette* 10 June 1916
[287] Captain Gilbert Jessop, 14/Manchesters, Service Record TNA WO 339/15674-C577072
[288] Brodribb, *The Croucher*, p.180
[289] *Newcastle Journal* 12 August 1918
[290] *Gloucester Journal* 31 August 1918

Photograph 25. No.13 Platoon, D Company, 1/5th Gloucesters: This photograph is one of a series taken of the different platoons outside of the same building near Ovillers in July 1916. In the front row, second from the left is Lance Corporal **William Washbourne** (GRFC) who would win the Military Medal in October 1916 and on his left is Sergeant **Sydney Millard** (GRFC) who would be killed in action at Pozières on 23 July 1916. (*Roger Hlam*)

For the majority of the rugby players, as well as some of the cricketers, this would be *their* testing time and although none would be involved on 1 July their services would be called upon in the following days as Day One objectives remained unsecured and the support and reserve formations were moved up to 'have a go'. On the Somme the rugby players and cricketers were in three of the divisions, the 17th (Northern) Division (including 9/Northumberland Fusiliers, 52 Brigade), the 19th (Western) Division (including 10/Worcesters and 8/Gloucesters, 57 Brigade) and the 48th (South Midland) Division (including the 5/Gloucesters, 145 Brigade); all three divisions were in support on 1 July.

Orders were issued prior to the assault to all attacking and support units which warned that "*...too much credence should not be given to the opinions of wounded men* [and that] *assisting a wounded man to the rear is a court martial offence...*"[291] The previous war involving Britain, the Boer War (1899-1902), would result in the deaths of 21,312 soldiers in just over two-and-a-half years; on 1 July Britain would lose almost that number over a period of twelve hours.[292]

In the last week of June all three divisions gradually moved into their support positions ready for the 'Big Push'. The southernmost division, the 17th (Northern) Division included Captain **Oswald**

---

[291] Battalion War Diary, *11th Battalion, Suffolk Regiment 1 July 1916 (Battalion Orders)*, WO95/2458
[292] Zero hour on 1st July was 7.30 am and the last bulletin of the day sent by Fourth Army Headquarters was at 6.50 pm although some units continued operations for a while longer depending on their situation.

Wreford-Brown (GCCC) serving with the 9/Northumberland Fusiliers. On 30 June the battalion was entrenched at the XV Corps Reserve Line near Morlancourt, but at 8.30 pm on 1 July the 17th (Northern) Division was ordered to take over the 21st Division front line sector opposite Fricourt (Day One objective) (See Map 2).[293]

Photograph 26. John Price's (GRFC) Postcard: Coloured embroidered postcards created by the French were a favoured means for the British soldiers to send messages home. Private **John Price**, 10/Worcesters, sent this one to his wife, Laurel, at Tredworth Road, Gloucester, with a message written on the back which read, *"To my dearest wife and son from your dearest husband Jack and I hope you will have a good time from your ever loving husband Jack. Good night and God bless you both, Kiss to you both xxxxxx"*. Owing to their delicate nature these post cards were usually send within an envelope and as such no date is available for this postcard. (*Mike Kean-Price*)

A similar situation awaited the men of the 19th (Western) Division (the 'Butterfly' Division) which included the 8/Gloucesters and 10/Worcesters.[294] On 16 June the 8/Gloucesters with the rugby players Sergeant **Arthur Saunders**, **William Nelmes**, Lieutenant **Hugh Thomas**, **Frank Ayliffe**, **Harry Cook**,[295] **Ernest Hall**, **William Dix**, **Arthur Goddard** and **William Sysum** moved to Rainneville, thirteen miles west of Albert and spent the next ten days practicing physical drills and honing their battle skills (See Map 2). On 27 June the Battalion moved to Franvillers Wood for further training. The

---
[293] James Edmonds, *History of the Great War. Military Operations France and Belgium 1916 Vol I: Douglas Haig's Command to 1st July: Battle of the Somme* (London: Macmillan, 1932), p.367
[294] The 19th (Western) Division was known as the 'Butterfly' Division because of its divisional emblem. The memorial to these men erected in the 1920s at La Boisselle is known as the Butterfly Memorial.
[295] Harry Cook would be invalidated out of the Army on 3 July 1917 after being wounded in the hand.

10/Worcesters with Privates **John Price** (GRFC) (see Photograph 26) and **Harry Collins** (GRFC) had also moved initially into the same area but then onto Dernancourt, just south of Albert, for its additional training. By 8.30 pm on 30 June both battalions had marched the final few miles and filed into the III Corps Reserve Line assembly trenches at Millencourt within sound of the seven day long British artillery bombardment of the German lines. The following morning with the explosions of the vast mines at La Boisselle and Y Sap reverberating around the countryside, the battalions moved closer to the front.

The 8/Gloucesters and 10/Worcesters moved first to the Intermediate Line, north of Albert near Aveluy and by 10.00 pm to the Tara-Usna Line, 900 yards from La Boisselle (Day One objective), where they remained throughout 2 July. As they moved up throughout 1 July they became all too aware of the increasing casualties suffered by the British as the wounded travelled in a continuous convoy back to the Casualty Clearing Stations; these men were the 'lucky' ones. Unlike the men who went over the top on 1 July, the men of the 57 Brigade were now under no illusions of what would greet them as soon as they left the comparative safety of their trenches. Although they had been ordered not to give "...*too much credence to the opinions of wounded men*...", they were now more than capable of forming their own opinions!

On 2 July the XV Corps Commander, Lieutenant General Sir Henry Horne ordered the 17th (Northern) Division to capture Fricourt, the scene of heavy fighting the previous day. The assault was scheduled for 12.15 pm after a seventy-five minute bombardment. However early in the morning patrols reported that Fricourt was now lightly held following a German retirement and at noon with relative ease the 17th (Northern) Division captured the village.

At 1.30 am on 3 July the 8/Gloucesters and 10/Worcesters moved into the front line opposite La Boisselle. At 2.15 am the attack commenced with the 10/Worcesters covering the right flank which resulted in the capture of the village at 3.15 pm. The 8/Gloucesters, commanded by Lieutenant Colonel Adrian Carton de Wiart, attacked from St Andrew's Trench in what was described as a soldiers' battle where "....*the fighting was hand to hand and at point blank range, with bombs, bullets or cold steel*..."[296,297] Throughout the following day the men consolidated their positions utilising the old German dugouts, in readiness to repulse the inevitable German counter-attack. As the last Germans were forced out of La Boisselle they fired red flares as a signal to their artillery, which had pre-registered on the dug outs in the village, that there was no German infantry left in La Boisselle only British 'Tommies'.[298] The battle for La Boisselle cost the lives of Private **John Price** (GRFC) and Private **Harry Collins** (GRFC), the latter sheltering in a dugout during the German

---

[296] H. FitzM Stacke, Captain, *The Worcestershire Regiment in the Great War* (Kidderminster: Cheshire and Sons, 1928), pp.169-171 (reprinted by The Naval and Military Press Limited)

[297] Lieutenant Colonel Adrian Carton de Wiart (1880-1963) in 1916 was attached to the Gloucestershire Regiment. Having lost an eye and his left hand in 1915 he famously threw grenades at La Boisselle by pulling out the pins with his teeth. He was awarded the Victoria Cross for his actions at La Boisselle when he took command of three other battalions whose commanders had become casualties. He was shot through the skull and ankle on the Somme, through the hip at Passchendaele, through the leg at Cambrai and the ear at Arras. He survived the war only to fight again in the Second World War including being taken prisoner after the plane he was in crashed into the sea.

[298] 'Tommy' was the slang for an ordinary British soldier and was the generic name used by the War Office showing how to fill out a Soldier's Pocket Book. There are various explanations put forward for this choice of name, one being that the Duke of Wellington after the Battle of Boxtel (1794) asked the name of a dying soldier ; he replied Private Thomas Atkins who explained away his fatal wounds as '*all in a day's work*'.

bombardment. Although a pre-war Reservist Harry Collins had been discharged as "...*permanently unfit, fit only for light duties...*" and need not have been at the front. On 9 January 1915, Harry fighting with the 1/Worcesters had been shot in the hand as he passed his rifle to his Corporal as they were crossing a ditch. After twelve weeks in hospital and several operations which included the amputation of his 'trigger' finger he was discharged, but somehow he taught himself to shoot and bayonet fight with his 'wrong' hand despite the unavailability of left-handed rifles and subsequently returned to France on 25 February 1916 with the 10/Worcesters. In letters sent back to Gloucester by surviving comrades these men were described as having,

"...*died like all True British Blood Heros* [sic] *in the past for King and Country and...dear ones at home...* "[299]

All of the rugby players in the 8/Gloucesters survived the capture of La Boisselle with Sergeant **Arthur Saunders** (GRFC) recommended for the Military Medal after leading his machine gun team through the brutally contested ruins. On 5 July the 57 Brigade moved back towards Albert into billets near the railway station where the men spent the following day cleaning their equipment and re-organising their units to compensate for the gaps in their ranks; the fight for La Boisselle cost the 8/Gloucesters twenty Officer casualties and 282 amongst the Other Ranks. On 7 July the men were treated to the luxury of a bath before they returned to Millencourt.

For the 17th (Northern) Division, its tasks were not finished with the capture of Fricourt for beyond lay Mametz Wood and although patrols had reported that the German defences in the wood were at best non-existent and at worst only lightly manned, advantage was not taken of this situation. Lieutenant General Horne delayed his order for a surprise attack against the southernmost tip of the Mametz Wood, Wood Trench and Quadrangle Trench until 5 July. After a thirty minute bombardment the attack began at 12.45 am under the cover of darkness and in heavy driving rain. The leading battalions, including the 9/Northumberland Fusiliers, had, before zero hour, crept undetected to within one hundred yards of the enemy positions. They then "...*charged in securing Quadrangle Trench and Shelter Alley* [but] *German machine gun fire was too severe...*" and hampered by uncut wire Mametz Wood and Wood Trench were not secured.[300] During the capture of Quadrangle Trench Captain **Oswald Wreford-Brown** (GCCC) was severely wounded by shell fire and evacuated back to the Casualty Clearing Station near Corbie where he died of his wounds two days later (see Photograph 27).[301,302]

---

[299] Extract taken from a letter written by Private James E. Skidmore, 10/Worcesters, and sent to the Laurel Price, the widow of John Price, dated Thursday 6 July 1916.
[300] Wilfred Miles, *History of the Great War. Military Operations France and Belgium, 1916. Vol II 2nd July 1916 to the End of the Battles of the Somme* (London: HMSO, 1938), p.21
[301] **Oswald Wreford-Brown** (GCCC) was buried at the Corbie Communal Cemetery Extension.
[302] *De Ruvigny's Roll of Honour* Volume 3 (1922) p.39

Photograph 27. The The Grave of Oswald Wreford-Brown (GCCC): The photograph shows the original grave marker of **Oswald Wreford-Brown** in the cemetery at Corbie Communal Cemetery Extension before it was replaced by a GWGC headstone. Oswald died on 7 July 1916. Other designs for the original grave markers can be seen in the background (*www.19141918.moonfruit.com Tideway School*)

As the Somme Offensive developed other battalions, including the 5/Gloucesters, were brought in to replace the tired and badly depleted battalions previously engaged in the fierce fighting. The 5/Gloucesters (145 Brigade, 48th (South Midland) Division) had been engaged further north holding the line at Hébuterne where the enterprising local French population produced postcards of the location which they sold to the British troops and which conveyed the devastation wreaked on the towns and villages by Germans. These postcards were usually sent home by the Tommies and **Percy Simmons** (GRFC) sent large numbers to his wife, Violet, in Gloucester (see Photographs 28 and 29).

Photograph 28. Hébuterne - Percy Simmons' (GRFC) Postcard: A postcard sent from Hébuterne whilst the 1/5th Gloucesters held there the line there in July 1916 by Corporal **Percy Simmons** (GRFC), A Company, to his wife Violet in Gloucester. The postcard conveyed some of the destruction to relatives back home and showed that no building was immune from artillery shells. (*David and Jackie Brown*)

On 17 July the Battalion moved by motor lorries first to Couin and subsequently to Bouzincourt. The following day the Battalion dug new trenches east of Ovillers before moving into captured German trenches north-east of the village in preparation for an attack on the next obstacle the fortified village of Pozières. On 19 July it was ordered to capture the German defences in front of Pozières between Points 79 and 40 but found uncut wire and strong resistance. Further attacks were ordered in conjunction with the 1/4th Oxford and Bucks Light Infantry but were 'greeted' with heavy shell and machine gun fire and resulted in 115 casualties in the Gloucesters' A and C Companies, of which fifty-three were killed or missing. Under the cover of darkness B and D Companies had a go but the defenders were resolute and resulted in a further seven casualties. The attack by D Company had been,

> "…held up by machine gun fire [and on entering the German trenches the soldiers] *found a machine gun mounted at a barricade to fire directly down the straight length of the trench. Weather fine.*"[303]

On 23 July a major attack was launched in conjunction with other battalions from the 145 Brigade, with on its left the 4th and 6th Battalions (TF), Gloucestershire Regiment from the 144 Brigade, the former having Lieutenant **Horace Merrick** (GCCC) in its ranks and on its right the 1st Australian

---

[303] Battalion War Diary, *1/5th Battalion, Gloucestershire Regiment 21 July 1916*, TNA WO 95/2763

Division.[304] The 5/Gloucesters had to attack uphill, as the enemy trench line followed the contours, along the end of Mash Valley with the result that there were German defences to the front *and* on both sides of the 5/Gloucesters' attack![305] After a preliminary bombardment the attack went in at 12.30 am but as the infantry advanced the,

> "...*German machine guns* [along the light railway track] – *for the most part unharmed by the British bombardment – opened with deadly effect. In the 144th Brigade the 1/6th Gloucestershire was literally mown down* [while] *the 1/5th Gloucestershire fared little better...*"[306,307]

The attack resulted in 156 casualties including five Gloucester rugby players who were initially reported as missing – Sergeant **Syd Millard**, Lance Corporal **Sidney Sysum**, Corporal **Melville Lewis**, Lance Corporal **Tom Lewis** and Private **James Griffiths**.[308] In the aftermath of the attack there was confusion and in a letter to Syd's mother, Mrs Alice Millard, from the Reverend George Helm, the 5/Gloucesters' Chaplain, published in *The Citizen*, he reported that,

> "...*her son and several others were seen to jump down into a German trench from which they did not return.*"[309]

There was no further news of the men, posted as killed in action in the Official Casualty List issued on 8 September, despite Mrs Millard's desperate quest for information through the pages of the *Cheltenham Chronicle and Gloucestershire Graphic* in which Syd's photograph appeared with the caption,

> "...*Sergt. Sydney Millard, Gloucestershire Regt., missing since going into action July 23rd. Son of Mrs Millard, Pincote Farm, Upton St. Leonards, Glos., who would be grateful for any information of him.*" [310]

It would be ten years before further details publically emerged. At a memorial service on 11 April 1926 at All Saints Church for Sidney Brown, who had served with 7/Gloucesters and who died following an injury sustained in a game for Gloucester against Aberavon, the Reverend Helm recalled the events of 23 July 1916,

> "...*no one was surprised when the whole of the Gloucester Fifteen joined up at the outbreak of war. Many of them enlisted in the 5th Gloucesters and they paid a heavy toll in that battalion alone. It would take* [me] *a long time to tell all their exploits but* [I can] *recall that sterling forward Sidney Millard and also Tom and Melville Lewis, whose names are inscribed on the war memorial in the Lady Chapel of* [All Saints Church]. *The Gloucester Fifteen were doubtless proud of the fact that of the four men who reached a German trench beyond Ovillers-La Boisselle* [i.e. Pozières] *in July 1916 after three days of terrible fighting, three were members of the Gloucester Fifteen and were the three men*

---

[304] This was the opening of the Battle of Pozières Ridge, 23 July -3 September 1916.

[305] Using the contemporary trench maps it is apparent that the 5/Gloucesters attackers had to cross on average about 230 meters of No Man's Land up an incline which rose by about fifteen to twenty meters.

[306] Wilfred Miles, *History of the Great War. Military Operations France and Belgium, 1916. Vol II 2nd July 1916 to the End of the Battles of the Somme* (London: HMSO, 1938), p.144

[307] To the left of the 5/Gloucesters, between it and the 6/Gloucesters ran the route of the light railway from Ovillers to Longueval and along this line were several previously undetected German machine gun emplacements.

[308] Over a five day period, 19-23 July, at Pozières, the 5/Gloucesters suffered 278 casualties

[309] *The Citizen* 31 July 1916

[310] *Cheltenham Chronicle and Gloucestershire Graphic* 30 September 1916

[I have] *named. Sid Sysum scored his last try* [as his body was found on the German parapet, killed as he attempted to jump down into the trench]..."[311]

The fifth player to be killed, Private **James Griffiths,** died in No Man's Land and like his comrades whose bodies were never found he is commemorated on the Thiepval Memorial (see Photograph 30).[312] The attack also resulted in the serious wounding of a number of other players including Second Lieutenant **William Pearce**, Corporal **Percy Simmons**, Sergeant **Fred Webb**, Lance Corporal **Alec Lewis**, the brother of **Melville** and **Tom Lewis**, and Private **Albert Cook**. The latter was hit in the knee by what he would describe for the rest of his life as an exploding bullet which resulted in the amputation of his leg.[313]

Photograph 29. Doullens - Percy Simmons' (GRFC) Postcard: A postcard sent from Hébuterne whilst the 1/5th Gloucesters held there the line there in July 1916 by Corporal **Percy Simmons** (GRFC), A Company, to his wife Violet in Gloucester. The postcard shows the Maire of Doullens being escorted by German troops on their way to 'requisition' motor vehicles watched by the local inhabitants in September 1914. (*David and Jackie Brown*)

The attack at Pozières on 23 July had the same effect as similar attacks had on recognised Pals Battalions for although the 5/Gloucesters had soldiers from various areas across Britain, the

---
[311] *The Citizen* 12 April 1926
[312] The German trenches were captured on 24 July 1916 after the defenders withdrew and although it would appear from the Reverend Helm's account that the bodies of the men killed were found and identified on 24 July, the battlefield would see further bloodshed in 1918 and it has to be assumed that during this period their graves were lost and hence they are all commemorated amongst the Missing on the Thiepval Memorial.
[313] Personal Communication: Terry Short, grandson of Albert Cook. (The use of exploding or expanding bullets had been outlawed under the Hague Convention 1899).

concentration of men from the Gloucester Rugby Club made it almost inevitable that an attack of this nature would have a devastating effect on a small local community. In Gloucester the news touched more than just the immediate relatives as the rugby men were well known throughout the city. With large gaps in its ranks, the 5/Gloucesters retired to Albert on 24 July and began a twelve day period at Cramont of training and the incorporation of 121 new drafts into its ranks

Also on the 23 July the 8/Gloucesters, two miles further down the line having pushed on from La Boisselle, assaulted the German Switch Line running through High Wood.[314,315] The attack launched at 1.00 am resulted in 200 casualties including Lance Corporal **William 'Jack' Nelmes** (GRFC) whose body was never recovered and identified. Within a week his mother and stepfather in Lydney received a letter from Sergeants Pollard and **Arthur Saunders** (GRFC) explaining that their son had been hit by a shell fragment after only joining the machine gun section on the day of his death; Arthur Saunders was well-known to the Nelmes family as they lived opposite each in Albert Street, Lydney.[316] Jack is commemorated on the Thiepval Memorial (see Photograph 30).[317] The 8/Gloucesters was taken out of the line for a short rest but within a week was back in the same area preparing for an attack on Bazentin-le-Petit. At 10.00 pm on 30 July A and B Companies of the 8/Gloucesters attacked the German Intermediate Line, but the attack stalled caught by enfilade machine gun fire and concealed snipers on their right from the direction of High Wood. The attack resulted in 174 casualties including Lieutenant **Hugh Thomas** (GRFC) and Sergeant Harold Pollard whose letter of condolence to Jack Nelmes' parents was one of the last he wrote. Hugh Thomas' body was never found and his name was also added to the Thiepval Memorial. Sergeant Pollard is buried in Caterpillar Valley Cemetery.

The 8/Gloucesters had been "*...engaged in some of the hottest fighting...*"[318] but on 1 August it moved off the Somme and ten days later relieved the 8/North Staffs between Wytschaete and Messines, near Ypres. The sector was described as 'quiet' although the Battalion War Diary frequently recorded German Minenwerfer Bomb and Trench Mortar activity each day between 4.00 and 6.00 pm. Despite the 'quiet' Sergeant **Arthur Saunders** (GRFC) was wounded on 12 September although had sufficiently recovered by 23 October when the Battalion took over dug outs in the old German front line north of Ovillers, back on the Somme.

Despite the battles raging across the Channel, life in Britain continued and on 31 July Second-Lieutenant **Frank Wicks** (GCCC), 22/Manchesters, recovering from broken ribs sustained in France, married Miss Phyllis Elaine Coulsting. His best man was an old sporting friend, Lieutenant Frank L. Hall, 4/Gloucesters, who he had met recently in Somerville Hospital, Oxford where both men were recovering from woundings; Lieutenant Hall had been wounded by shrapnel in the head and hand.[319,320] Frank would now be invalided out of the Army and awarded a Silver War Badge.

---

[314] A trench system would consist of at least two parallel lines of trenches. If part of the first trench line was captured by the enemy, a 'switch' trench would be dug to connect the second trench line to the still held part of the first trench line. A trench system with a switch trench would also render attack particularly difficult as enfilade fire would be possible because the trench would now be at an oblique angle to the line of the attack regardless of the direction it came from.

[315] High Wood is the British name for the wood, the French name being Bois des Fourcaux

[316] Both the houses now no longer exist and have been replaced by modern buildings.

[317] Also killed during this attack was Lieutenant Stanley Priestley the brother of Lance Corporal **Donald Priestley** (GCCC), 28/London, who himself was killed in action on 30 October 1917.

[318] *Gloucester Journal* 18 November 1916

[319] *Western Daily Press* 1 August 1916

There was good news for the GCCC as it was reported that,

> "…when the war is over the County Club will be able to resume free from debt [as] in the course of two seasons, the sum of £600 had been raised in subscriptions without a ball being bowled…"[321]

Cricket matches were also taking place on a regular basis usually involving military sides and sides made up of men ineligible for military service and in the absence of First Class cricket generally attracted "… *a large number of spectators.*"

August:

Lieutenant **George Holloway** (GCCC), 9/West Yorkshires, was reported as missing on the night of 10 August whilst on patrol in No Man's Land at Agny, south of Arras, but by mid-September news had reached Stroud that he had been wounded and taken prisoner. George's wound, caused by a shell fragment hitting his arm, was initially treated at a dressing station followed by ten days of treatment and recovery at Douai before he was transferred to a POW Camp. By September George was able to write home from Gütersloh Prisoner of War Camp, Germany, "*…I am quartered here and well treated. My wound is much better.*"[322] He was held captive for two years at Gütersloh before transfer to Crefeld and Ströhen POW camps. On 12 October 1918 under a reciprocal agreement with the German Government he was interned in Holland before being repatriated to Britain on 19 November 1918; in the same month he would have to justify his capture to the British Army's Standing Committee of Enquiry to convince it that this had not been a deliberate act to escape the fighting.[323] Whilst in camp George, a noted escapee and known by the name 'Little Man' "*…suffered rather severely at the hands of the Hun…*";[324,325] it is thought that George Holloway wrote the account of the escape attempts at Ströhen POW Camp which Will Harvey included in his book, *Comrades in Captivity*.[326]

September:

On the night of the 3/4 September for his actions Captain **Hugh Jones** (GCCC) was awarded the Military Cross with the 13/Gloucesters, the pioneer battalion of the 39th Division. Some of his men had lost their way coming back across No Man's Land, hindered by gas helmets, as they sought the relative safety of their trenches during a German gas barrage. To guide them back to safety Hugh, despite presenting himself as a prominent target to German infantrymen, machine gunners and snipers alike, stood on top of the parapet and flashed his torch to show them the right direction and

---

[320] Lieutenant Frank Leslie Hall was killed in action on 27 August 1917 in the Ypres Salient. His body was never identified and he is commemorated amongst the Missing on the Tyne Cot Memorial, Panel 72 to 75.
[321] *Western Daily Press* 31 July 1916
[322] *Gloucestershire Chronicle* 16 September 1916
[323] All officers taken as prisoners of war had to justify their capture after the war to the War Office's Standing Committee of Enquiry and George Holloway's account is reproduced later in the section dealing with November 1918.
[324] The identity of 'Little Man' as George Holloway has been established by Roger Deeks (F.W. Society) and is explained in an appendix (commentary) which accompanies the 2010 edition of F.W. Harvey's 1920 book *Comrades in Captivity* recently published by Douglas McLean Publishing, Coleford, Gloucestershire.
[325] F.W. Harvey, *Comrades in Captivity* (Coleford: Douglas McLean Publishing, 2010) p.214
[326] Harvey, Comrades in Captivity, pp.205-214

with encouragement got them all back except two who were hit but were subsequently rescued by Hugh.[327] His citation read,

> "For conspicuous gallantry during operations. While clearing trenches with his company after an attack, the enemy opened a heavy bombardment. He displayed the greatest courage whilst standing in the open under shell fire for two hours assisting his men to get into safety. Later he went by himself, under heavy shell fire, and fetched two stretchers for his wounded"[328]

Lieutenant Colonel Aubrey Holmes Boulton commanding the 13/Gloucesters wrote that, "*…a braver or more generous character I never met*" while a fellow officer recalling the incident wrote that,

> "Hugh was in charge of the company one night, when the Germans put up a terrific gas shell barrage. Some of his men having lost their in the gas helmets, Hugh got out of the trench at very great risk, and by flashing his torch and pushing and pulling them along, he got them all back to the trench with only two fatalities. Then he walked over the open to an artillery dugout, and brought back two stretchers"[329]

It was not uncommon for the Army to erect two fixed lamps along sections of trenches which were lit after an attack or raid to guide the men back to their own trenches in the dark across often featureless landscapes where all sense of direction would be lost. Likewise it was not uncommon for the Germans also to light two fixed lamps in the hope that British infantrymen would make their way across to the German lines either to be shot or taken prisoner. It is obvious that Hugh's actions were different as a moving light could only have been operated by a man who would have made a perfect target in the dark. Sadly Hugh Jones would not live to see the end of the war. In April 1918 he was wounded in both legs and was transferred back to Britain. Despite making a good recovery he contracted pneumonia and died on 10 November 1918 at the Fort Pitt Military Hospital, Chatham.

On 3 September Lieutenant **Sidney Kitcat** (GCCC), RNVR, witnessed the shooting down of the first Zeppelin over the British mainland. The training establishment HMS *Crystal Palace* where he was an instructor had been a particularly vulnerable target for air raids, until the nearby railway tunnels were used as an air raid shelter. Before that orders had been issued that in the event of an air raid all personnel had to scatter over the grounds and lie low to minimise casualties. On 3 September Sidney and a few other officers were standing on the main terrace at Crystal Palace after the air raid alarmed had sounded amazed at the silence and stillness as the men lay prone and lifeless hidden from view by the darkness. But above them Lieutenant William Leefe Robinson, 39 Squadron, RFC had engaged a Zeppelin on a bombing raid,

> "Suddenly the heavens flared and all the faces of the scattered men hidden in the darkness showed up white. From somewhere beyond the North Tower came the startling reflection of an almost blinding light…it was the sudden ignition of the Zeppelin's gas-bag in the sky over twenty miles away."[330]

Lieutenant William Leefe Robinson was the first British pilot to shoot down a Zeppelin and for his actions he was awarded the Victoria Cross for what was a hazardous action as the exploding helium

---

[327] *Dean Forest Mercury* 13 October 1916
[328] *London Gazette* 20 October 1916 p.10185
[329] W.A. Sibley and Jack D. Newth, *Wycliffe and the War. A School Record* (Gloucester: John Bellows, 1923), p.61. W.A. Sibley was the Headmaster of the Senior School and Jack Newth CBE, BDS was the Chair of Governors (1914-1922).
[330] *The Singapore Free Press and Mercantile Advertiser* 7 July 1931

gas could easily engulf the attacking aircraft.[331] The crew of Zeppelin SL11 were all killed. On 16 October 1959 an agreement was reached for all German nationals buried in Britain to be re-interred in a central location and on 10 June 1967 following the work of the Volksbund Deutsche Kriegsgraberfursorge (the German War Graves Commission), the Cannock Chase German Military Cemetery was opened; it contains almost 5,000 graves including the communal grave of the crew of Zeppelin SL11.

On 25 September the objectives for the renewed offensive across the Somme included the capture of the three fortified villages of Geudecourt, Morval and Lesboeufs. The capture of Morval was assigned to the 5th Division including Bristol's Own, the 12/Gloucesters (95 Brigade) while Lesboeufs was the responsibility of the Guards Division which included the 1/Grenadier Guards (3 Guards Brigade) with Lance Corporal **Harry Lane** (GRFC).[332]

At 12.35 pm the infantry advanced behind a steadily and methodically advancing artillery barrage where the losses incurred were variable depending on the sector. In front of Lesboeufs the 1/Guards Brigade come up against three belts of uncut wire and the *"...officers and men began to fall fast."*[333] However with the wire cut by hand and covered by it's own marksmen and bombers to ensure that the German infantry 'kept their heads down' the Guards pushed on to the enemy trench and captured it. By 3.30 pm Lesboeufs was under British control as the supporting units of the 1/Grenadier Guards advanced through their comrades to the next objective. Just south at Morval a similar tale unfolded as an equally determined advance captured the village with the 12/Gloucesters going in at 2.35 pm in the final assault.[334] With the two villages now in British hands the Germans began a heavy bombardment on their pre-registered targets forcing the British to withdraw all but a small number of troops to minimise casualties whilst still retaining control. For his part in the storming of Lesboeufs, Harry Lane was awarded the Distinguished Conduct Medal [DCM]. His citation in the London Gazette read,

> *"For conspicuous gallantry in action. He led his machine gun team forward with great courage and determination, reaching the second objective. Later, he pushed on to the third objective and accounted for large numbers of the enemy."* [335]

Harry however in a letter to his parents had a different view of the award,

> *"I have received heaps of congratulations and also drank a fine drop of Scotch with the Company officers. There is a cash consideration attached to this medal - the second highest it is possible for an NC officer or man to win. I am feeling in the pink at present and hope to remain so. It looks like another winter here but 'Bill' must know he's up against it now. Of course he's mad, but he will have to give the game up sooner or later*

---

[331] Lieutenant William Leefe Robinson would survive the war after being taken prisoner in April 1917 but his health was affected in captivity and died from influenza ('Spanish Flu') on 31 December 1918. He is buried at Harrow Weald (All Saints) Churchyard, Harrow.

[332] Dean Marks, *Bristol's Own, The 12th Battalion Gloucestershire Regiment 1914-1918* (Thatcham: Dolman Scott Ltd., 2011), pp.146-150

[333] Miles, *History of the Great War. Military Operations France and Belgium, 1916. Vol II* p.374

[334] Although the 12/Gloucesters initially had three cricketers in its ranks by 25 September 1916 there were none. Captain **Hugh Jones** has gained a commission in the 13/Gloucesters, Second Lieutenant **Frank Wicks** had been invalided out of the Army in July 1916 and Private **Solomon Levy** was receiving treatment for a GSW to the chest; on recovery in March 1917 he was posted to the 7/Gloucesters in Mesopotamia but was discharged in January 1918 as unfit for service following a shrapnel wound to the chest.

[335] *London Gazette* 14 November 1916

because we shall simply smash him up if he continues to hang on. We lost some good lads in the last battle, but 'Bill' didn't get off scot free...May my good fortune continue. In less than fortnight I shall have been out here two years - rather a good record isn't it? It is getting very cold now; sharp frost this morning, but it is better than rain." [336,337]

Sadly Harry's good fortune would not continue and he was killed in action on 30 March 1918 on the Somme during the German Spring Offensives.

Lance Corporal **Alec Lewis** (GRFC) following his recovery from his wounding on 23 July at Pozières with 5/Gloucesters, had gained a commission as a Second Lieutenant with the 6th Battalion, Royal Berkshire Regiment. Within weeks of joining his new battalion and regiment he was awarded the Military Cross [MC],

"For conspicuous gallantry in action. He assumed command of a company of another unit, reorganised bombing sections and successfully dealt with the enemy at a critical time. He set a splendid example" [338]

The Citizen reported that,

"...his two younger brothers [**Melville** and **Tom Lewis** (GRFC)] *fell in action in the early operations in the Somme offensive* [while] *he was twice wounded though not seriously...Lieut. Lewis has taken part in some of the most desperate fighting, and his decoration was gained in the battle for one of the enemy's most strongly-fortified positions on the Somme."* [339,340]

As a reflection of the high officer mortality rates and the desperate need for replacements, it had taken just over sixty days from the time that Alec was wounded as a Lance Corporal at Pozières to winning the Military Cross as a Second Lieutenant. It was subsequently reported, not surprisingly, that *"...Lieut. Lewis has been given a well-earned and necessary rest."*[341] Alec would gain a Bar to his Military Cross (i.e. a second Military Cross) in December 1917.[342]

Also distinguishing himself with gallant action Corporal **William Washbourne** (GRFC), one of the players whose enlistment back in August 1914 had inspired his fellow Gloucester citizens, was now awarded the Military Medal [MM]. William informed his family in one of his letters home but only as a modest aside with the brief mention providing no real details of his actions.[343,344] It was not

---

[336] *The Citizen* 26 October 1916
[337] Harry Lane refers to the DCM as the second highest gallantry order for Other Ranks (ORs) to win. The highest order was the Victoria Cross which indicates just how prestigious was the DCM. In the Great War the DCM and DSO (the officer equivalent of the DCM) were considered as 'near misses' for a Victoria Cross.
[338] *London Gazette* 11 December 1916
[339] *The Citizen* 13 December 1916
[340] The fortified position was probably the imposing Schwaben Redoubt on the Thiepval Ridge which the 6/Berkshires, 53 Brigade, 18th (Eastern) Division, attacked on 29 September (Battle of Thiepval Ridge, 26-28 September)
[341] *The Citizen* 13 December 1916
[342] Alec Lewis died at Meriden, Warwickshire in 1941 and at the request of his employers was accorded a funeral with full military honours.
[343] *Gloucester Journal* 28 October 1916
[344] The *London Gazette* carried the actual citations for all gallantry awards except the Military Medal and Mentioned in Despatches. As a result is now difficult to determine why these medals were awarded. The 5/Gloucesters Battalion War Diary and its trench newspaper the *Fifth Gloucester Gazette* acknowledge the award but provide no further details.

uncommon for the volunteer soldiers of both Clubs to be modest over their considerable achievements.

October:
The wounded soldiers at home in Gloucester played the return rugby match against the orderlies at the Kingsholm ground raising funds for the Voluntary Aid Detachment [VAD] Equipment Fund. The soldiers were triumphant by 11 points to six in a game which was again kicked off by the Mayor, Sir James Bruton. The soldiers were supported by **Arthur Hudson** (GRFC) on leave from the Royal Navy and **George Romans** (GRFC and GCCC) while the orderlies were ably reinforced by **Fred Ashmead** (1/Gloucesters) (GRFC) and **J. Jewell** (GRFC).

November:
At the end of October the 8/Gloucesters did another front line tour east of Thiepval and the Stuff Redoubt where it was frequently subjected to heavy shelling which from 24 to 27 October resulted in sixty-six casualties. On 1 November its front line duty was temporarily at an end and the Battalion found itself back in the old German dug outs at Ovillers but were still within range of the German guns. A direct hit killed Sergeant **Arthur Saunders** (GRFC) only a few days after he had written to his mother, Mrs Sarah Thorne in Lydney, telling her that his award of the Military Medal won for his actions four months earlier at La Boisselle had been confirmed.[345] Within days of receiving his letter, Sarah was informed by her other son Charlie that Arthur had been killed in action.[346] On 11 July 1917 Sarah Thorne accepted Arthur's Military Medal from Brigadier General Grove in the presence of the Mayor of Bristol and 300 soldiers in a ceremony on College Green. The Brigadier General in paying tribute addressed the soldiers and said that,

> "...they, as soldiers, knew pretty well what they had to go through, but [I am] *afraid that the outside world was little aware of the hourly danger those men were in and the tremendous hardships they had to go through both by night and by day...*"[347,348]

Eleven days later Lance Corporal **Oscar Walwin** (GRFC) would become the eleventh and last Gloucester Football Club player to die on the Somme in 1916. Oscar, along with his brother Hugh who was now a Turkish prisoner, having been captured at Katia in April, had enlisted in the RGH but Oscar had been attached to the 2/Worcesters. On 1 November, near Le Transloy, the 2/Worcesters and the 9/Highland Light Infantry came under heavy shell fire before they advanced at 3.30 pm "...*up to the waist in slime...*" against the Boritska Trench which had previously resisted all attempts to capture it.[349] With the light fading the battalions were forced to withdraw due to exhaustion and the continuing heavy machine gun fire from Le Transloy cemetery; the ground which was swept by the machine guns was described as "...*the terrain of the machine gunner's dream.*"[350] Amongst the

---

[345] Arthur's mother Sarah was widowed in 1896 when her husband John Saunders was drowned whilst fishing in Lydney Docks. She subsequently married William Thorne who adopted Arthur.
[346] Charlie Saunders, Canadian Field Artillery, died of wounds on 6 September 1917. Both Arthur and Charlie are commemorated on the gravestone of their father, John, at St Mary's Churchyard, Lydney.
[347] *Western Daily Press* 4 July 1917
[348] At the same ceremony Lance Corporal A.H. Tucker, Somerset Light Infantry, was also presented with a Military Medal won at Guedecourt on 2 October 1916.
[349] Miles, *History of the Great War. Military Operation France and Belgium 1916 Vol II*, p. 469
[350] Dunn, *The War the Infantry Knew*, p.276

casualties was Oscar Walwin who was seriously wounded and quickly transferred to a base hospital in Rouen. He recovered sufficiently to send a standard field postcard on 3 November to his parents, Walter and Annie Walwin, informing them of his wounds and that he was "...*going on well.*" However at midday on Monday 13 November his parents received a telegram as his condition had deteriorated and that they could and probably should visit him in Rouen.[351] Both of them set out immediately from Gloucester for France via Southampton but two hours later a second telegram arrived stating that he had died, aged 21 years; his parents were contacted at Southampton before they departed.[352] The 2/Worcesters captured Boritska Trench on 5 November 1916.

December:

On 26 December the final sportsman to die in 1916 was Captain and Flight Commander **John Nason** (GCCC), 46th Squadron, Royal Flying Corps [RFC]. John had joined the RFC in January 1916 from the 14/Royal Sussex and had graduated from the Royal Aero Club as a Flying Officer on 22 September 1916.[353,354,355] He was described as "...*an extremely useful pilot...*" but was killed after only three months by enemy action on 26 December during a flight over the Ypres Salient. John and his observer, Lieutenant C.A.F. Brown, were in a Nieuport 12 (serial number A3294) on a photographic patrol when the aircraft was attacked by a German Roland aircraft over Railway Wood, east of Ypres towards Menin; the aeroplane was brought down with the crash killing both men; John Nason was buried in Vlamertinghe Military Cemetery.[356,357,358]

With the introduction of conscription (Military Service Act, 27 January 1916) came the recognition that for the first time Britain was engaged in 'total war' where civilians and military personnel were needed to support the war effort. The Act effectively meant that all fit young men were now part of the war effort whether engaged in vital war industries ('starred' occupations) or part of the Armed Forces; the engagement of women in war industries was a further indication that 'total' warfare had arrived in Britain. Conscription had now removed the 'unpatriotic' barrier which had been levelled at non-military rugby matches and on Boxing Day the Gloucester Football Club organised a game at Kingsholm against Cinderford. The Gloucester XV, included Lieutenant **Lindsay Vears** (Royal Field Artillery) (full back), **Arthur Hudson** (Royal Navy) (wing, captain), **George**

---

[351] In general the Government paid only half the fare for hospital visits by parents and wives to wounded soldiers in hospital. Charities were set up to fund the difference as the cost generally was too great for the relatives. In the Forest of Dean the Miners Association set up a specific fund to enable these visits with no financial burden on the relatives (*Dean Forest Mercury* 12 November 1915).
[352] *Gloucester Journal* 18 November 1916
[353] *De Ruvigny's Roll of Honour* Volume 3 (1922) p.204
[354] *Cheltenham Chronicle and Gloucestershire Graphic* 6 January 1917
[355] *Flight* 19 October 1916
[356] Trevor Henshaw, The Sky Their Battlefield: Complete List of Allied Air Casualties from Enemy Action in WW1 (London: Grub Street, 1995). The loss of the aircraft was claimed by Vizefeldwebel [Senior NCO] A. Ulmer, Jagdstaffel 18.
[357] John Nason's RFC Service Record, Casualty Card and Certificate of Graduation from the Royal Aero Club were provided courtesy of the Royal Air Force Museum, London.
[358] The official Casualty Card reported that John's observer Lieutenant C.A.F. Brown was also killed in the crash but details of his grave have not been reported on the CWGC database.

Collingbourne (centre),[359] Private **Ernest Hall** (8/Gloucesters) (centre) and Private **Frederick Ashmeade** (1/Gloucesters) (centre/wing).[360] The half backs were **William Hall** (outside half) and Private **Jim Stephens** (5/Gloucesters) (scrum half) while the pack consisted of **Gordon Vears** (starred occupation), **Norman Hayes**, ex-Lance Corporal **George Halford** (1/Gloucesters), Sergeant **J. Lee** (10/Worcesters), Private **George Lane** (5/Gloucesters), **J. Jewell**, Assistant Paymaster **Hubert Kingscott** (Royal Naval Reserve) and Sergeant **W. Jennings** (5/Gloucesters). The majority of the players were home on leave and between them they had played 1,643 games for Gloucester which resulted in a sixteen points to six victory for the Club.[361] Although the games were now acceptable the gate receipts, still a contentious issue, were always donated to the local Red Cross Hospitals rather than used to alleviate the Club's mounting debt. This game raised £61 6s which was handed over to the Commandant, Mrs T.P. Parnell, of the Hillfield and the Palace VA Hospitals in Denmark Road and at the Bishop's Palace, Gloucester, respectively.[362,363] At the start of the war a large number of British Red Cross hospitals were opened across the country which were an important part in the recuperation of wounded British, French and Belgian soldiers. Wounded soldiers were usually stabilised at CCS and Base Hospitals before crossing the Channel for treatment in the major British hospitals including the Bristol and Gloucester Royal Infirmaries. After this the servicemen were transferred for nursing care to local Red Cross VA hospitals which were staffed by Volunteer Aid Detachment [VAD] personal under the supervision of a Nursing Sister and a Doctor. These hospitals were dependent on local communities 'adopting' them and raising sufficient funds for medical supplies and food; fund raisers for Red Cross Hospitals, of which the rugby match was one, were common throughout Great Britain. One of the medical Officers at the Gloucester Voluntary Aid (Red Cross) Hospital was Dr Arnold Alcock (Gloucester Football Club President, 1924-1969). Throughout the war the Gloucester Football Club would organise a number of matches raising funds for the Gloucester Royal Infirmary and the two Red Cross Hospitals in the city.

---

[359] G. Collingbourne played three games for the Gloucester Football Club, one for the First XV, but in retirement he became one of the administrative staff at the Club.

[360] F. Ashmead(e) – *The Citizen* refers to him in reports as both H. Ashmead and F. Ashmead. In 1949 when Frederick Ashmead died, he was referred to as "…*a well-known sportsman…*" and the youngest of the Gloucester 'Old Contemptibles' to have fought in the Great War (*The Citizen* 25 March 1949).

[361] Before the war Lindsay Vears represented the Club 73 times 1901-09, Arthur Hudson 242 times 1902-14, Ernest Hall 108 times 1904-11, William Hall 155 times 1907-13, Jim Stephens 321 times 1894-1911, Gordon Vears 295 times 1902-13, Norman Hayes 128 times 1908-14 George Halford 214 times 1907-14, J. Jewell 91 times 1901-06 and Hubert Kingscott 17 times 1912-14; Messrs Hudson, Hayes and Halford would continue to play for the Club after the war.

[362] £61 6s represents a substantial amount and indicates that a large crowd had watched the game as the estimated average pre-war gate receipt had been £32 16s.

[363] The Hillfield VA Hospital building is now home to the Gloucester Trading Standards Service and the Registration and Coroner Services.

Photograph 30. Thiepval Memorial to the Missing of the Somme, 1916: The 140 feet tall Thiepval Memorial was unveiled on 1 August 1932 by the Prince of Wales in the presence of the President of France. It commemorates and lists the names of 72,203 men who died in the Somme sector before March 1918 and who bodies were never found and identified. Amongst them are the names of ten Gloucester Rugby players, **Henry Collins, James Griffiths, Melville Lewis, Tom Lewis, Syd Millard, Jack Nelmes, John Price, Arthur Saunders** and **Sidney Sysum**. (*Authors*)

For Club, King and Country

4

1917: DEATH AND GLORY

"...angry and determined to get revenge...he rushed the position and fired his Lewis Gun up through the ceiling into the room above..."

Charles Cook's (GRFC) actions which resulted in the award of the Military Medal

Following a disastrous year for the Allies, the French Government lost faith in its Commander-in-Chief, Général Joseph Joffre and dismissed him in December 1916, appointing Général Robert Nivelle, the 'hero' of Verdun, in his place. Nivelle formulated a plan to end the war within four months and was sufficiently persuasive to convince the French Government and the British Prime Minister, David Lloyd George, of the efficacy of his plan. Nivelle's persuasiveness was sufficient to convince Lloyd George that the British Army should be placed under French command although political pressure in Britain prevented this becoming a reality.

The Nivelle Plan, launched in April consisted of the main attack coming from the French Army on the Chemin des Dames, north east of Reims, with the British Army in a subsidiary role conducting diversionary attacks at Arras. The latter gained significant tracts of territory but the French Offensive was a disaster with large numbers of casualties and subsequently the French soldiers ('poilu') in open mutiny refusing to go on the offensive although they would defend their positions in the event of a German attack. Nivelle was subsequently dismissed as the French Government appointed its third Commander-in-Chief, Marshal Phillippe Pétain, who immediately addressed the issues raised by the mutineers. Amidst this uncertainty and with the French Army trying to conceal the extent of the mutiny, Field Marshal Sir Douglas Haig now pursued his aim of a Flanders offensive which would come to dominate British thinking in 1917, with the 'Battle of Passchendaele' coming to be one of the enduring symbols of the Great War (see Map 2).

For the players of both Clubs the year would bring more deaths and more recognition of their gallant efforts with many medals for bravery awarded.

March:

On 20 March the 1/Gloucesters began an extended period of training, support and specialised tasks including tunnels repairs.[364] During this time the Battalion XV, the Officers XV and the 'Soccer' XI played a number of games against other battalions. The Battalion XV also took part in the [1st] Divisional Rugby Competition beating the 2/Welsh in the second round by six points to nil, the 1/South Wales Borderers in the third round 13 points to nil and in the semi-final the 2/King's Royal Rifle Corps by thirteen points to nil. However the Battalion War Diary does record how the Battalion XV fared in the final because it had gone back into the line and the final probably had to be cancelled.

Photograph 31. Soldiers in a Trench: The soldier nearest the camera is Sergeant **Hubert Charles Barnes** (GRFC), 1/5th Battalion, Gloucestershire Regiment who was awarded the Military Medal for gallantry on 4 April 1917. (*SoGM, GLRRM:05835.1*)

April:

The 5/Gloucesters, now in the line at south of Cambrai, was joined at the beginning of the month by Second Lieutenant **Charles Barnett** (GCCC) who had enlisted at a recruitment office in Cheltenham

---

[364] Battalion War Diary, *1st Battalion Gloucestershire Regiment 20 March-7 November 1917*, TNA WO 95/1278

on 18 December 1916 in the Inns of Court Officer Training Corps [OTC] based in London. After a period of training he came across the Channel on the troopship *Berkhamsted* on 29 March and joined the 5/Gloucesters.[365]

On 4 April the 5/Gloucesters (145 Brigade) held the left flank of the 144 Brigade's night attack near Epehy, south of Cambrai, with C and D Companies tasked with the capture of objectives at Lempire and Maye Copse (see Map 2). The companies assembled west of a railway embankment using it to conceal their assembly but with a heavy covering of snow and a cloudless moonlit night, the movement was spotted and a heavy barrage was directed at the attacking soldiers. Fortunately the shells consistently fell behind the rear companies causing few casualties. By 6.00 am their objectives had been taken together with nine POWs, two machine guns and a number of dead although at a cost of fifteen killed and forty wounded, two of whom subsequently died of wounds. That night the 5/Gloucesters won one Distinguished Conduct Medal and six Military Medals including one that awarded to Sergeant **Bert Barnes** (GRFC) (see Photograph 31).[366]

Photograph 32. Pack Horse Train, Salonika: A pack horse train marching across the snowy landscape carrying the supplies of the 2nd Battalion, Gloucestershire Regiment in Salonika, Greece, 1916. These conditions were also typical of those experienced by Lance Corporal **Edwin Wootton** (GRFC) serving with the 9th Battalion, Gloucestershire Regiment. (*SoGM, GLRRM:04802.6*)

---

[365] There are discrepancies between the dates on Charles' Medal Index Card and his Service Record – the dates used here are in accord with the latter. The 5/Gloucesters' Battalion War Diary does not record him joining the Battalion.
[366] Battalion War Diary, *1/5th Battalion Gloucestershire Regiment 4/5 April 1917*, TNA WO 95/2763

The Allied attacks on the Central Powers were not confined to the Western Front. In October 1915 the Greek Prime Minister, Eleftherios Venizelos, requested assistance for the Serbs against the combined forces of Austro-Hungary and Bulgaria in a move that would provide protection for Greek sovereignty. On 21 October a joint Franco-British force landed at Salonika (Thessaloniki) but its intervention came too late to save the Serbs and despite subsequent Greek pressure to leave the Allies decided to remain and a new theatre the Salonika Front (or Macedonian Front) was opened to pressurise Germany's main ally and counter the threat posed by the Bulgarian Army.

The 9/Gloucesters (78 Brigade, 26th Division), with Lance Corporal **Edwin Wootton** (GRFC) amongst its ranks, had arrived on the Western Front on 21 September 1915. Less than seven weeks later the Division was on the move initially travelling for two days in cattle trunks from Longeau Station in Amiens to Marseilles where it arrived on 11 November. After a six day sea voyage on board HMS *Mars* the Division arrived in Alexandria, Egypt, and with very little rest re-embarked for Salonika. By the 25 November the men were in camp at Lembet where conditions were extreme and *"on the 27th and 28th a severe blizzard with frost, snow and intense cold caused much discomfort in the camp."*[367] Amidst harsh conditions the Division spent the next eighteen months supporting the Advanced Line, moving from camp to camp (see Photograph 32). The moral status of the men of the 9/Gloucesters during this period however was of concern to the newly arrived commander, Lieutenant-Colonel J. Fane, who almost immediately concluded that there were discipline problems which manifested themselves in a *"...slackness in saluting."* and he placed out of bounds to all ranks the establishments known as *"... 'Odeon', 'Moulin Rouge', 'Alhambra', 'Folies Begères', 'Bar Americain', 'Renaissance', 'Britannia' and 'Mon Plaisir'..."*[368,369]

The 9/Gloucesters, camped at Pearse Ravine, was on high alert and on the night 23/24 April 1917 was ordered to support an attack by the 11/Worcesters against Bulgarian forces. The Gloucesters assembled in Senelle Ravine but immediately came under *"...enemy artillery fire [that] was intense and very accurate"*.[370] At ten minutes past midnight 78 Brigade Headquarters ordered A Company forward to reinforce the left of the assaulting battalion and at 2.05 am B Company was also sent forward, commanded by Captain Walter E.L. Griffiths and supported by Lance **Corporal Wootton** (GRFC).[371] At 4.15 am Captain Griffiths sent a message to Battalion HQ that B Company was pinned down in Ravine XI by heavy rifle, machine gun and bomb fire; he was ordered to retire back to the trench line but during this manoeuvre Edwin Wootton went missing and in a letter from his platoon officer, his wife Alice was informed that,

> *"...on the night of April 24 we were ordered over the top. Your husband was exceedingly cheerful and responsible for the men's splendid spirit during the attack. He was last seen helping a wounded comrade, so perhaps he was hit and unconsciously wandered into the enemy's lines but I fear the worst has befallen him and that he has made the supreme sacrifice. His name has been sent forward for a decoration for his most conspicuous bravery and devotion to duty."*[372,373]

---

[367] Battalion War Diary, *9th Battalion Gloucestershire Regiment 6 November 1915*, TNA WO 95/4873
[368] Battalion War Diary, *9th Battalion Gloucestershire Regiment 3 March 1917*, TNA WO 95/4873
[369] It has not been recorded what activities went on in these establishments!
[370] Battalion War Diary, *9th Battalion Gloucestershire Regiment 23/26 April 1917*, TNA WO 95/4873
[371] Captain Walter Edward Lambourn Griffiths was killed in action on 26 April 1917 and is buried at Karasouli Military Cemetery.
[372] *Gloucester Journal* 14 July 1917

Despite the recommendation for a gallantry award, Edwin's unselfish actions went unrecognised and in August 1918 Alice Wootton was officially notified that her husband was now classified as having been killed in action on 25 April 1917; his body was never found.[374] Although a rugby player Edwin had a passion for cricket and was captain of the 9/Gloucesters XI whilst in training in 1915 (see Photograph 33).[375]

At the end of the month Second Lieutenant **Frank Stout** (GRFC), 20/Hussars, who had previously won the Military Cross the previous year, became a casualty and was wounded in three places although the *Gloucester Journal*'s readership was re-assured that his wounds were slight. Sadly the 'slight' nature of these wounds would affect Frank for the rest of his life and he died an invalid in 1926 as a direct result of these injuries.[376]

Lieutenant and Quartermaster **George Dennett** (GCCC), as a Boer War veteran had enlisted in the early months of the war with his old regiment but had subsequently gained a commission with the 1st (Garrison) Battalion, East Yorkshire Regiment in October 1915. The Battalion had been transferred to India in February 1916 and was on Empire garrison duties when news arrived that George's only son, Maurice, aged nine years had died.[377]

In Bristol the newspapers reported on the case of **Charles Lucas Townsend** (GCCC) who as a solicitor appealed against the ruling of the Stockton Military Tribunal that he was eligible for military service which granted him a one month's conditional exemption. His appeal at the Durham County Appeal Tribunal confirmed the conditional exemption but extended the exemption period to six months after which he would be liable for service.[378] This case is unusual in that all people appearing before a Military Tribunal were granted anonymity with only their occupations identified in the newspapers.

June:
Captain **Horace Merrick** (GCCC) serving with the 4/Gloucesters in the 144 Brigade, 48th (South Midland) Division south-west of Cambrai was awarded the Military Cross; his citation read,

> "*For conspicuous gallantry and devotion to duty. He showed great coolness and bravery when in command of his company and displayed great energy in organising the whole position captured, having had to assume command of the other company meanwhile.*"[379]

Further it was announced that Major **Ernest English** (GCCC), 1/King's Shropshire Light Infantry, was awarded the Distinguished Service Order [DSO] and Captain **James Horlick** (GCCC), Coldstream Guards, the Military Cross for "*...distinguished service in the field...*", while Second Lieutenant **John Healing** (GCCC), 2/Royal Warwicks in 22 Brigade 7th Division, was awarded the Military Cross "*...for valuable services rendered in connection with the war...*".[380,381] These awards were in addition to the previously announced DSO for Captain **Percy Robinson** (GCCC), Royal Field Artillery (February 1917).

---

[373] The recommendation would have been for the award of the Military Medal for gallantry
[374] *Gloucester Journal* 17 August 1918
[375] *Cheltenham Chronicle and Gloucestershire Graphic* 25 September 1915
[376] *Gloucester Journal* 28 April 1917
[377] *Cheltenham Chronicle and Gloucestershire Graphic* 7 April 1917
[378] *Cheltenham Chronicle and Gloucestershire Graphic* 28 April 1917
[379] *London Gazette* 18 June 1917 p.5995
[380] *London Gazette* 4 June 1917 p.5469

Photograph 33. 9/Gloucesters Cricket Team: No.5 Platoon, B Company, 9/Gloucesters Cricket XI went undefeated against all-comers during training. The team was captained by Private **Edwin Wootton** (GRFC) (1887-1917) (middle seated on ground). (*CCGG*)

The Great Western VA Hospital kept up its new tradition of cricket matches with a couple of games against the Palace Red Cross Hospital. The recovering 'boys' and orderlies from the Great Western triumphed in both matches with the away match on the Palace Ground being won by seventy-one runs.[382]

July:

Haig's favoured Flanders offensive, the Third Battle of Ypres (Passchendaele), was launched on 31 July and would have eight recognisable phases, the first of which was the Battle of Pilckem Ridge (31 July – 2 August). The northern sector of this battle was assigned to the XIV, XVIII, XIX and II Corps with the advance against the ridge in the direction of the town of Langemarck. The northernmost part of this sector was allocated to 3 Guards Brigade (Guards Division, XIV Corps) which included the 4/Grenadier Guards with Private **Alfred Purton** (GRFC) in its ranks; on their immediate left were units of the French Army. Alfred had been wounded in October 1916 and after a period of recovery in Britain he returned to France on Easter Monday 1917.

---

[381] *London Gazette* 1 June 1917 p.5480
[382] *Gloucester Journal* 30 June 1917

1917: Death and Glory

The first objective, the Pilckem Ridge, seventy feet above the surrounding ground, had 'commanding' views over the flat land of the Salient. Orders were issued that the Grenadier Guards officers had to wear a Private's uniform and carry a rifle and bayonet although as a concession to their officer status they were allowed to carry their revolvers provided they were concealed in the right hand pocket of their tunics.[383] These measures recognised the targeting of British officers by enemy snipers although at this stage of the war NCOs and even Private soldiers were capable of assuming 'command' in the absence of an officer; all ranks had knowledge of the objectives, the ground, the area maps and German defences. For this attack each man carried four empty sandbags, 170 rounds of Small Arms Ammunition [SAA], two Mills Bombs [hand grenades], one flare and 70% of the men would carry a shovel, 10% a pick and the remaining 20% a wire cutting tool. In addition each man would carry one day's ration, one Iron ration, one lemon and two water bottles of rum and tea.

At 9.00 pm on 30 July the Battalion left its bivouacs and marched to the assembly trenches which it reached by 1.20 am despite heavy shelling.[384] At 3.50 am the British barrage opened along the whole front and at 4.28 am as the barrage lifted (i.e. moved forward) to its next objective the attacking troops went 'over the top' only to be met by a German retaliatory barrage which had started the instant that the British barrage had lifted.[385] The German machine gunners began to sweep No Man's Land and during this stage,

> "...all companies found it difficult to recognise landmarks and compass bearings had to be resorted to. There was a marked tendency to mistake [objectives]. Concrete emplacements were rapidly outmanoeuvred, and the occupants of the dug-outs immediately came out and surrendered, only in a few isolated cases was it found necessary to bomb them."

During the attack, Alfred Purton received gunshot wounds to his head and one of his legs; in the aftermath of the attack the Battalion War Diary identified the casualties but due to the 'fog of war', Alfred's name does appear amongst them. After initial stabilising treatment at the CCS, Alfred was moved to the Base Hospital at Boulogne, prior to transfer to a hospital in Britain. But Alfred never became sufficient stable for this move and in mid-August his wife, Florence, was granted permission to visit him in Boulogne. She spent a period of time there, but he never returned home and died on 27 August 1917 from his wounds shortly after Florence had returned home to Gloucester.[386]

Chance meetings in the trenches gave old rugby colleagues the opportunity to swap gossip. Lance Corporal **George Griffiths** (GRFC), 10/Gloucesters, writing home mentioned that he had bumped into Colonel **Cornelius Carleton** (GRFC), now commanding the 6/Welsh, coming out of dug out and had an interesting chat with him.[387,388] The newspaper commented that rugby had "...*evidently not lost its attraction*..." as George mentioned that they were playing another battalion of the Gloucesters although "...*it is something like 90 in the shade!*" George added that "...*last March at __[censored]__ he had played a few games with* **Charlie Cook** (GRFC) *and* **William Parham** (GRFC)";

---

[383] Battalion War Diary, *4th Battalion Grenadier Guards 27 July 1917*, TNA WO 95/1223
[384] Battalion War Diary, *4th Battalion Grenadier Guards 31 July 1917*, TNA WO 95/1223
[385] See Appendix B note 4: Artillery Barrages
[386] *Gloucester Journal* 8 September 1917
[387] *Gloucester Journal* 14 July 1917
[388] George Griffiths and Cornelius Carleton played together seven times for the Gloucester First XV between 1909 and 1911

within three months William Parham would be dead and George Griffiths would die in less than a year (April 1918). The sporting activity of the various regiments away from the front line continued to be reported and included an article in the *Sportsman* written by Captain **Michael Green** (GCCC), 1/Gloucesters, not on cricket but on rugby played within the battalion which between March and July was undefeated in eight matches.[389] Michael decided not to supply any names but did indicate that several of the players were "...*well-known in Gloucestershire.*" [390]

The Great Western Road VA Hospital 'Boys' cricket XI consisting of recovering soldiers and orderlies played a strong Gloucester XI at the Kingsholm ground. For the Gloucester XI Captain H.G. Norman gathered some of his men from the Gloucester Volunteer Corps, including **Arthur Paish** (GCCC) while **George Romans** (GRFC and GCCC) assisted the Boys who lost by sixty runs.[391]

August:

Captain **Percy Stout** (GRFC), Motor Machine Gun Corps, now emulated his brother Frank and won an award, the Distinguished Service Order [DSO], for gallantry. His citation read,

"*For conspicuous gallantry and devotion to duty. At a critical moment, when a number of armoured cars were in danger of being cut off, he led the attack to their relief, and after two hours' heavy fighting gained the objective, after inflicting heavy losses upon the enemy.*" [392]

Later in the month Second-Lieutenant **Ernest Alderwick** (GCCC), 11/Suffolks (The 'Cambridge' Suffolks), after only two months at the front, having joined his battalion on 19 June, was killed in action at Hargicourt on 26 August whilst leading his men in a night attack from Sunken Farm trench.[393] It was reported that Ernest had endeared himself to all his comrades regardless of rank not only by his cheery nature but also by an unselfish act when on a long and tiring march he had carried the pack of one of his men who was in distress.[394,395]

Having fought across the Somme battlefield the 5/Gloucesters was now transferred to the Ypres Salient to take part in another major offensive of the war, the Third Battle of Ypres. After a period of training at Pommier near Arras, the Battalion arrived at Ypres at 11.30 am on 22 July 1917 where the 48th (South Midland) Division now became part of General Sir Hubert Gough's Fifth Army. The Battalion now had alternating periods of rest and training near Vlamertinghe with periods of front line trench duty in the Salient. On 6 August the Battalion held the line east of Ypres near the Steenbeek where it was subjected to"...*hostile shelling...*" which resulted in numerous casualties including Second Lieutenant **James Winterbotham** (GCCC) who had been wounded for the second time when he was hit by a shell fragment which embedded itself in his leg after it had burst near the entrance of the dug out in which he was sheltering.[396] After the wound was stabilised he was

---

[389] In 1917 the identity of the battalion had been censored but it is now known to be the 1st Battalion, Gloucestershire Regiment
[390] *Cheltenham Chronicle and Gloucestershire Graphic* 21 July 1917
[391] *Gloucester Journal* 21 July 1917
[392] *Edinburgh Gazette* 20 August 1917
[393] *Gloucester Journal* 8 September 1917
[394] *Western Daily Press* 6 September 1917
[395] His younger brother Second Lieutenant Frances Ralph Alderwick served for six months with the Gloucesters before relinquishing his commission through ill health (*Gloucester Journal* 8 September 1917)
[396] Battalion War Diary, 1/5th Battalion Gloucestershire Regiment 6 August 1917, WO 95/2763

transferred to a hospital at Epsom for an operation.[397] The Royal Army Medical Corps had set up a chain of medical posts through which a wounded soldier passed with each post designed either to treat the wound or to stabilise the wounded man in order to pass him on to the next post. After each stage triage decided whether the man was treatable and if not he was simply made as comfortable as possible. Nearest the front were the Regimental Aid Posts which passed the man to the Field Ambulance, the Casualty Clearing Stations [CCS], the Base Hospitals, usually hospitals near the Channel ports or far behind the lines before transfer across the Channel to a British hospital.[398] Once treated the man would be sent to a local Red Cross VA Hospital before going home for a period of convalescence and a subsequent return to active duty; in Gloucester there were three VA Hospitals while there were eleven in Bristol.[399]

The Battalion's next task was to secure the right hand flank of the attack at the Battle of Langemarck (16-18 August). On the 15 August the Battalion once more left its camp and marched through Ypres in a north-east direction to St Julien where it deployed for an attack on the Green Line which the Germans, as a remedy for the high water table in the Salient, had strengthened with concrete strong points or 'pill boxes' which the Battalion encountered for the first time.[400] The first and second waves of the attack would consist of C Company on the right and A Company on the left while the third and fourth waves would deploy D Company on the right and B Company on the left. On the 16 August the Battalion War Diary recorded that,

"...at ZERO hour, 4.45 a.m. the Attack commenced with a barrage. The first objective, namely BORDER HOUSE, Gun Pits on S and N sides of ST. JULIEN – WINNIPEG road was soon gained. Machine guns in JANET FARM and in positions in rear prevented any further advance. A house containing a M.G. was still held by the enemy. This was cleared with Rifle Grenades and a Lewis Gun & was occupied. By this time the barrage had left us behind & many casualties had been caused. The Battalion therefore dug in its present position. A weak counter-attack was stopped with Lewis Gun & rifle fire. During the day enemy snipers were very active & caused us some casualties"[401]

Amongst the attacking soldiers in B Company was Corporal **Charles Cook** (GRFC) who for his actions that day was awarded the Military Medal [MM] for gallantry. Although there are no citations published for the MM, his daughter, Majorie Reade, would recall years later that the Company was,

"...attacking a machine gun position in a farm cottage when his [i.e. Charles Cook's] friend, next to him, was shot. He was angry and determined to get revenge so he rushed the position and fired his [Lewis] Gun up through the ceiling into the room above [where

---

[397] *Cheltenham Chronicle and Gloucestershire Graphic* 25 August 1917
[398] The Regimental Aid Posts [RAP] were set up as near to the front line as possible and were staffed by the Battalion Medical Officers and the battalion orderlies and stretcher bearers. The RAPs tried to stabilise the fresh open wounds to ensure the immediate survival of the soldier and the possibility of more sophisticated life saving treatment further down the line. The proximity of the RAPs to the front line ensured that the medical staff worked in hazardous, primitive conditions and were frequently shelled by the enemy artillery.
[399] In Gloucester there were three hospitals, the Great Western Road Voluntary Aid [VA] Hospital, the Hillfield VA Hospital and the Palace VA Hospital. In Bristol there were eleven hospitals including those at Kingsweston, Aston Court and Almondsbury.
[400] The attack objectives were marked on the maps by a series of coloured lines (green, yellow, red, blue black, purple); intermediate coloured lines were also used on the map to indicate reporting lines. In the instance cited above the green line probably marks the first objective of the attack.
[401] Battalion War Diary, 1/5th Battalion, Gloucestershire Regiment 16 August 1917, TNA WO 95/2763

the German machine was placed]. *The four man German machine gun team immediately came down the stairs with their hands up and shouting 'Kamerad'."* [402]

The 5/Gloucesters was relieved by the 8/Warwicks on the 17 August but remained in support until the evening when it returned to Dambre Camp having suffered casualties of one officer killed, one missing and six wounded together with 209 Other Ranks (killed, missing and wounded).

September:

The 5/Gloucesters Battalion War Diary recorded that following a recommendation after 16 August the award of the Military Medal for **Charles Cook** had been confirmed by the War Office.[403]

October:

The next phase of Third Ypres, the Battle of Broodseinde (4 October 1917), was led by 143 Brigade, with the 1/5th Gloucesters (145 Brigade) in reserve. The Battalion was billeted at Reigersburg Camp on the Ypres-Brielen Road but moved closer to the front on 3 October. However it was gradually drawn into the fight and at 3.30 pm on 3 October it was directed to move up to Arbre to provide closer support but by 5.00 pm these orders had been superseded and it was ordered to attack along with the 143 Brigade at 6.00 am on 4 October (see Map 4). It's orders indicated that,

> "B, C and D Companies, in that order from right to left, were to attack Adler Farm, Inch Houses and Vacher Farm respectively: A Company, with Battalion Headquarters, were in reserve at Albatross."[404]

When the attack commenced and the men left the comparative safety of the trenches, it was obvious that the British artillery barrage had ranged too far ahead with the shells falling harmlessly in the area behind the German machine gun emplacements. Hence along with the mud and the water and unmolested machine guns, the British troops struggled to make progress in the face of overwhelming enemy fire power and,

> "Owing to the barrage being too far ahead and heavy rain the line was advanced only 200 yds, where the position was established. Casualties were light but the total was 2 Officers killed and wounded and 125 OR" [405]

Amongst the 'light' casualties suffered by the 5/Gloucesters were Corporal **Charles Cook** MM (GRFC) and Lance-Corporal **William Parham** (GRFC), the latter who had survived injury on the Somme the previous year was not so fortunate this time. William had been at the front since March 1915, although he had returned home in March 1916 for his wedding to Eveline Cook. In September 1917 he was granted home leave again along with his friend Charles Cook but by the start of October both men had re-joined their battalion in the Ypres Salient. It was soon reported in Gloucester that on 4 October 1917, fighting alongside each other in the same action, Charles Cook had been seriously wounded in the face, losing an eye and that William Parham had been killed.[406] By January 1918 the

---

[402] Personal Communication: Marjorie Read (daughter of Charles Cook) speaking to Graham Gordon (SoGM) 2013; the quote is not *verbatim*. Although it is not possible to determine the exact situation, the Battalion War Diary entry for 16 August 1917 probably identifies the situation when Charles Cook won his MM.
[403] Battalion War Diary, *1/5th Battalion Gloucestershire Regiment 30 September 1917*, TNA WO 95/2763
[404] Wyrall, The Gloucestershire Regiment in the War 1914-1918, p.227
[405] Battalion War Diary, *1/5th Battalion Gloucestershire Regiment 4 October 1917*, TNA WO 95/2763
[406] *Gloucester Journal* 27 October 1917

Hospital Visitors of the Gloucestershire Society were able to report that Charles had been transferred for treatment to the King George Hospital, London.[407]

The offensive was renewed with the final push towards Passchendaele on 26 October at 5.40 am by the Canadian Corps but to create the impression that this was a general offensive along the whole of the line there were simultaneous attacks both north and south to tie down the enemy's reserves. On the northern flank the Fifth Army attack met with little success and in a renewed effort General Gough sent in the 63rd (Royal Naval) Division from XVIII Corps, which included 1/28th (County of London) Battalion (Artist's Rifles) which as part of the 190 Brigade had Lance Corporal **Donald Priestley** (GCCC) in its ranks. The Battalion advanced up the valley of the Lekkerboterbeek but the knee-deep mud slowed the advance to a vulnerable crawl of less than a yard a minute. As the supporting British barrage became ineffective and the men's rifles became useless and clogged with mud, the soldiers attempted to fall back to their starting positions. But the mud which made their advance painfully slow equally hindered or prohibited their return. Fortunately Donald Priestley did make it back to 'safety' but on 30 October the Battalion resumed its attack despite heavy losses (see Map 4). Again the attack floundered in knee-deep mud which prevented the soldiers keeping up with their artillery barrage and they were caught in the open and subjected to a severe German bombardment,[408]

> "The Artist's Rifles (28/London) suffered particularly severely, and the casualties in the brigade amounted to nine hundred all ranks."[409]

Donald Priestley died in this second attack, trapped in No Man's Land with no cover and no hope of a safe return and subjected to an intense German artillery bombardment. Amongst the mud of Passchendaele the bodies of William Parham and Donald Priestley were not found and both are commemorated amongst the 35,000 Missing on the Tyne Cot Memorial (see Photograph 34).[410]

November-December:

In an attempt to draw off German reserves from Flanders the British decided to mount what would become the first mass tank attack of the war. However before the attack could be launched the Third Battle of Ypres was closed down but despite this the Battle of Cambrai (20 November – 7 December) was launched. Almost five hundred tanks were assembled in secret under strict security and took the Germans completely by surprise.[411] The front between Gonnelieu and Boursies was pushed forward in some sectors by nearly six miles and such was the elation that for the first time in three years church bells rang out across Britain. However the jubilation was short-lived as the tanks exceeded their effective range which enabled the Germans to re-group and mount massive counter-attacks across the whole of the front which regained a lot but not all of the territory taken by the British.

---

[407] *Gloucester Journal* 19 January 1918
[408] See Appendix B note 4: Artillery Barrages
[409] James E. Edmonds, *History of the Great War. Military Operations France and Belgium 1917 Vol II 7th June – 10th November. Messines and Third Ypres (Passchendaele)* (London: HMSO, 1948) p.355
[410] Donald's brother Lieutenant Stanley Priestley was killed in action on 23 July 1916 with the 8/Gloucesters during the same attack that **William Nelmes** (GRFC) was killed.
[411] Davies, *Conceal, Create, Confuse,* pp.133-141. Detailed description of how 500 were brought together in secret.

Photograph 34. Tyne Cot Commonwealth War Graves Commission Cemetery and Memorial: The largest GWGC cemetery in the world with 11,956 burials of which 8,369 are unidentified. The memorial which forms the back drop to the cemetery lists the names of 35,000 servicemen who died in the Ypres Salient after August 1917 and who have no known grave and includes **William Parham** (GRFC) and **Donald Priestley** (GCCC). A number of German blockhouses or pill-boxes are incorporated into the cemetery. (*Authors*)

Holding the line in front of La Vacquerie was with the 2/5th Battalion, Gloucestershire Regiment with Lieutenant **William Pearce** (GRFC) amongst its ranks (see Photograph 35).[412] On 2 December the Germans launched a large counter-attack in the area between Epehy and La Vacquerie. The Official History states that,

> "*At 3pm the enemy came on in considerable numbers east and south-east of the village, and, although the advance over the open was everywhere checked and driven back by fire, the bombing attacks* [forced the British line] *back almost to the eastern outskirts of La Vacquerie*" [413]

---

[412] The 2/5th Gloucesters was part of the 184 (2nd South Midland) Brigade, 61st (2nd South Midland) Division, III Corps, Third Army.
[413] W. Miles, *History of the Great War. Military Operations France and Belgium, 1917 Vol.III The Battle of Cambrai* (London: HMSO, 1948), p.250

After recovering from his wounding at Pozières with the 1/5th Battalion, Lieutenant William Pearce, *"...a forward of real merit, being fast, clever and resourceful..."*, was transferred to A Company, 2/5th Battalion and was killed defending La Vacquerie.[414] When war was declared William was working in the Midlands and immediately enlisted in the 5/South Staffordshire Regiment but was soon promoted to Sergeant having had experience in the South African Mounted Police which he had joined in 1903.[415] He rapidly gained a commission in August 1915 with the 1/5th Battalion, Gloucestershire Regiment and was back amongst his friends and former team mates, although he left them for the last time in July 1916 when he was wounded during the attack on Pozières. Early in December his wife, Margery, received a letter from a brother officer, Lieutenant H.G. Knight who informed her that *"...his death was practically instantaneous, I am glad to say"*.[416] Sadly the war had not quite finished with William - he was buried at Villers-Plouich Communal Cemetery, just over a mile west of La Vacquerie but with the turbulence of war the cemetery itself became a 'casualty of the war' and as a result the exact location of his actual grave is unknown. As a consequence William's headstone bears the all too common inscription *'Known to be Buried in this Cemetery'*.

Photograph 35. Lieutenant William 'Billy' Pearce (GRFC): Lieutenant **William Pearce**, 2/5th Battalion, Gloucestershire Regiment was killed in action on 2 December 1917 at La Vacquerie. The photograph taken *circa* 1916 shows William holding his daughter, Monica (1915-1993) who would have a nursing career in Great Britain and Paris and become the Matron (1961-1973) at the Birmingham General Hospital. After her retirement she founded St Mary's Hospice, Selly Oak (opened in 1979) and founded the first hospice in Poland at Gdansk in 1989; she was awarded the OBE and honoured by the Pope. *(Gwen Johns)*

Captain **Alec Lewis** (GRFC), 6/Royal Berkshires, 53 Brigade, 18th (Eastern) Division in the Ypres Salient, again distinguished himself and was awarded a Bar to his Military Cross, that is, a second Military Cross:

---

[414] *Gloucester Journal* 15 December 1917
[415] *Gloucester Journal* 15 December 1917
[416] *Gloucester Journal* 15 December 1917

> *"...for conspicuous gallantry and devotion to duty in carrying out the duties of brigade intelligence officer. During some reconnaissances made under heavy shell and rifle fire, he gained most valuable information regarding the ground and our dispositions. On one occasion he made a reconnaissance along the front line in close proximity to the enemy under fire from their snipers."*[417]

Alec's experience as a brigade intelligence officer would result in a posting to the 4/Intelligence Corps and a promotion to Major. The Intelligence Corps had been formed in August 1914 specifically to analyse prisoner of war and refugee debriefings and later analysis of aerial photographs, all to assist the Army in the disposition of its units; the Corps was disbanded in 1929.

For the men of the rugby and cricket clubs 1917 had indeed been 'death or glory' as six had died during the year and eight were awarded medals for gallantry.

---

[417] *Gloucester Journal* 27 April 1918

5

1918: THE END OF THE GREAT ADVENTURE

"…he did not know what fear was…"
A Guard's Officer writing on the death of **Henry Lane** (GRFC)

"He destroyed a great many groups of hostile machine guns…"
Herbert Tayler (GCCC) on the award of the Distinguished Conduct Medal [DCM] and Medaille Militaire

This year would see the end of the Great War but with a surge in the casualty rates as mobile warfare returned to the Western Front. With the ever-looming prospect of an army from the United States of America of one million men being ready to take to the field before the end of 1918, the German commanders Field Marshal Paul von Hindenburg and General Erich von Ludendorff devised a high risk offensive, the Kaiserschlacht - the 'Kaiser's Battle' - designed to drive a 'wedge' between the British and French Armies, drive the British back to the Channel ports and force the surrender of the French Army. The German Spring Offensive, a series of five co-ordinated attacks along the Western Front would commence on 21 March with Operation Michael targeting the British Fifth Army at its junction with the French Army.

January:

Captain **James Winterbotham** (GCCC), 5/Gloucesters, was awarded the Military Cross announced in the 1918 New Year Honours' List issued on 31 December 1917 (see Photograph 36).[418,419,420,421]

Photograph 36. An Oil Painting by Frederick Roe: Entitled *'A relieved Platoon of the 1/5th marching in from the trenches past Headquarters at Hébuterne 1916'*. The 1/5th Gloucesters held the line at Hébuterne immediately before the Somme Offensive. The painting includes the officers from left to right, Captain C. Winterbotham (War Poet, killed in action 27 August 1916), Reverend G.F. Helm (Chaplain 1/5th Gloucesters) and Captain **J.P. Winterbotham** MC (GCCC). (*SoGM, GLRRM:02936*)

March:

On 21 March the Germans launched the first of their five offensives, initially targeting the British Fifth Army and VI and IV Corps from the Third Army along a forty-three miles front running between Arras, St Quentin and La Fère (see Map 5).[422] Using Stormtroopers (Sturmtruppen) to spearhead the attacks, the British were driven back along on the whole of the attack front, forcing the retirement of

---

[418] Battalion War Diary, *1/5th Battalion Gloucestershire Regiment January 1918*, TNA WO 95/4251
[419] *Gloucester Journal* 5 January 1918
[420] Quoted in his obituary *The Citizen* 2December 1925.
[421] His brother Lieutenant Cyril Winterbotham, the war poet, also serving in the 5/Gloucesters had been killed in action on 27 August 1916; the two brothers had served together since the beginning of the war
[422] The British Third Army consisted of four corps – north to south XVII, VI, IV and V Corps. Initially the Germans only targeted the VI and IV Corps with simple holding actions against the XVII and V Corps..

the remaining Third Army Corps (XVII and V) rather than run the risk of isolation and annihilation. On 30 March the British Official History highlighted this German strategy and testified to the intensity of the fighting,

> "The right and left divisions of the VI Corps passed a quiet day, but the Guards Divn, in the centre, had to sustain the heaviest attack made upon it since it went into the line, the enemy, no doubt, hoping to cut off the troops...At 8 a.m. a heavy bombardment was opened on the 3rd Guards Bde, and it soon spread southwards to include the 1st. Shortly after 10 a.m. when a British barrage was dropped on the attackers...the Germans increased the rate of their gun fire. Three-quarters of an hour later, their infantry (234th Division), with packs on, advanced against the 3rd Guards Bde (1/Grenadier and 1/Welsh Guards), under cover of a barrage provided by machine guns and fourteen aeroplanes dropping bombs. They were everywhere stopped by devastating fire before reaching the outer belt of wire, except at one spot where fifty broke in, but were dealt with by immediate counter-attack. The 1st Guards Bde (2/Grenadier Guards) was similarly successful, although, when a second attack was made upon it, a few Germans gained a footing in the line. These intruders were likewise overwhelmed by counter-attack."[423]

The assault by the German 234th Division resulted in the death of Lance Corporal **Harry Lane** (GRFC) whose bravery in 1916 had been recognised with the award of the Distinguished Conduct Medal. Harry, a Reservist who had been at the front since 8 November 1914, was buried at Bucquoy Road Cemetery, Ficheux, about three miles directly behind the line he was defending, close to the 20th and 43rd Casualty Clearing Stations, which remained at Boisleux-au-Mont throughout March 1918 despite the advancing Germans (see Map 5). At the start of March he had been promoted to Lance Corporal in the divisional troop unit, the 4th Battalion, Guards Machine Gun Regiment which was formed on 1 March 1918. Early in April Harry's mother received a letter from Sergeant J.W. Hill which conveyed the news that he had been killed in action on the morning of 30 March 1918.

> "...I can assure you he suffered no pain whatever, his death being instantaneous. Myself and all the section join in with you in the loss of such a gallant and noble son...I myself shall miss him a great deal as he has been in my section ever since he came out in 1914 and was the best Corporal I had."[424]

The Citizen reprinted a letter from a Guards officer to Henry's wife which agreed that he had been "...killed instantaneously by an unlucky shell which came straight down the mouth of a deep dug-out" and he testified to Harry's character by adding that "...he did not know what fear was..." [425]

For Harry's mother, Elizabeth Lane, this was a particularly sad time as two days after Harry's death, his father, William Lane died.

April:

As the German Army's advance engulfed Harry Lane and the Guards Division, further south its progress was unrelenting as it crossed the old Somme battlefields, which having taken the British

---

[423] J.E. Edmonds, *History of the Great War. Military Operations France and Belgium, 1918 Vol II March-April: Continuation of the German Offensive* (London: Macmillan & Co.,1937), p.97
[424] *Gloucester Journal* 20 April 1918
[425] *The Citizen* 23 April 1918

Army 142 days to capture in 1916, were lost to the Germans in two days in 1918. British Army units were driven back so fast that they had great difficulty establishing any sort of defensive line that would halt or even slow down the German advance. On 25 March the German front line was near Bapaume but by 27 March the line had advanced twelve miles and Albert was in German hands (see Map 2). The British Army pulled back fighting rearguard actions the whole of the way, taking a heavy toll on the advancing Stormtroopers and ordinary infantryman alike. Every able-bodied British soldier was pressed into action from cooks to Officer's servants. Pioneer battalions were no exception and, although accustomed to using their rifles, were now fighting alongside infantry units to stem the German onslaught.[426] Lance Corporal **George Griffiths** (GRFC) now transferred to the 13/Gloucesters (Pioneers) was killed on 4 April 1918 somewhere between Bapaume and Albert.[427] His body lay behind German lines and with their rapid advance the time and manpower devoted to burying the British and German dead in marked graves was low. As a consequence George's body was never found and he is commemorated on the Pozières Memorial to the Missing of the Somme, 1918.[428] George Griffiths, "...*a rattling forward...*", was an 'old soldier' who had served with the 1/Gloucesters guarding Boer prisoners on the island of Ceylon.[429] He had re-joined his old regiment in France on 20 January 1915 but was invalided home in April. After recovery he was transferred to the 10/Gloucesters, returning to the Western Front in August 1915; subsequently he was transferred to the 13th Battalion after the 10/Gloucesters was disbanded in February 1918.[430] In the same action Captain **Hugh Jones** (GCCC), fighting alongside George Griffiths in the 13/Gloucesters, received extensive but not life threatening wounds to both legs and was transferred to a London hospital for treatment; four machine gun bullets had pierced his thighs.[431,432] Hugh never returned to front and sadly in November, the same year, he succumbed to influenza.

On 9 April, the Germans launched their next assault of their coordinated offensive, the Battle of the Lys (Operation Georgette), in an area which stretched from La Bassée to north of Ypres. In this area the 8/Gloucesters were defending the line near Mount Kemmel as the Germans swept over the region (see Map 2). By the middle of the month Ellen Dix was officially notified that her husband Private **William Dix** (GRFC), 8/Gloucesters, had been missing since 15 April 1918.[433] In June she was relieved to receive a reassuring postcard from him which indicated that he, together with thirty of his comrades, was now a prisoner of war in Germany.[434] Although the newspapers reported his

---

[426] The recruitment advertisements for men to join Pioneer battalions stressed the fact that they must be accustomed to using spades and shovels. A major task for the Pioneers was to consolidate newly captured enemy trench systems but with the ever present danger of German counter-attacks they were expected to down their spades and pick up their rifles to stem the attack. The training that the Pioneers received reflected these dual activities.
[427] Although George at the time of his death is listed on the CWGC Database as a member of the 10/Gloucesters, it was disbanded on 14 February 1918 and the men transferred primarily to the 13th (Service) Battalion (Forest of Dean), Gloucestershire Regiment.
[428] On the Somme, the Missing from the 1916 battles are commemorated on the Thiepval Memorial while those missing in the 1918 battles are commemorated on the Pozières Memorial. The two memorials are within sight of each other
[429] *The Citizen* 19 December 1908
[430] *Cheltenham Chronicle and Gloucestershire Graphic* 17 April 1915
[431] *Gloucester Journal* 6 April 1918
[432] Sibley and Newth, *Wycliffe and the War. A School Record,* p.61
[433] *Gloucester Journal* 18 May 1918
[434] *Gloucester Journal* 1 June 1918

whereabouts in Germany he actually remained in Belgium forced to work behind the German front lines and was eventually liberated at Turnout, near the Dutch border on 11 November. After the Armistice William, as a prisoner, unlike a lot of his Gloucester team mates, was quickly demobilised and by the end of November he was back in Gloucester and ready to assist the Club in playing its first few matches despite having lost a stone in weight due to the scanty rations, "...*chiefly horseflesh and beans – provided by the enemy.*"[435]

As the German advances made progress across the Western Front the situation became critical for the British and French Armies and Field Marshal Sir Douglas Haig issued his special order, dated 11 April, to his forces,

> "….*There is no course open to us but to fight it out. Every position must be held to the last man: there must be no retirement. With our backs to the wall and believing in the justice of our cause each one of us must fight on to the end.*"

Meanwhile the career of **Cornelius Carleton** DSO (GRFC), 2/Welsh, had blossomed after being promoted to Temporary Major. Initially he had been given command of the 6th (Glamorgan) Battalion, Welsh Regiment (June 1916-March 1917) and subsequently four months commanding the 8th (Service) Battalion, Berkshire Regiment (March-July 1917) before returning to the 6/Welsh. On 9 April now with the rank of Acting Lieutenant-Colonel, he took command of his own battalion, the 2/Welsh; from Lieutenant to Acting Lieutenant-Colonel, such were the fortunes of war. His stint as commanding officer was but short-lived as after four days he was wounded, for the second time, in the right arm, and transferred to the Prince of Wales' Hospital in Marylebone, London.[436] The History of the Welsh Regiment stated that:

> "*On 11th April "A" and "B" Companies went up in support of the Cameron Highlanders on the La Bassée Canal where they came in for a good deal of shelling, Lieutenant-Colonel Carleton being wounded for the second time…*"[437]

The ferocity of the fighting during this stage of the war was never truly conveyed to or appreciated by the civilians on the home front in Gloucestershire. The *Gloucestershire Chronicle* reported that "...*near a lock on the canal some Gloucestershire men fought on after they had been cut off and surrounded for some 12 hours...*"[438] This statement however failed to express the desperate nature of the fighting as the Germans tried to break the Allied line. The Battalion War Diaries portray a different story. On 15 April the 1/Gloucesters had taken over the sector in the vicinity of the La Bassée Canal but within days a captured German soldier revealed details of a forthcoming attack and immediately "...*all ranks* [were] *warned of what was coming.*" On 18 April following a hour-and-half bombardment which included mustard gas shells ("yellow cross"), the Germans attacked at 8.15 am in thick fog with visibility down to less than 50 yards.[439] The fighting was ferocious and as the Germans got to within one hundred yards of B Company's position, one Lewis Gun team alone exhausted 1,400 rounds of ammunition to hold the advance. But the Germans were breaking through the various positions and the Gloucesters were forced to fight from shell hole to shell hole. As the Gloucesters' reserves were pushed up to secure positions and check the enemy's advances,

---

[435] *The Citizen* 2 December 1918
[436] *Gloucester Journal* 27 April 1918
[437] Thomas O. Marden, Major General Sir, *The History of the Welch Regiment 1914-1918*, (1932) p.452 (Reprinted and available from Naval and Military Press).
[438] *Gloucestershire Chronicle* 11 May 1918
[439] Battalion War Diary, *1st Battalion Gloucestershire Regiment 18 April 1918*, TNA WO 95/1278

the "...*machine gunners, runners and stretcher bearers were shot down as fast as they appeared on the road...*" Reinforcements became exhausted as all available men were deployed into the firing line. Battalion Headquarters was subject to "...*severe shelling by 5.9s coupled with severe machine gun fire...*" and communication with it became impossible – at 11.00 am Sergeant Major Biddle (D Company) did get through and requested further reinforcements only to be told that there were none.[440] Nothing escaped the enemy onslaught. As the wounded men were brought back to the Dressing Station by the surviving stretcher bearers, it too was hit by a 5.9" shell which "...*killed and wounded several of the medical staff and casualties...*" But the ferocity of the enemy assault was matched by an equally ferocious defence by the Gloucesters which was prepared to fight "...*to the last man.*" By midday the attack had been held and the Germans driven back. That action by the Gloucesters resulted in fifty-six men killed and 128 wounded and thirty-three gallantry medals won.

May:

In Gloucester the announcement of the death of Lieutenant **Ronald Grist** (GRFC) would have challenged the memory of most of the rugby supporters for he had played for the Club in 1888-89 season.[441] In 1914 at the age of forty-six years Ronald had volunteered for active service and after being passed fit by the military doctors, joined the 18/Rifle Brigade. He was assigned to garrison duties in order to release younger soldiers for active combat and in November 1915 he was initially sent to India but soon transferred to the military garrison at Rangoon (Burma). Sadly after two years he fell ill and died on 15 May 1918, aged forty-nine years and was buried in the Rangoon Cantonment Cemetery.[442] In May 1945, after the re-capture of Rangoon from the Japanese in the Second World War, the CWGC established the Rangoon War Cemetery and three years later in 1948, thirty-six soldiers from the Great War, including Ronald, were re-interred in the Rangoon War Cemetery.

June:

After over three months of bitter fighting, the German Spring Offensive gradually lost momentum as Haig's men made their 'last stand' and took an extremely high toll on the elite German forward units who out-distanced their supply trains. The logic of using their best troops as Stormtroopers seemed initially to make sense but was a gamble which was fatally flawed; the British and French defences were never breached and, as the Allies fell back, they retained the ability to inflict massive casualties. The result was that the German Army had expended its best troops and would now have to rely on troops who, for the most part, lacked combat experience; fortunately the Allies still had experienced troops remaining who could form the nucleus of the units for the remainder of the war.

In the King's Birthday Honours, Major (Acting Lieutenant Colonel) **Gilbert Collett** (GRFC), 5/Gloucesters, was awarded the Distinguished Service Order [DSO] for "...*distinguished service under*

---

[440] For his action CSM W. Biddle would be awarded a Bar to his DCM

[441] In the 1888-89 season Ronald represented the Club on the wing in eighteen of the twenty-three games played that season, scoring nine tries. In the match reports in *The Citizen* Ronald was 'man-of-the-match' in all his games with the newspaper bemoaning the fact that he was too often ignored by his team mates. Ronald was also one of a handful of players to enhance his reputation when he represented Gloucestershire against the touring New Zealand Maoris and was more than a match for their defence. Ronald would have undoubtedly played more games for Gloucester but his work took him away from the city.

[442] *Gloucester Journal* 25 May 1918

fire..."[443] This award was not for any one specific act but for leadership of A Company 1/5th Gloucesters and for his periods in command of the 1/5th and 2/5th Gloucesters.

July:

By the end of June the British had stabilised their front line and began the fight back against the now over-extended German forces. At Le Hamel on 4 July the line was straightened in an action which involved Australian, British and American troops and the all-important British Tank Corps.[444] On 23 July further south at Moreuil the French 3rd and 152nd Divisions d'Infantrie launched an attack towards Sauvillers-Mongival (see Map 5). To directly support the French infantry British tanks from the 9th Battalion, Tank Corps were attached to and under the command of the French 3rd Division with each tank provided with an English speaking French soldier. Amongst the tank crews was Sergeant **Herbert Tayler** (GCCC), who for his actions that day was awarded the Distinguished Conduct Medal [DCM] and the French Medaille Militaire for conspicuous gallantry and devotion to duty during the operations when in the absence of a tank commander,

> "*He commanded a tank with great success during the whole of an action, fighting it with much skill and the utmost bravery. He destroyed a great many groups of hostile machine guns, and brought away several guns complete with spare parts. On his own initiative he advanced through our protective barrage and patrolled far in advance of the infantry, thus greatly assisting their action. He set an admirable example of cheerfulness and resolute determination.*"[445,446]

The French Medaille Militaire was awarded "*Pour leur grande bravoure pendant le combat du 23 juillet 1918*". For their actions that day the 9th Battalion, Tank Corps was awarded two DCMs, ten Military Medals and twelve Medailles Militaire; Herbert was one of four tank crew to receive both a British and a French gallantry award.

At the end of July 1917 Lieutenant **Michael Arthur Green** (GCCC), 1/Gloucesters, was assigned to the 30 (Infantry) Brigade, promoted to Captain with the role of Brigade Major. The Brigade Major was in constant contact with the front line battalion and played a key role in the planning and execution of brigade operations. During one of Michael's visits to the front line following a successful attack he adjusted the line in readiness for the next operation. For his actions he was awarded the Military Cross with a citation that read,

> "*For conspicuous gallantry and devotion to duty. He went forward after a successful attack to reconnoitre and adjust the new line in full view of the enemy and under very heavy artillery and machine gun fire. He showed marked ability in carrying out this work, and obtained valuable information which enabled dispositions to be made to ensure the line against immediate counter-attacks*"[447]

---

[443] *London Gazette* 3 June 1918 p.6458
[444] This action saw the introduction for the first time of the new Mark V tank, a more manoeuvrable, reliable and better armed and armoured model than previous. Also it now became standard practice for infantry sections to 'adopt' tanks so that the tanks and the infantry fought as more cohesive units.
[445] *London Gazette* 29 October 1918 p.12840
[446] *London Gazette* 5 November 1918 p.13117
[447] *London Gazette* 26 July 1918 p. 8864 and *Western Daily Press* 1 August 1918

August:
On 8 August at Amiens the British launched a well prepared attack supported by tanks against the German lines (see Maps 2 and 5). The latter were taken by surprise and the British pushed through on what Ludendorff would describe as the 'Black Day of the German Army'.[448] Although there was still a large amount of fighting to be done and at a high cost in casualties, the Battle of Amiens (8-12 August) began what became known as the *'Final Hundred Days'*. The lack of a flexible and reactive logistics system had cost the Germans dearly in their Spring Offensives but the British had employed Sir Eric Geddes to re-organise the Army's Logistics Corps which provided Haig with the ability to switch points of attack safe in the knowledge that the infantry would not go short of food and military supplies. Between 8 August and 11 November all the British Armies were able to mount coordinated attacks along the whole of the British sector switching points of attack which for the Germans resulted in huge problems regarding the deployment of their reserves and reinforcements. Further south the French Army were also exerting the same kind of pressure on the German line.

September:
In the days preceding the Battle of the Canal du Nord (27 September-1 October 1918) the 56th (1st London) Division was advancing towards the heavily fortified canal which was part of the defences of the German Army's much vaunted and supposedly impregnable Hindenburg Line (Siegfried Stellung) comprising of concrete bunkers, machine gun emplacements with overlapping fields of fire and deep belts of barbed wire; the whole was designed to create killing zones which would take a heavy toll on the approaching British Army. In order to ensure that the latter had a 'fighting chance' the Divisional Train, part of the Army Service Corps [ASC], kept it supplied with materials and munitions. Although not an 'active' combat unit, the work of the Divisional Train was extremely hazardous as it attracted the close attention of the German artillery and machine gunners in an attempt to cut off the vital supplies. In the 56th Divisional Train Second Lieutenant **Thomas Archibald Truman** (GRFC and GCCC) died on active service on 13 September at the No. 1 Canadian Casualty Clearing Station [CCS] at Etrun, not from enemy action but from pneumonia and peritonitis after only three days illness which was testimony to the harsh conditions prevailing in the battle zone (see Map 2) (see Photograph 37). Thomas was buried in the cemetery attached to the CCS which is now known as Duisans British Cemetery; his fellow rugby player, **Arthur Russell** (GRFC) is buried in the same cemetery. Thomas was described as one of "*...the best all round athletes in Gloucester...*" although his job meant that his representative appearances were limited.[449]

On 26 September Captain **William Grant** (GCCC), 5/Cameron Highlanders (9th (Scottish) Division, 26 Brigade (Highland)) was killed in action at Passchendaele during the Fourth Battle of Ypres as the British Second Army advanced the line. In 1917 at a high cost in casualties the British Army had waged a 103 day-long campaign and captured the town of Passchendaele with its commanding views over the Ypres Salient but in April 1918 the German Spring Offensive regained most of the captured ground within eighteen days.[450] Since 8 August 1918 the Allied armies advanced re-

---
[448] Erich Ludendorff, *My War Memories* (London: Hutchison & Co., 1919)
[449] *The Citizen* 18 September 1918
[450] The Third Battle of Ypres (Passchendaele) lasted from 31 July until 10 November 1917 while the Battle of Lys (2-29 April 1918) in front of Ypres lasted from 9-27 April 1918 and the Germans recovered the ground lost in 1917.

capturing the ground lost during the German Spring Offensives. Early in September William had been awarded the Military Cross as on two occasions he had,

> "...made a reconnaissance under heavy artillery fire, bringing back a full account of the situation. He went round the line while fighting was in progress encouraging his men."[451]

At the beginning of the war William was still a scholar at Clifton College although had passed the Cambridge University entrance examination. But keen to enter service he had applied for a commission on 6 August 1914 with the Leicestershire Regiment and on the 11 August with the Gloucestershire Regiment; as he was under 21 years old his mother had to grant permission. He was accepted into both regiments.[452] He opted for the Gloucesters but was soon transferred to the Worcestershire Regiment. In January 1916 he was wounded in the left knee after the collapse of a dug out in which he was sheltering and subsequently contracted scarlet fever, both conditions attributed to active service by the Medical Board at the Military Hospital in Sterling; he was passed fit to resume active service on 29 May 1916. William made a will on 22 January 1918 which was contained in a letter addressed to his mother in which £100 from his estate valued at £1,022 2s 11d was left to his sister and the remainder to his servant Private Herbert York, 5/Cameron Highlanders, who "...*has pulled me through a lot...and* [is] *more my friend than servant...*". He asked his mother not to lose touch with Herbert York and to "...*do what you can for him.*"[453,454]

After five months recuperation from his wounding in April, Lieutenant Colonel **Cornelius Carleton** (GRFC) resumed command of the 2/Welsh, but typical of the man who seemed to be in the 'thick of the action', within two weeks, he was wounded again for the third time, this time in the wrist, and again left his command to be hospitalised in London.[455] Cornelius would not return to take command of the 2/Welsh as by the time that he recovered the war had finished; Cornelius Carleton managed to survive in France from 13 August 1914 until the end of the war, hospital stays aside.

October:

Although the war was in reality in its final weeks this was not the view either politically or from the trenches where the fighting remained ferocious and the casualty rates high. Wounded three times and a survivor from the 5/Gloucesters, **Percy Simmons** (GRFC) in March 1918 had gained a commission as a Second Lieutenant in the 2/Wiltshires (58 Brigade, 19th (Western) Division).[456] Percy was killed in action at St Aubert, near Cambrai during the Battle of the Selle (17-25 October), by friendly fire on 20 October as the British artillery launched a bombardment immediately prior to the Wiltshires attacking the German lines (see Map 2).

---

[451] *Dundee Courier* 26 September 1918
[452] Captain William Grant, 5/Cameron Highlanders, Service Record, TNA WO 339/21990-C579836
[453] Private 18740 Herbert York, 5/Cameron Highlanders, survived the war
[454] The rest of William Grant's letter contains personal messages to his mother which will not be reproduced here – the Army chose to open this private letter much to the annoyance of the family and their solicitors
[455] *Gloucester Journal* 28 September 1918
[456] The 2/Wiltshires had gone to war in September 1914 as part of 21 Brigade, 7th Division but in December 1915 the brigade moved to the 30th Division. In May 1918 the regiment moved to the 58 Brigade, 19th (western) Division.

"At 0200 hours the barrage opened 200 yards in front of the Railway Embankment, where it remained for 44 minutes [but] several of these shells burst short with the result that the Battalion suffered several casualties from our own barrage. Lieut JHF RAMSDEN being wounded, 2nd Lieut PJ SIMMONS being killed..."[457,458,459]

Photograph 37. End of the Match: Thomas Truman (GRFC and GCCC) strides off at the end of his first County match against Warwickshire. In a low scoring match he failed to score in both innings as did **Charles Barnett**, **William Brown**, **Richard Godsell** and **Gilbert Jessop** in the first innings. In the background **George Dennett** (left) and **Jack Board** are in discussion with one of the umpires. Thomas Truman died on 13 September 1918 at Etrun. Jack Board who was 47 years old when war broke out supported the war effort through charity cricket matches while George Dennett (East Yorkshire Regiment) the survived the war and resumed his County Cricket career. (*CCGG*)

The last rugby player to die on the Western Front was Second Lieutenant **Arthur Charles Russell** (GRFC). Initially serving as a Private in the 3/Gloucesters and the Army Service Corps, he gained a

---

[457] Battalion War Diary, *2nd Battalion Wiltshire Regiment 20 October 1918*, TNA WO 95/2329
[458] A not uncommon complaint amongst the infantry was the artillery 'shorts' – British artillery shells which for a variety of reasons fell short of their intended target, the German positions, and landed amongst attacking British infantry soldiers resulting in significant casualties.
[459] After the war Percy Simmons' wife, Violet was eventually re-married to Gunner Francis Potter, DSC, who was the Director-General on board HMS Iron Duke, Admiral Jellicoe's flagship at the Battle of Jutland 1916. Francis' task was to aim and fire all the 13.5" guns and on 1 June 1916 he wrote a report his actions at Jutland.

commission on 5 November 1917 with the 6th (Reserve) Battalion, Rifle Brigade (The Prince Consort's Own). In October 1918 he was attached to the 2nd Battalion and was in the line at Estrun about three miles north-west of **Percy Simmons** and the 2/Wiltshires. On 16 October he was hit by a bullet which penetrated his right lung and although transferred to the Canadian CCS at Etrun he died there twelve days later on 28 October from his wounds.[460] He was buried at Duisans British Cemetery along with fellow Club player, **Thomas Truman** (GRFC and GCCC)

Major (Brevet Lieutenant Colonel) **Arthur Du Boulay** (GCCC) DSO, Royal Engineers, a professional soldier and veteran of the Boer War, was taken ill and moved to the 6th Stationary Hospital at Fillièvres, thirty miles west of Arras. He died on 25 October from influenza (Spanish Flu) as the pandemic began to spread across Europe.[461,462]

November:

As Germany sued for peace and the Great War drew to a close, the Allies pushed the Germans back as far eastwards as possible to exert the maximum amount of political gain during the Armistice negotiations. The Battle of Valenciennes (1-2 November) witnessed the last officially recognised act of gallantry by a Gloucester Rugby player (see Map 2). On 1 November at 7.15 am, the 2/5th Gloucesters (182 Brigade, 61st Division) had entered Maresches, four miles south east of Valenciennes, but were rapidly driven out by a strong German counterattack as the fighting remained ferocious and unabated up to the very end of the war. But at 7.30 pm the 182 brigade launched a night attack which re-captured the village but further advances stalled in the face of strong machine gun emplacements.[463] One of a number of these strongly fortified enemy positions was captured by a small group of men from the 2/5th Gloucesters which included Sergeant **Albert Barnes** (GRFC) who for his actions was awarded the Distinguished Conduct Medal [DCM]. His citation read,

> "For gallantry and devotion to duty. At Maresches, during a night attack on 1st November 1918, he was acting C.S.M. The advance was held up in one sector by a strong enemy post, and he, with his company commander and a few men, rushed the post. He bayoneted two of the enemy and knocked another out with his fists. His fine courage and example inspired the confidence of all ranks." [464]

With the enemy positions at Maresches over-run by the 2/5th Gloucesters and the 2/4th Ox and Bucks, the following morning they pushed on eastwards as part of the continuing divisional advance, destroying enemy posts moved beyond St Hubert.

---

[460] *The Citizen* 1 November 1918

[461] Arthur Du Boulay was acknowledged as one of the Army's finest batsmen and held the run record at 402 not out scored for the School of Military Engineering against the Royal Navy in July 1907; he also took eight wickets in the same match (*Newcastle Daily Journal* 26 July 1916 and www.cricketarchive.com)

[462] The Spanish Flu pandemic of 1918 killed an estimate 50-100 million people worldwide. The Great War soldiers were considered particularly vulnerable owing to the harsh deprived of the battlefields

[463] The ferocious nature of the warfare was maintained by German machine gun crews whose fanatical and often suicidal defence would be renowned during this phase of the war.

[464] *London Gazette* 2 December 1919

Photograph 38. Captain Hugh Jones, MC (GCCC) (1888-1918): Captain **Hugh Jones**, 13/Gloucesters, was awarded the Military Cross for standing in the open and flashing his torch to guide his men back to the safety of the trenches. Hugh died of pneumonia in November 1918. (*Wycliffe College*)

Earlier in the year, in April, Captain **Hugh Jones** MC (GCCC), 13/Gloucesters had been wounded in both legs and on recovery in July had been transferred to the 3rd Battalion (Depot) – the Gloucesters reserve battalion - at Sittingbourne. However at the end of October he was admitted to Fort Pitt Military Hospital at Chatham suffering from influenza and whilst there pneumonia rapidly developed and he died two weeks later on 10 November (see Photograph 38). His body was brought back to Lydney and was buried in St Mary's Churchyard with the private grave stone being inscribed with the badge of the Gloucestershire Regiment. Hugh, a pupil at Wycliffe College, had shown great aptitude for cricket and featured regularly in the school magazine, *The Wycliffe Star*, between 1902 and 1904.[465] Sadly his real potential was never realised as after only one game for Gloucestershire CCC in 1914 the war intervened. An obituary written in 1923 for the publication, *Wycliffe and the War. A School Record*, recorded that he was a modest man who when recommended for the Military Cross protested to his Colonel who politely told him to mind his own business; Hugh subsequently requested his parents *"Please don't shout about it"*.[466,467] Hugh was the last cricketer to die during the war

The Armistice which would effectively end the Great War came into effect at 11.00 am on 11 November 1918 as Big Ben rang out across London in the same way as it had signalled the start of

---

[465] The relevant copies of *The Wycliffe Star* and *Wycliffe and the War* were supplied courtesy of Catherine Roberts, Wycliffe College.
[466] Sibley and Newth (eds), *Wyclffe and the War. A School Record*, pp. 60-65
[467] The chapel spire and the clock tower at Wycliffe School were built as memorials to the former students who died in the Great War.

the war on 4 August 1914. However the Armistice was not the end of hostilities but *merely* a ceasefire and as a consequence both sides tried to consolidate their positions and for the Allies training was maintained until the war was officially ended by the Treaty of Versailles signed on 28 June 1919.[468] As a consequence, the war would deal one final blow to the Rugby Club.

The Royal Naval Air Service (RNAS) and the Royal Flying Corps (RFC) had been amalgamated into the independent Royal Air Force [RAF] on 1 April 1918.[469] To meet the potential of renewed hostilities the RAF maintained a programme training new pilots. Amongst the Flight Cadets was **William Henderson** (GRFC) who had emigrated to Canada in 1911, fought with the Canadian Infantry before joining the RFC in 1917 and ultimately the RAF in 1918. Sadly, on 28 November 1918, a week after being on leave in Gloucester visiting relatives, he was killed in a flying accident in Scotland. Whilst practising acrobatic combat manoeuvres in a Sopwith Camel, his lap strap snapped and William flew out of the cockpit and, in the absence of a pilot's parachute, fell to the ground.[470] His body was brought back to Gloucester and was interred at Gloucester Old Cemetery in a CWGC grave.[471]

By the end of the Great War, forty-seven players from the two clubs had died, twenty-nine from the rugby club, seventeen form the cricket club and one who played for both.

At 3.00 pm on Thursday 21 November Lieutenant **George Holloway** (GRCC), West Yorkshires, set foot on the GWR Station at Gloucester having been a prisoner of war at Gütersloh in Germany for the past two years. He had been released from the German camp and interned in Holland on 12 October as part of a prisoner exchange scheme on condition that he did not re-join the war effort.[472] With the signing of the Armistice he was repatriated to Britain and on 26 November was transferred to the POW Reception Centre at Ripon where he was recommended for two months leave before reporting to the Reserve Battalion at Whitley Bay.[473] However on 4 December he received a letter from the War Office requesting details of his capture to be provided to the Army Council's Standing Committee of Enquiry which, as an officer, required him to explain and justify his capture by the Germans. In his testimony George wrote,

"I went out on patrol on the night of August 6th 1916 with a Sergt. and two men about 1 am with orders from Brigade to reconnoitre the G[erman] wire and if possible get a prisoner. The men carried rifles and 2 Mills [bombs] each, myself revolver and 2 Mills. I arranged with my Coy Commander...to have Very Lights fired every ¼ hour if not back again by 2 am. We found the G. wire intact opposite our Coy front (about 300 yards away) and after listening for a working party of their's and hearing none, decided to return about 2 am. By this time a dense ground fog had come on and it was v. difficult to

---

[468] This date is significant in that it is five years to the day, 28 June 1914, that the Archduke Franz Ferdinand was assassinated in Serejvo by Gavrilo Princip, an event which started the chain of events which led to the Great War.

[469] The Royal Naval Air Service (RNAS) and the Royal Flying Corps (RFC) had been the flying arms of the Royal Navy and the British Army respectively. However on 1 April 1918 the RNAS and the RFC amalgamated into the Royal Air Force which became the third arm of the British Forces and an 'independent' service in its own right.

[470] Bob Brunsdon, 'Flight Cadet William Douglas Henderson, Royal Air Force, 32nd Training Depot Station, Montrose', *The Sentinel* Volume 1 Issue 15 (October 2012), pp.6-8. (*The Sentinel* is the journal of the Cheltenham and Gloucester branch of the Western Front Association).

[471] *The Citizen* 4 December 1918

[472] *Cheltenham Chronicle and Gloucestershire Graphic* 23 November 1918

[473] Lieutenant George Holloway, 8/Northumberland Fusiliers, Service Record TNA WO 339/23456-C572864

see anything – no stars were out. At the same time we hit some wire which we took to be ours and I crawled in to the trench only to find it wired in top to bottom. After consultation we agreed it was probably our line, though v. likely another part, since the wire, staples, uprights, etc were same as ours. After proceeding along the outside I again tried the trench, only to find the same again. I neither heard or saw any sentry groups. Accordingly I took the men through the wire and over the trench to the other side, my idea being that if our trench as expected it made no difference which side we came in from, where as if G[erman] trench we might v. likely find out something useful. I left the men in the wire and myself crawled along the parados side of the trench until I heard a man cough: when I got within a few yds of him, not being able to see, I challenged 'Are these W. Yorkshire lines?' Some whispering followed and I challenged again: This time I got the reply 'Hands up Englander'. I shouted to the men to get back and at the same time he fired but missed: I returned his shot and heard him fall down but whether dead or not I don't know as I plunged into the wire and worked back towards their lines since I had no chance of getting over their front line back, as they started to fire on us heavily and to bomb and traverse their wire with M[achine] G[un] fire. A quarter of an hour or so later the firing ceased and I crawled into a shell hole just inside their wire and close to their 2nd line, cut a good deal and with a bomb wound in my right arm but otherwise alright. I remained there quite 3 hours close enough to hear the Gs talking and having breakfast: with any luck I hoped to get back that night, but about 9 am two Germans came out and walked about just behind where I was hidden without any arms or equipment and eventually they came up and peered over: I could of course have shot both as I had a Mills left and 5 chambers to my revolver but I had a trench and two lots of wire to cross so gave in. They dressed my wound in their dressing-station, sent me to B.H.A. from which I went by motor to Vitry and then by ambulance to Hospital at Douai. The men, I heard after, got back next night after lying up in No Mans Land by day, but the Sergt. was only found some days later and in a v. weak state but unwounded."[474]

On 10 May 1919 George received a letter from the War Office which explained that the Army Council considered that *"…no blame attaches to him in this matter."*

December:

With the cessation of open hostilities the various battalions rapidly reverted to their 'normal' state holding formal parades with the full complement of troops. On 7 December the 1/Gloucesters held a ceremonial parade at Foy-Notre-Dame, two miles east of Dinant, Belgium, displaying the King's Colour and the Regimental Colour which had arrived in France the previous day having been brought across the Channel by a specially chosen Colour Party; at the start of the war the regimental Colours of the various battalions had been secured in Britain for safe keeping usually under the responsibility of the local mayor.[475] The parade was possibly a welcome break in the Battalion's march to the Rhineland as part of the Army of Occupation. The march had begun at Beugnies on 18 November and would end thirty-seven days later at Palmersheim (A and B Companies) and Odendorf (C and D Companies) after 170 miles. Although the Battalion only marched on nineteen of the thirty-seven

---

[474] Lieutenant George Holloway, 8/Northumberland Fusiliers, Service Record, TNA WO 339/23456-C572864
[475] Battalion War Diary, *1st Battalion Gloucestershire Regiment 6-7 December 1918*, WO 95/1278

days (nine miles per day), the other days were rest days during which they mostly practised route marches![476]

The end of the war did not materially affect the Gloucestershire County Cricket Club but as it came about six weeks into the normal rugby season it gave the Gloucester Rugby Club a chance to start attacking the £530 debt which had built up over the four war years; the Club was also keen to bring rugby back to their supporters in Gloucester.[477] Gloucester Rugby Club swiftly organised two fixtures for the Christmas period against the 4th (Reserve) Battalion, Gloucestershire Regiment, part of the Tyne Garrison, stationed at Seaton Delaval, Northumberland, and the 3rd Battalion, Gloucestershire Regiment, which was based at Maidstone; the games were organised in the knowledge that a keen but anonymous supporter would financially underwrite both games.[478]

The 3/Gloucesters, the first opponents on 18 December, came with a formidable rugby reputation which attracted a large crowd that was still trying to get into the Kingsholm Ground at kick-off time. Gloucester was able to field a team with **Charles Cook** MM, **William Washbourne** MM, **Arthur Hudson**, **E. Bowen**, and Lieutenant Fraser in the three-quarters, **William Dix** and **Harry Cook** at half back and a pack of forwards including **Norman Hayes**, **Arthur Hall**, A. Redding, **John H. Webb**, A. Ward, Sergeant **J. Lee** and **L. Taylor**; some of this team comprised men in starred occupations, others were home on leave while William Dix as a former prisoner of war had been demobilised as a matter of priority and despite the deprivations of prisoners he was sufficiently fit to put is name forward as being available. Another of the old Gloucester players, **George Cook** had also arrived back in the city after spending over four years as a prisoner of war but his playing days were now over. Gloucester edged the game by nine points to six.[479]

The 4/Gloucesters represented an attractive fixture as many of its players were from Gloucester and the surrounding area and included Corporal **Fred Webb** (GRFC) (captain), Lance Corporal **William Dovey** (GRFC), Lance Corporal **Jesse Beard** (GRFC) and Lance Corporal **William Rigby** (GRFC) the latter, although released for munitions work, was still a member of the Battalion.[480] For Gloucester Sergeant **Tom Voyce** (2/5th Gloucesters) replaced Lance Sergeant **Harry Cook** (8/Gloucesters) and **J. Daniels** replaced **Arthur Hall**. Gloucester won by seventeen points to three.[481,482]

Encouraged by the success of the Christmas period games, evident from the large crowds, the Gloucester club decided to organise a series of fixtures for the remainder of the season, from January to April 1919. The Club announced a twelve match programme on the basis that a consistent squad of Gloucester players would be available to represent the Club.[483] However the Club

---

[476] Battalion War Diary, 1st Battalion, Gloucestershire Regiment, 18November-24 December 1918, TNA WO 95/4251
[477] The £530 debt was equivalent to approximately the profits from five regular season based on the last regular season financial report published in June 1914
[478] The Citizen 15 November 1918
[479] The Citizen 21 December 1918
[480] Despite William Rigby working at the Gloucester Wagon Works, he was still a member of the Reserve Battalion, Gloucestershire Regiment and liable for re-call to the Colours in the event of an emergency.
[481] The Citizen 27 December 1918
[482] On 1 February 1919 Tom Voyce gained a commission as Second Lieutenant in the 3/Royal West Kents
[483] The fixture programme included Leicester, R.N. Depot Devonport, Cardiff, New Zealanders, Monmouthshire, RAF, Canadians and 3/Gloucesters (The Citizen 3 February 1919). Although twelve games were scheduled it appears that only eleven were actually played (Personal Communication: Chris Collier, Rugby Heritage Project).

underestimated the military demands which would still be placed on its players as the military authorities aware of the volatile situation only slowly demobilised servicemen until the peace treaty (Treaty of Versailles) was signed; men were kept on active service as part of the Army of Occupation and as a resource required to help civilians populations return to normal and to clear the former battlefields. The latter task was particularly hazardous, with large amounts of dangerous live munitions and scrap metal to be collected and corpses, many now no more than skeletons, to be removed, either through exhumation or simply by 'gathering up' exposed remains, for proper burial in the various military cemeteries. [484]

Although November 1918 brought an end to the 'Great adventure', in truth it never lasted more than a month into the war and by September 1914 the men were enlisting and fighting from a patriotic spirit and the desire to protect their homes and families from the enemy. The experiences of the Great War would stay with the men for the rest of their lives and many would suffer and continue to die, some years later, from wounds received or be inflicted with psychological effects for the rest of their lives. A return to 'normality' was encouraged by the Government but many would find that the life they had known before the war was gone forever. Men would soon start to meet together at battalion and regimental reunions to remember and drink a toast to 'Fallen Comrades'

---

[484] Although the Club had hoped for a stable squad, the team sheets showed that out of the twelve games, Arthur Hall played 7, George Halford 6, Arthur Hudson and J Lee 5 each, Tom Voyce, John Webb and Lionel Hamblin 4 each with the players between 1 and 3 games as Army and Navy demands impacted availability; Gloucester had to draft in other local players to fulfil the fixtures.

6

1919 AND BEYOND: THE AFTERMATH

"All honour to them for ever"
Sir James Bruton, MP, President of the Gloucester Football Club on the unveiling of the Club's Roll of Honour, 25 June 1920

Early In 1919 the general opinion favoured Britain rapidly getting back to 'normality' although from widely published newspaper photographs and soldiers' postcards it was generally acknowledged that in France 'normality' would take longer to achieve. However it was not generally appreciated that the servicemen would remain in the Army and Navy, carrying out various essential tasks, which was in addition to the logistical problem associated with demobilisation, as a plan had to implemented to return millions of men to civilian life using a priority system based on age, length of service and occupation. This plan was underpinned by the availability of transport ships which often resulted in congestion simply due to the numbers of troops involved. As the Army of Occupation moved into Germany under the terms of the Armistice, Allied prisoners of war were released and given priority within the demobilisation plan.

As the returning soldiers came home, the country developed a massive unemployment problem as the men 'flooded' the jobs market with the Government finding it difficult to invest in job creation schemes owing to a national financial crisis. The pre-war national debt had stood at £700,000,000 and Sir Eric Geddes who held various posts throughout the war related to logistics, estimated that Britain had property worth more than that currently on the Western Front.[485,486,487,488] It is now estimated that in total the war cost Great Britain £3,251,000,000.[489,490]

---

[485] Using The National Archives currency converter the pre-war National Debt would today (2005) be equivalent to £30,142,000,000.

There had been great promise and expectation, particularly in the autumn of 1914 that the soldiers, having done their duty, would return home to their old jobs *and* to a fairer better Britain. This message had been re-iterated throughout the war, the most prominent being that made by David Lloyd George who, as Prime Minister, had eloquently promised land reforms and that the men would return to "*...a fit country for heroes to live in*", but in reality there was significant unemployment and the sincere promises made by employers in 1914 had long evaporated as four Christmas Days had passed rather than the expected one.[491]

In addition to the 702,410 British soldiers who died during the Great War, there were 1,662,625 men who returned wounded.[492,493] The men of 1914 and beyond had suffered for King and Country and were promised a '*land fit for heroes*' upon their return but the reality of the post-war years was somewhat different. Jobs were scarce amidst economic conditions harsh and in 1919, in an effort to make companies do the '*right thing*', the King's National Roll Scheme was introduced which encouraged employers to employ at least 5% of their workforce as disabled soldiers, in return for which the company could display a crest and would be given preferential consideration in Government contracts.

In many respects the Gloucester Football Club and the Gloucestershire County Cricket Club were no different to other employers. During the war GRFC had created a debt of £530, an amount equivalent to five years of profits while the GCCC had had severe financial problems before the war and to some extent were financially 'saved' by the war. In October 1914 a members meeting of the latter had discussed the dissolution of the club but decided against it. Initially it was agreed to suspend all games for the 1915 season and this was ultimately extended for the remainder of the war. Both Clubs faced a financial crisis in 1919, a critical year for the survival of both clubs, especially as player availability could still not be guaranteed with the continuing military commitments.

At the Gloucester Rugby Club, the war had ended the careers of some players but for others it had represented an unwelcome break and for them further games were played - Lieutenant **Frank Ayliffe**, 8/Gloucesters, back row, 216 games, **Tom Burns**, Royal Field Artillery, half back, twenty-two games, Corporal **Charles Cook** MM, 5/Gloucesters, full back, thirteen games, Lance Corporal **William Dix**, 8/Gloucesters, (stand off) eighty-seven games, Corporal **George Halford**, 1/Gloucesters, second row, 122 games, **Arthur Hall**, starred occupation, forward, 200 games, Corporal **Joe Harris**,

---

[486] Despite being a civilian Sir Eric Geddes was appointed Director General of Military Railways and Inspector General of Transportation with the BEF in 1916. He is credited with revolutionising the logistics situation on the Western Front and is considered to one of the men 'who won the war' as he enabled the BEF to switch points at attack very rapidly as supplies and munitions could be moved quickly and efficiently.
[487] *The Citizen* 7 December 1918
[488] He estimated that there was enough British railway stock and materials in France to complete two of the world's biggest railways. Britain was also the world's largest owner of canal stock.
[489] www.bbc.co.uk/guides/zqhxvcw
[490] £3,251,000,000 in 1918 would be the equivalent of about £139,800,000,000 in today's market although the spending power would have been greater in 1918
[491] David Lloyd George speech at Wolverhampton 23 November 1918 (*The Times* 25 November 1918)
[492] This figure refers to soldiers who lived in Great Britain but the figure for the British Empire Forces which in addition to the British also included Australians, Canadians, Newfoundlanders, Indians and South Africans was 908,371 died and 2,090,212 wounded (Figures taken from *Statistics of the Military Effort of the British Empire during the Great War 1914-1920* (London: HMSO, 1922)).
[493] The wounded figure is difficult to estimate since although casualty returns show numbers wounded these figures would have included men wounded more than once. Further Pension Records show that not all wounds were serious enough for a man to be considered for a pension.

5/Gloucesters, front row, eighty-two games, **Arthur Hudson**, Royal Navy, wing, thirty-one games, Captain **Joseph Lawson**, Royal Gloucestershire Hussars, second row, fifty-one games, Major **Alec Lewis** MC and Bar, 4/Intelligence Corps, centre, eight games, **Tom Millington**, full back, 239 games, Sergeant **Sid Smart**, 5/Gloucesters, second row, 121 games, Corporal **William Washbourne** MM, 5/Gloucesters, wing, forty-six games, Lance Corporal **Fred Webb**, 5/Gloucesters, wing, sixty-six games and Private **John H. Webb**, 5/Gloucesters, front row, eighty-two games.

For the County Cricket Club the situation was similar. Of the thirty-three players who contributed to the 1914 season, thirteen played again after the war together with another six players who had been unavailable during the final pre-war season mainly due to military commitments. These players included Lieutenant **Charles Barnett**, 5/Gloucesters who played another thirty-one matches, Lieutenant **William Brown**, 5/North Staffs, seven matches, Lieutenant Colonel **Basil Clarke** twelve matches, Captain **George Dennett**, East Yorkshires, 147 matches, Private **Alfred Dipper** D Squadron RGH, 369 matches, Captain **Michael Green**, MC, 1/Gloucesters, sixty-two matches, Lieutenant Colonel **Douglas Robinson**, MC, King's Own (Royal Lancaster Regiment), 114 matches and Clerk **Charles Parker**, RAF, 487 matches.

Regardless of the prevailing situation, one of the 'features' of the immediate post-war period was the bestowing of honours not only by the British Government but also other governments aligned with the Allied cause in the war. As a reflection of the officer status of the men from the cricket club compared with the rugby club these honours were bestowed mainly on the former. The exception was **Percy Stout** (GRFC) who for a period, 1916-17, worked in the Intelligence Department in Cairo and was made an Officer of the Most Excellent Order of the British Empire [OBE] in January 1919 for valuable services rendered in connection with military operations in Egypt.[494] In December his contribution in Egypt was again recognised this time by His Highness the Sultan of Egypt who conferred on Percy the Order of the Nile 4th Class [495,496]

For the cricketers there were numerous post-war awards. In the King's Birthday Honours of June 1919, Lieutenant Colonel **James Horlick** (GCCC) was appointed an Officer of the Military Division of the Most Excellent Order of the British Empire [OBE] (Military Division) for services in Salonika. In the same Birthday Honours list Major **Eric Crankshaw** (GCCC) was appointed a Member of the Most Excellent Order of the British Empire [MBE] (Military Division) for rendering miscellaneous services. Further **James Horlick** was appointed the Chevalier Legion d'Honneur by the President of the French Republic in July 1919. In the same month the Greek Military Cross was bestowed on him by His Majesty the King of the Hellenes and he was further awarded by His Majesty the King of Serbia the Order of the White Eagle, 4th Class (with Swords) (1920). In July Lieutenant Colonel **Ernest English** (GCCC) was awarded the Croix de Guerre by the President of the French Republic. Lieutenant Colonel **Arthur Du Boulay** (GCCC) was awarded the Croix de Guerre (Belgium) (1919) and appointed as an Officier de l'Ordre de Leopold II (avec Palme) (Belgium) (1919), having previously been appointed as an Officer of the Order of Agricultural Merit (France) (1917)

---

[494] *London Gazette* 1 January 1919 p.53
[495] *London Gazette* 25 November 1919 p.14637
[496] The Order of the Nile was Egypt's highest state honour and was awarded for exceptional services to the nation.

February 1919:

Some early demobilisation of British soldiers took place but generally this represented the repatriation of prisoners of war. On 9 February for instance Lieutenant **George Holloway** (GCCC) was gazetted out of the Service (Service Category V) from No.2 Dispersal Unit, Chisledon with the *proviso* that in the event of an emergency he had to report immediately to Clipstone Camp.[497,498] As a postscript to the war, George's internment in Holland a month before the Armistice was probably forgotten until eighteen years later when he received a letter, dated 4 December 1936, from a fellow internee, ex-Second Lieutenant Saltoun. It suggested that a small donation would be appreciated towards a gift for Princess Juliana to celebrate her marriage and as a mark of be appreciation for the kindness received from the Dutch population whilst interned;[499,500] history does not record how George responded to this request.

The Gloucester Rugby Club's makeshift twelve match season kicked off in order to generate some much needed gate-receipt income. Although the Committee had decided that it could rely on a stable squad it soon became apparent that many of the men were still soldiers despite the cessation of hostilities. As the Armistice was technically just a cease-fire, the Army had issued a widely reported Order which made the position clear,

> "An Army Order issued on Tuesday [3 December 1918] night states that while the present military situation does not admit of the commencement of general demobilisation yet it is possible gradually to release from the Colours a number of soldiers who are urgently required for civilian life. As it cannot be said definitely that all risk of recrudescence of hostilities has passed it is necessary to make provision for the recall of men to the Army in the event of an emergency re-mobilisation becoming necessary. To meet the situation, the Army Council have decided to form a new class of Army Reserve, designated Class Z. Accordingly all men released from service with the Colours on the expiration of their demobilisation furlough will be passed to this class of Reserve except men such as are discharged physically unfit, etc"[501]

The fixtures were still honoured although the Club was forced to find additional local and available players to cover for the regular players who still had military commitments. However, despite these *ad hoc* games it was apparent that the gate receipts were insufficient to avoid a serious financial situation before the start of the first proper season in September 1919. As a result, a fund was opened for the benefit of the Club and the list of subscribers was regularly published in the papers.[502]

---

[497] Lieutenant George Holloway, 8/Northumberland Fusiliers, Service Record, TNA WO 339/23456-C572864
[498] The 'emergency' referred to is the resumption of hostilities which would remain a threat under the peace treaty, the Treaty of Versailles, was signed on 28 June 1919; in 1919 this threat probably was real but in reality both sides were exhausted and financially not in a position to resume hostilities for any lengthy period.
[499] Princess Juliana, the daughter of Queen Wilhelmina of the Netherlands, married Prince Bernhard of Lippe-Biesterfeld on 7 January 1937. She succeeded her mother to the throne on 6 September 1948.
[500] Holland remained neutral throughout the war and was used by both sides for prisoners of war to live on the understanding that they would not return home and re-join the armed forces. As a neutral country Holland financially benefitted throughout the Great War and did not suffer the same deprivations as the belligerent countries.
[501] The Citizen 7 December 1918
[502] *The Citizen* 15 March 1919

March 1919:

Prior to the start of the first cricket season for five years, Sir James Bruton presided over a meeting on 24 March at the Guildhall, Gloucester, to discuss raising funds for the Gloucestershire CCC. The Honorary Secretary, Walter Pearce informed the club that they were well on the way to meeting their target of £2,000 but would need to find winter employment locally for seven cricket professionals. The meeting further agreed that it was unfortunate that any appeal for funds by the GCCC would clash with a similar appeal from the Gloucester Rugby Club.[503] For the financially hard-pressed citizens of Gloucester who were also trying to recover from the deprivations of war, to be asked to contribute to a second fund could be too much and as a consequence it was decided that one of the trial games for GCCC would be played at The Spa on Easter Monday (21 April) in the hope of raising funds with something tangible for the spectators.

May 1919:

Six months after the end of the war the Gloucestershire County Cricket Club resumed activity and took part in the 1919 County Championship playing fifteen games, the first of which against Sussex was on 23 May at The Spa in Gloucester; Gloucestershire won by twenty-four runs. The team had a familiar look and included Lieutenant Colonel **Douglas Robinson**, Private **Alfred Dipper**, Second Lieutenant **Foster Robinson**, Major **Alison White** DSO, Sapper **Francis Ellis** and Clerk 3 (RAF) **Charlie Parker.**

Of the thirty-three players who had represented Gloucestershire in 1914 eight had died - **William Brownlee, Theodore Fowler, William Grant, Burnet James, Hugh Jones, Claude Mackay, John Nason** and **Francis Roberts** - which represented a 24% casualty rate. Of the eighty-five players who had played for the county and fought in the Great War, eighteen had died (21% overall casualty rate). It was also acknowledged that of those who had returned some were not the 'same men' who had left in 1914 - Lieutenant **Charles Barnett** (GCCC), 5/Gloucesters, resumed his cricketing career and played until 1926 but it was acknowledged that he was "...*greatly handicapped by several wounds in his leg...*" received during the war.[504]

June 1919:

At the Gloucester Rugby Club's players' meeting on 19 June, **George Halford**, now recovered from his wounds received in January 1915 and who had been elected captain for the 1913-1914 season, was unanimously re-elected to lead the team and as per 1914 **Lionel Hamblin** was re-appointed as vice-captain while **Fred Webb** was the Players' Representative.[505] At the Club's AGM held on 27 June the player positions and a thirty-five match programme for the 1919-1920 season were announced ; the fixture list included fourteen games against the old adversaries – the Welsh clubs. The Treasurer, George J. Collingbourne, produced a financial statement for the 'missing' seasons 1914-1919 which showed a total income of £1,696 0s 5d while total expenditure was £1,421 5s 8d, producing a balance of £274 14s 9d. The major part of the income, £1,225 14s (72%) was generated

---

[503] *Gloucestershire Chronicle* 29 March 1919
[504] *Cheltenham Chronicle and Gloucestershire Graphic* 4 October 1919
[505] *Gloucester Journal* 21 June 1919

from gate receipts from the twelve matches organised after Christmas. It would be several more months before a regular income from gate receipts could be guaranteed.[506]

July 1919:
On 1 July Gloucester, including the Gloucester Football Club, celebrated the return to the City of the cadre of the 1/5th Gloucesters which was greeted by the same large enthusiastic crowds which cheered them on their way to war on 5 September 1914; amongst its ranks were many of the remaining rugby players yet to be demobilised. The last soldiers of the 1/5th Gloucesters returned to Barracks almost five years after they had left for the Isle of Wight, Swindon and Chelmsford and nearly four-and-a-half years after they had landed at Boulogne.

August 1919:
The first full cricket season finished with the County Cricket Club showing better form having won four and drawn five of their sixteen games, which meant that it finished eighth in the County Championship, compared with last (sixteenth) in its previous full season in 1914. The Cheltenham Cricket Festival also resumed and normality returned, especially as the cricket was severely disrupted by bad weather! Only three full days' play was experienced at the Festival and, for consecutive festivals, proved financially disastrous for the Club. The wet weather exacerbated an already catastrophic situation as the canvas screen along the railings to "...*forestall the patrons of the 'free gallery'*..." was only erected after the weather became inclement by which time these 'free gallery patrons' had already taken shelter elsewhere and the expense was unjustified.[507,508]

September 1919:
The first full season after the war for the Gloucester Football Club kicked off on 13 September with a thirteen points to three victory over Lydney with **Fred Webb** scoring three tries and **Lionel Hamblin** adding two conversions. The statistics for the season show that the Gloucester Football Club won nineteen matches and lost twelve whilst scoring 384 points and conceding 222 points (see Photograph 39). The teams, as well as containing some familiar names, now contained a new generation of players who would become household names in Gloucestershire, including **Stanley Bayliss** (Royal Field Artillery), **Sidney Brown** (7/Gloucesters), **Norman Daniell** (Royal Field Artillery), **Frank Mansell** (5/Gloucesters) and **Tom Voyce** (5/Gloucesters and the Royal West Kents) On 27 January 1920, the Five Nations Championship witnessed the first game at Swansea, between Wales and England which Wales won by 19 points to 5; selected for England were the Gloucester Football Club players **Sidney Smart** (back row) and **George Halford** (second row); after the war neither player went back to France for an international match although the first match on the resumption of the Five Nations Championship was played in Paris with France being defeated by five points to nil by Scotland on 1 January 1920.[509]

---

[506] *Gloucester Journal* 28 June 1919
[507] *Cheltenham Looker* On 23 August 1919
[508] The pitch for the Festival was prepared by William Woof the former GCCC player and veteran of the Boer War
[509] *Gloucester Journal* 24 January 1920

Photograph 39: Gloucester Football Club: Gloucester First XV 1919-1920: Players left to right. Standing: J. Harris (in suit) (5/Gloucesters), F. Mansell (5/Gloucesters), T. Voyce (5/Gloucesters and Royal West Kents), N.L. Hayes, J. Webb (5/Gloucesters), S. Smart (5/Gloucesters), C. Mumford, J.F. Lawson (7/Northants and RGHY). Seated: G. Welshman, W. Washbourne MM (5/Gloucesters). A. Hall (starred occupation), A. Hudson (Royal Navy, submarines), G. Halford (1/Gloucesters), F.W. Webb (5/Gloucesters), S.A. Brown (7/Gloucesters), F.W. Ayliffe (5/Gloucesters), F.Ward. On ground: W. Dix (8/Gloucesters), T. Millington (Royal Field Artillery). (GRHP)

November 1919:

The legacy of the war persisted well beyond the date of the Armistice. **Arthur Penduck** (GCCC) had enlisted on 14 November in Bristol and despite being a Footman by trade was assigned to a Royal Army Medical Corps [RAMC] Hospital and served overseas. He remained with the RAMC until June 1916 when at his own request he transferred to the Royal Field Artillery,[510] and subsequently in May 1919 to the Royal Air Force Reserve [RAFR]. In November he was medically examined in consideration of a pension and it was found that an old knee injury, from 1912, had been aggravated by active service causing a 20% disability; there was a risk that the knee could suddenly give way.[511,512]

Other soldiers were not so 'lucky' – **Percy Bell** (GCCC) having survived the rigors of war succumbed to the influenza epidemic ('Spanish Flu') and died on 2 December 1920, while **Frank Stout** (GRFC), the Gloucester, England and British Isles back row forward, spent his last years as an invalid from wounds received and died on 30 May 1926.

---

[510] *Dursley, Berkeley and Sharpness Gazette* 3 June 1916
[511] The injury had been assessed during his medical examination on 14 December 1914 and after finding no medical problems Arthur had been medically passed as A1
[512] Arthur Edward Penduck Service Record

December 1919:

The Directors of the Gloucester Football and Athletic Ground Company Limited met at the New Inn Hotel in Gloucester. The financial discussions centred on the disposable balance for the year of 9s 5d which they thought was "...*considerable*..." as very little rugby – their main source of income – had been played. They also agreed that the rent to the Gloucester Rugby Club for the 1919-1920 season should be reduced from £375 per year to £250 provided the Club paid them 33% of the its profits for the season.[513]

Photograph 40. Gloucester Rugby Football Club Roll of Honour: The Gloucester Rugby Football Club Roll of Honour, made in carved oak, was inscribed with the words, "To the memory of those members of this club who made the supreme sacrifice in the Great War 1914-19".The inscription on the bottom reads, "They greeted the unseen with a cheer – and so they passed over – and the trumpet sounded for them on the other side". There are eighteen names on the Roll – **H.Berry, H. Collins, C. Cummings, G. Griffiths, H. Hancock, W.D. Henderson, S. Millard, W. Parham, W.J. Pearce, T. Powell, J. Price, A. Purton, P. Roach, A. Russell, A. Saunders, P. Simmonds, S. Sysum and E. Wootton**. The memorial which currently is in the Lions Den, was unveiled by the President of the Club Sir James Bruton MP on 25 June 1920. (*Malc King, GRHP*)

March 1920:

On 2 March 1920 the City High Sheriff, Mr H.G. Norman invited fifty members of the Gloucester Football Club to a dinner at the Guildhall. In his after dinner speech Mr Norman considered that the football club was:

---

[513] *Cheltenham Chronicle and Gloucestershire Graphic* 20 December 1919

"...a very valuable asset to the city. [He also] asked to be allowed to say how pleased he was to see the Cook brothers present that evening. Had it not been for the misfortunes of war, they would have been playing for the First Fifteen today. [He was pleased in the way that the players in general had responded to the call for men at the outbreak of war and that] they certainly did not wait for conscription." [514]

June 1920:
On 25 June the Gloucester Football Club's carved oak Roll of Honour listing the names of eighteen players who had fallen in the Great War was unveiled by Sir James Bruton, MP, President of the Gloucester Football Club, in the presence of many of the relatives of the fallen, with the words, *"All honour to them for ever"*. The Roll of Honour now hangs in the Lions Den at Kingsholm Stadium (see Photograph 40).

Photograph 41. The 5/Gloucesters War Memorial, Gloucester: The War Memorial to the 5th Battalion, Gloucestershire Regiment stands outside Gloucester Park. It was unveiled on 28 March 1925 by Field Marshal Lord Plumer who commanded the Second Army during the Great War. It is inscribed with the names of 1,065 soldiers who made the supreme sacrifice. The wall behind the memorial is Gloucester War Memorial which is a series of bronze panels which bear the names of 1,253 Gloucester servicemen who died in all units of the Army and Navy. (*Authors*)

March 1925:
On 28 March the 5th Battalion, Gloucestershire Regiment's War Memorial was unveiled by Field Marshal Lord Plumer who had commanded the Second Army during the Great War. The memorial is

---
[514] *Gloucester Journal* 6 March 1920

situated next to Gloucester Park (the Spa) and lists the names of 1,065 servicemen (see Photograph 41).[515]

Photograph 42. Frank Stout MC (GRFC), Stanined Glass Window Memorial: The stained glass memorial window commemorating Captain **Frank Stout**, 20/Hussars, in the Church of St Philip and St James, Hucclecote, Gloucester. Frank, depicted as the knight St George, survived the war but spent his last years as an invalid owing to wounds received and die in 1926. The inscription reads, *"In loving memory of Frank Moxon Stout M.C. Born Feb. 21. 1877. Died. May. 30. 1926"* (*Authors*)

---

[515] In 1921 the official statistics for the men who were killed in the Great War although this number would continue to rise over several years as men succumbed to their wounds. The official statistics for the Gloucestershire Regiment were, 1st Battalion – 983; 2nd Battalion – 324; $1/4^{th}$ Battalion – 333; $1/5^{th}$ Battalion – 557; $2/5^{th}$ Battalion – 481; $1/6^{th}$ Battalion – 469; $2/6^{th}$ Battalion – 296; 7th Battalion – 692; 8th Battalion – 931; 9th Battalion – 131; 10th Battalion – 625; 12th Battalion – 754; and 13th Battalion – 293 (*Dean Forest Mercury* 27 January 1921).

May 1926:

The effects of the war were long lasting and not all of the servicemen who fought in the Great War 'died between 1914 and 1918. Captain Frank Stout MC, 20th Hussars (GRFC) who had won fourteen England international caps and seven caps for the British Isles (*aka* British Lions) had been wounded in April 1917. Although he 'recovered' and returned to duty, he would spend his last years as an invalid; he died on 30 May 1926. He was commemorated in a stained glass window at the church of St Philip and St James, Hucclecote (see Photograph 42).

Photograph 43. The Bristol War Memorial: The Bristol War Memorial in Colston Avenue was unveiled on 26 June 1926 by Field Marshal Sir William Birdwood, Commander of the ANZAC forces. The memorial designed as a cenotaph has no names inscribed upon it. (*Authors*)

June 1932:

On 26 June the Bristol War Memorial erected on Colston Avenue was unveiled by Field Marshal Sir William Birdwood GCB, GCSI, GCMG, GCVO, CIE, DSO, in the presence of such a large crowd that the adjoining streets had to be closed by the police two hours beforehand.[516] Sir William Birdwood was the Commander of the Australian and New Zealand Army Corps [ANZAC] in Gallipoli and Commander-in-Chief, Fifth Army on the Western Front during the closing stages of the war. The

---

[516] *Western Daily Press and Bristol Mirror* 27 June 1932

Bristol War Memorial was designed as a cenotaph and although there are no names inscribed upon it, it commemorates the 6,000 local men who died during the war. At the ceremony there were representatives from various Army and Navy units including men from the 4th, 6th, 8th and 12th Battalions, Gloucestershire Regiment (see Photograph 43).[517]

October 1933:
On 21 October the City of Gloucester's War Memorial was unveiled by the Duke of Beaufort. The memorial situated next to the 5/Gloucester's Memorial on the edge of Gloucester Park, lists the names of 1,253 servicemen on a series of bronze panels from all battalions of the Gloucestershire Regiment as well Gloucester men that served with other units in the Army and Navy. On 30 June 1949 additional panels were unveiled listing the Gloucester men who died during the Second World War.

September 2013:
On 12 September the Kingsholm Stadium War Memorial was jointly unveiled by Lieutenant General Tim Evans, Commander of the Allied Rapid Reaction Corps [ARRC] and Stephen Vaughan, CEO Gloucester Rugby. The Memorial is situated on the outside of Kingsholm Stadium and commemorates the thirty players who fell in the Great War; the memorial also commemorates the one player who fell in the Boer War and the nine players who fell in the Second World War (See Photograph 44).[518]

---

[517] *Western Daily Press and Bristol Mirror* 22 June 1932
[518] The additional names of players who fell in the Great War compared with those listed on the 1920 Roll of Honour is as a result of recent research conducted at the Gloucestershire Archives which has been published in the book, *'They played for Gloucester and fought for their country'* by Martin and Teresa Davies which is available from the Gloucester Rugby shop and Hudsons Sports.

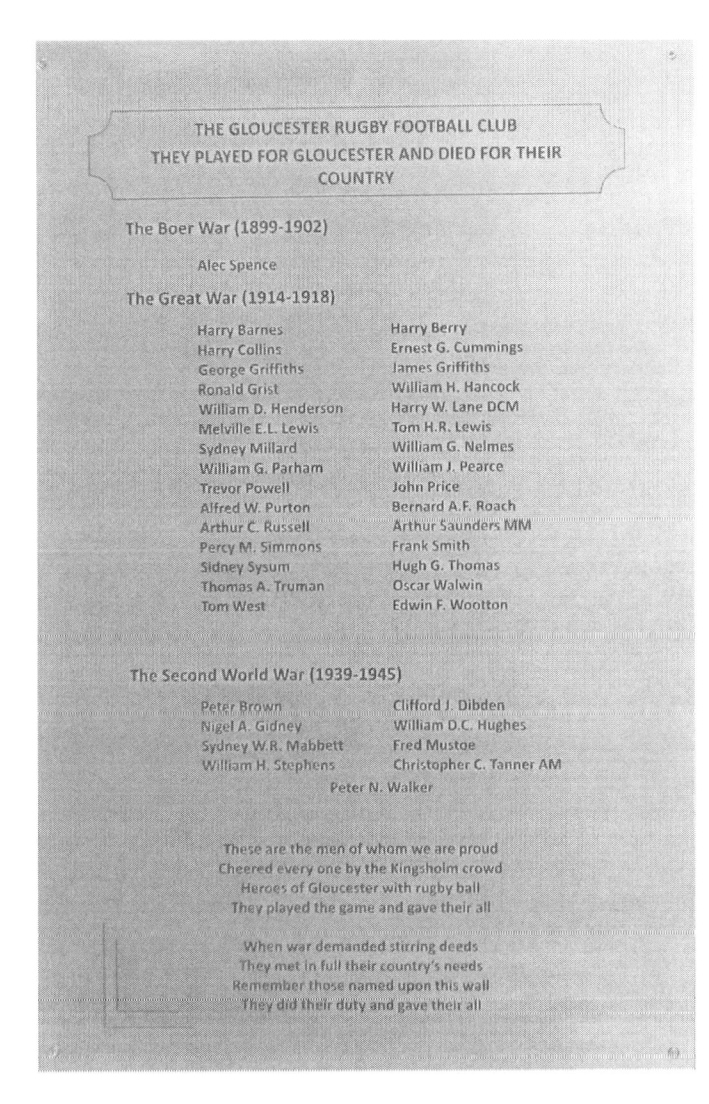

Photograph 44. The Kingsholm Stadium War Memorial: The Kingsholm Stadium War Memorial was unveiled on 12 September 2013 by Lieutenant General Tim Evans, Commander of the Allied Rapid Reaction Corps (ARRC) and Stephen Vaughan, CEO, Gloucester Rugby. The memorial, erected near Main Reception, bears the names of thirty players who fell in the Great War. Also inscribed is the name of one player who died in the Boer War and nine who died in the Second World War. (*Authors*)

POSTSCRIPT: It would appear that the Gloucestershire County Cricket Club did not erect a memorial which commemorated the men who had played for the Club and who lost their lives in the Great War. In the minutes of Annual General Meeting of 1920 the President, Lord Beauchamp, KG, is recorded as acknowledging the Club's contribution to the war effort and the supreme sacrifice by the men of the Gloucestershire County Cricket Club.[519]

---

[519] Personal Communication: Roger Gibbons. Lord Beauchamp in the President's address at the 1920 AGM recorded that sixty-four players had served with the Colours of which fourteen had died on active service and a large number had been wounded.

For Club, King and Country

7

THE ROLL OF HONOUR

"We've watched you playing cricket

And every kind of game

At football, golf and polo

You men have made your name

But now your country calls you

To play your part in war

And no matter what befalls you

We shall love you all the more…"

A Great War song written by Paul A. Rubens in 1914 and performed in the music halls by Phyllis Dare.[520]

---

[520] Max Arthur, *When this bloody war is over. Soldiers' Songs of the First World War* (London: Judy Piatkus (Publishers) Ltd, 2001), pp.6-8

Players Died on Military Service

ALDERWICK, Ernest (GCCC), Second Lieutenant, 11/Suffolks, 26 August 1917
BARNES, Harry (GRFC), Private, 1/Gloucesters, 9 May 1915
BERRY, Harry (GRFC), Corporal, 1/Gloucesters, 9 May 1915
BROWNLEE, Wilfred (GCCC), Second Lieutenant, 3/Dorsets, 12 October 1914
CHARTERIS, Hugo, Lord Elcho (GCCC), Captain, Royal Gloucestershire Hussars, 23 April 1916
COLLINS, Henry (GRFC), Private, 10/Worcesters, 4 July 1916
CUMMINGS, Ernest (GRFC), Private 1/5th Gloucesters, 26 April 1915
DU BOULAY, Arthur, DSO, CG* (GCCC), Lieutenant Colonel, Royal Engineers, 25 October 1918
FOWLER, Theodore (GCCC), Corporal, 1/Honourable Artillery Company, 17 August 1915
GRANT, William, MC, CG* (GCCC), Captain, 5/Queen's Own Cameron Highlanders, 26 September 1918
GRIFFITHS, George (GRFC), Lance Corporal, 13/Gloucesters, 4 April 1918
GRIFFITHS, James (GRFC), Private, 1/5th Gloucesters, 23 July 1916
GRIST, Ronald (GRFC), Second Lieutenant, 18/Rifle Brigade, 15 May 1918
HANCOCK, Walter (GRFC), Corporal, 1/Gloucesters, 29 October 1914
HENDERSON, William (GRFC), Flight Cadet, Royal Air Force, 28 November 1918
JAMES, Burnet (GCCC), Second Lieutenant, 7th Squadron RFC, 26 September 1915
JONES, Hugh, MC (GCCC), Captain, 13/Gloucesters, 10 November 1918
LANE, Henry, DCM (GRFC), Lance Corporal, 4/Machine Gun Guards, 30 March 1918
LEWIS, Melville (GRFC), Corporal, 1/5th Gloucesters, 23 July 1916
LEWIS, Tom (GRFC), Lance Corporal, 1/5th Gloucesters, 23 July 1916
MACKAY, Claude (GCCC), Second Lieutenant, att. 2/Manchesters, 7 June 1915
MARSDEN, Edmund (GCCC), Captain, 64th Pioneers, Indian Army, 26 May 1915
MILLARD, Sydney (GRFC), Sergeant, 1/5th Gloucesters, 23 July 1916
NASON, John (GCCC), Captain, 46th Squadron RFC, 26 December 1916
NELMES, William (GRFC), Corporal, 8/Gloucesters, 23 July 1916
PARHAM, William (GRFC), Corporal, 1/5th Gloucesters, 4 October 1917
PEARCE, William (GRFC), Lieutenant, 2/5th Gloucesters, 2 December 1917
POWELL, Trevor (GRFC), Private, 1/5th Gloucesters, 3 February 1916
PRICE, John (GRFC), Private, 10/Worcesters, 3 July 1916
PRIESTLEY, Donald (GCCC), Lance Corporal, 1/28th London Regiment, 30 October 1917
PURTON, Alfred (GRFC), Private, 4/Grenadier Guards, 27 August 1917
ROACH, Bernard (GRFC), Private, 2/Grenadier Guards, 25 December 1914
ROBERTS, Francis (GCCC), Captain, 9/Rifle Brigade, 8 February 1916
RUSSELL, Arthur (GRFC), Second Lieutenant, 2/Rifle Brigade, 28 October 1918
SAUNDERS, Arthur, MM (GRFC), Sergeant, 8/Gloucesters, 1 November 1916
SIMMONS, Percy (GRFC), Second Lieutenant, 4/Wiltshires, 20 October 1918
SMITH, Frank (GRFC), Sergeant, 7/Gloucesters, 21 April 1916
SYSUM, Sidney (GRFC), Lance Corporal, 1/5th Gloucesters, 23 July 1916
THOMAS, Hugh (GRFC), Second Lieutenant, 8/Gloucesters, 30 July 1916
TRUMAN, Thomas (GRFC and GCCC), Second Lieutenant, ASC, 14 September 1918

TURNER, Ronald (GCCC), Second Lieutenant, 1/5th Essex, 15 August 1915
WALWIN, Oscar (GRFC), Lance Corporal, 2/Worcesters, 12 November 1916
WEST, Thomas (GRFC), Rifleman, 10/King's Royal Rifle Corps, 29 September 1915
WILLIAMS, John (GCCC), Private, Auckland Regiment, NZEF, 25 April 1915
WOOTTON, Edwin (GRFC), Lance Corporal, 9/Gloucesters, 25 April 1917
WREFORD-BROWN, Oswald (GCCC), Captain, 9/Northumberland Fusiliers, 7 July 1916
YALLAND, William (GCCC), Lieutenant, 1/Gloucesters, 23 October 1914
  *CG=Croix de Guerre

Roll of Honour

ALDERWICK, Ernest Ewart Gladstone (1886-1917) (Cricketer)

Born on 4 April 1886 at Montpelier, Bristol and killed in action on 26 August 1917 at Peronne, France aged 31 years. He was buried at Hargicourt Communal Cemetery Extension, grave A.2. Ernest, a Clerk for a Chocolate Manufacturer, was the son of Francis Robert and Emily Alderwick and in 1909 he married Florence Annie Stevens and together they had four children. Before the war the family lived at 857 Fishponds Road, Bristol. He served with 15/Gloucesters (Private, 30580); 93rd Training Reserve (TR) Battalion (Private, TR/4044); 2/Dorsets (L/Corporal, 24522) and finally as a Second Lieutenant in the 11/Suffolks (Cambridgeshire). He landed in France on 19 June 1917 and was awarded the campaign medals - 1914-15 Star, British War Medal and the Victory Medal. Ernest played two matches for Gloucestershire County Cricket Club as a right-hand batsman in 1908.

BARNES, Albert Edward DCM (1890-1950) (Rugby player)

Born in 1890 at Gloucester and died on 4 September 1950 at the Royal Hospital, Great Western Road, Gloucester aged 59 years; his funeral was held at St Paul's Church, Cheltenham. Albert, a Professional Soldier, was the son of William and Mary Jane Barnes (née Bowkett). He married May Victoria Barnes and together the couple had two children. Albert had joined the Royal Marine Light Infantry in 1911 and the census for that year shows that he was on board HMS Kent in the China Sea. He served throughout the Great War as a Sergeant (241211) in the 2/5th Battalion (TF), Gloucestershire Regiment. He landed in France on 23 May 1916 and was wounded in January 1918. He was awarded the campaign medals - British War Medal and the Victory Medal and won the Distinguished Conduct Medal [DCM] (November 1918) for gallantry. Albert's citation for his DCM reads: "*For gallantry and devotion to duty. At Maresches, during a night attack on 1st November 1918, he was acting C.S.M. The advance was held up in one sector by a strong enemy post, and he, with his company commander and a few men, rushed the post. He bayonetted two of the enemy and knocked another out with his fists. His fine courage and example inspired the confidence of all ranks.*"

Before demobilisation he was transferred to the Military Foot Police (Sergeant, P/18172). His older brother **Harry Barnes** (GRFC) was killed in action on 9 May 1915. Albert played nine games for the Gloucester Rugby Club at forward between 1909 and 1910.

BARNES, Herbert Henry ('Harry') (1888-1915) (Rugby player)

Born in 1888 at Gloucester and killed in action on 9 May 1915 at Aubers Ridge, aged 27 years. Harry has no known grave and is commemorated amongst the Missing on the Le Touret Memorial, Panel 17. Employed by Arnold, Perrett and Company, Gloucester, he was the son of William and Mary Jane Barnes (née Bowkett). Before the war he had served with the British Army and as a Reservist he was recalled to the Colours in 1914 and served with the 1/Gloucesters (Private, 8424) and landed in France on 13 August 1914. He was awarded the campaign medals - 1914 Star with clasp and rose ('*Old Contemptible*'), British War Medal and the Victory Medal. Harry is commemorated on the Gloucester War Memorial, the Memorial at All Saints Church, Gloucester and the Kingsholm Stadium War Memorial. He played sixty games for the Gloucester Rugby Club at centre between 1908 and 1911, thirty-eight of which were for the First XV. His younger brother **Albert Barnes** (GRFC) won the DCM during the war with the Gloucestershire Regiment.

BARNES, Hubert Charles ('Bert') MM (1891-1961) (Rugby player)

Born in 1891 at South Hamlet, Gloucester and died on 22 April 1961 in hospital at Cheltenham, aged 69 years; his funeral was held at St Paul's Church, Cheltenham. A Brewer with Arnold, Perrett and Company, Wickwar, he was the son of Charles Thomas and Julia Annie Barnes (née Curtis) and in 1915 he married Clementina Williams and the couple had three children; before the war they lived at 8 Clegram Street, Gloucester. He enlisted in August 1914 and was promoted to a Sergeant (2374, 240525) in the C Company, 1/5th Battalion (TF), Gloucestershire Regiment. He landed in France on 29 March 1915 and was awarded the campaign medals - 1914-15 Star, British War Medal and the Victory Medal. He was won the Military Medal for gallantry in April 1917. He played five games for the Gloucester Rugby Club at full back between 1912 and 1913.

BATEMAN-CHAMPAIN, Hugh Frederick CMG, MiD(1) (1869-1933) (Cricketer)

Born on 6 April 1869 at Ashford, Middlesex and died on 7 October 1933 at Swinley Park, Ascot, aged 64 years; his funeral was held at Sunningdale Church with a memorial service at Holy Trinity Church, Sloane Street, London. Hugh, a Professional Soldier, was the son of Colonel Sir John Underwood and Harriet Sophia Bateman-Champain (née Currie) and in 1904 he married Dorothy Gertrude Arbuthnot and the couple had two children. He was educated at Cheltenham College and the Royal Military Academy, Sandhurst and joined the West Yorkshire Regiment in 1889 before transferring to the

Indian Army and the 1st Gurkhas in 1891. In 1912 he was appointed as Military Secretary to His Excellency the Governor of Bengal. In the Great War he served in France, Gallipoli, Mesopotamia and North Persia with the Royal Army Ordnance Corps (Lieutenant, Acting Captain), the Indian Army (Major, Brigadier-General), 2/9th Battalion, Gurkha Rifles (Lieutenant-Colonel, Acting Brigadier-General) and finally as a Brigadier-General in the Gurkha Rifles (Staff Corps). He landed in France on 15 August 1915 and was awarded the campaign medals, 1914-15 Star, British War Medal and the Victory Medal. He was Mentioned in Despatches once. During his lifetime he was awarded the Companion of the Order of St Michael and St George (CMG) (August 1918) in connection with his service in Mesopotamia, the Order of the Lion and Sun (1st Class) (Persia) (January 1920) and was appointed as an Esquire of the Grand Priory of the Order of the Hospital of St John of Jerusalem in England (January 1925). Hugh played eleven matches for Gloucestershire County Cricket Club as a right-hand batsman between 1888 and 1902. Whilst still a pupil at Cheltenham College he was personally chosen by W.G. Grace to play for Gloucestershire CCCC and he died playing the game he loved. After retiring from the Army in 1921 Hugh became General-Secretary of the British Red Cross Society until his death in 1933.

BERRY, Henry ('Harry') (1883-1915) (Rugby player)

Born on 8 January 1883 at St Mark's parish, Gloucester and killed in action on 9 May 1915 at Aubers Ridge, aged 32 years. Harry has no known grave and is commemorated amongst the Missing on the Le Touret Memorial, Panel 17. An Innkeeper, he was the son of James and Hannah Berry (née Harding) and in 1910 he married Beatrice Eveline Arnold and the couple had two children; before the war they lived in St Catherine Street, Gloucester. Harry joined the Gloucestershire Regiment in 1899 and served in the Boer War (1899-1902) with the 4th, 2nd and 1st Battalions and was awarded the Queen's South Africa Medal with three clasps, Cape Colony, Orange Free State and South Africa 1902. In 1907 he retired from the army and eventually joined the National Reserve. He was recalled to the Colours in August 1914 and served as a Corporal (5711) with the 1/Gloucesters. He landed in France on 2 February 1915 and was awarded the campaign medals - 1914-15 Star, British War Medal and the Victory Medal. Harry is commemorated on the Gloucester Rugby Football Club Roll of Honour, the Kingsholm Stadium War Memorial, the Gloucester War Memorial and the Roll of Honour St Mary de Lode Church, Gloucester. He played 144 games for the Gloucester Rugby Club at wing forward between 1907 and 1913, 135 of which were for the First XV. Harry won eleven Gloucestershire County Caps and four England International caps in 1910, scoring two tries and playing in the inaugural game at Twickenham against Wales.

BROWNLEE, Wilfred Methven (1890-1914) (Cricketer)

Born on 18 April 1890 at Cotham, Bristol and died on 12 October 1914 from meningitis whist in training at Wyke Regis, Dorset, aged 24 years. He was buried at Bristol (Arnos Vale) Cemetery (grave

G.436). Wilfred, a School Master, was the son of William Methven and Anna Eleanor Brownlee (née Dunlop). He enlisted in August 1914 initially as a Private in D Company, 6th Battalion (TF), Gloucestershire Regiment but within weeks was awarded a commission as a Second Lieutenant in the 3rd Battalion, Dorsetshire Regiment. Wilfred is commemorated on the War Memorial at Corpus Christi College, Cambridge University and the War Memorial Arch, Clifton College. He played thirty-two matches for Gloucestershire County Cricket Club as a right-hand batsman and right-arm fast-medium bowler between 1909 and 1914.

CARLETON, Cornelius Asgill Shaw, DSO, MiD(4) (1884-1964) (Rugby player)

Born on 1884 at Newnham, Forest of Dean and died on 20 December 1964 at Farnham, Surrey, aged 81 years. Cornelius, a Professional Soldier, was the son of Dr John Shaw and Rose Anne Carleton (née Carter) and married Jane Playfair Chrystal Menzies in 1936. Cornelius joined the Gloucestershire Regiment in May 1901 and after promotion to Corporal he gained a commission in December 1905 as a Second Lieutenant in the 2nd Battalion, Welsh Regiment. In August 1908 he was seconded for service to the Northern Nigerian Regiment, West African Frontier Force before returning to his regiment in 1912 and serving with it in Egypt (1913). He returned to England in late 1913 and took up an appointment at the Hythe School of Musketry, returning to the 2/Welsh on the outbreak of war. He initially served with D Company, 2/Welsh (Lieutenant, Captain, Temp. Major) followed by command of the 6th (Glamorgan) Battalion, Welsh Regiment (June 1916-March 1917 and August 1917-March 1918)), the 8/Royal Berkshire Regiment (March-July 1917) and finally as an Acting Lieutenant-Colonel commanding his own battalion, the 2/Welsh (April-September 1918). He landed in France on 13 August 1914 and was awarded the campaign medals - 1914 Star with clasp and rose ('*Old Contemptible*'), British War Medal and the Victory Medal. He was also awarded the Distinguished Service Order [DSO] (September 1914) for gallantry and Mentioned in Despatches (4 times). His citation for the DSO reads: "*For daring and successful reconnaissance on several occasions, on the last of which, on 15th September, he was severely wounded*". He was wounded on three occasions - September 1914, April 1918 and September 1918. He played twenty-three games for the Gloucester Rugby Club at back row forward between 1909 and 1913 of which twenty were for the First XV. He also played rugby for the British Army and the Harlequins RFC, won three Gloucestershire County caps and gained an England trial in 1912.

CHARTERIS, Hugo Francis Wemyss, Hon. (Lord Elcho) (1884-1916) (Cricketer)

Born on 28 December 1884 at Wilbury House, Salisbury and killed in action on 23 April 1916 at Katia, Egypt, aged 32 years. Hugo was commemorated on the Jerusalem Memorial, Panel 3 (Missing). Hugo, a Solicitor, was the son of the Earl of Wemyss, Hugo Richard, and Countess of Wemyss, Mary Constance Charteris (née Wyndham) and married Lady Violet Catherine Manners in 1911; the couple had two children. He served as a Lieutenant and Captain with A Squadron, 1/1st Royal

Gloucestershire Hussars Yeomanry. He landed Egypt in May 1915 but did not travel with the RGHY to Gallipoli on 7 August 1915, remaining in Egypt with the rear party minding the regimental horses. He was awarded the campaign medals - 1914-15 Star, British War Medal and the Victory Medal. He was wounded twice at Katia in April 1916 and after each treatment went back into the fighting line until he was killed. Hugo is commemorated on the Aberlady Chapel War Memorial, the Aberlady War Memorial, the Royal Gloucestershire Hussars Yeomany Memorial, College Green, Gloucester, the Houses of Parliament War Memorial, the Stanway War Memorial and the Stanway House Memorial. Hugo played once for Gloucestershire County Cricket Club as a right-hand batsman in 1910. His younger brother, Lieutenant Ivo Alan Charteris, Grenadier Guards, was killed in action at Sailly la Bourse on 17 October 1915, aged 19 years.

COLLETT, Gilbert Faraday DSO, MiD(3) (1879-1945) (Rugby player and Cricketer)

Born on 18 July 1879 at Wynstone Place, Gloucester and died on 25 February 1945 at Hucclecote, Barnword, Gloucester, aged 66 years. Gilbert, a Chemical Manufacturer (a family business), was the son of John and Sarah Anne Collett (née Dosson) and married Dorothy Lawrence Millar in 1926; the couple lived at Wynstone Place, Brookthorpe near Gloucester. Gilbert was a pre-war Territorial soldier with the 5/Gloucesters and landed in France on 29 March 1915 commanding A Company; his brother Lieutenant Colonel John Henry Collett was the Commanding Officer of the 5/Gloucesters. He served initially with 1/5th Battalion, Gloucestershire Regiment (Captain, Major) and finally as a Lieutenant-Colonel commanding the 2/5th Battalion, Gloucestershire Regiment (April 1917-March 1918). He was awarded the campaign medals - 1914-15 Star, British War Medal and the Victory Medal. He was also awarded the Distinguished Service Order (DSO) (June 1918) for gallantry and was Mentioned in Despatches three times (including May 1918). He was wounded in November 1916. Gilbert played nine matches for Gloucestershire County Cricket Club as a right-hand batsman between 1900 and 1914 and played forty-eight games for the Gloucester Rugby Club on the wing between 1897 and 1905, all of which were for the First XV.

COLLINS, Henry ('Harry') (1879-1916) (Rugby player)

Born in July 1879 at St Nicholas, Gloucester and killed in action on 4 July 1916 at La Boisselle, aged 37 years. Harry has no known grave and is commemorated amongst the Missing on the Thiepval Memorial, Pier and Face 5A and 6C. Harry, an Engine Driver at Priday, Metford and Co. Ltd., Gloucester, was the son of Daniel and Acquilla Collins (née Stone) and married Florence Edith Eldridge in 1907; the couple had three children and lived at 2a Clare Street, Gloucester. Harry enlisted in the 3rd (Militia) Battalion, Gloucestershire Regiment in 1894 but was transferred to the 1st Battalion, Gloucestershire Regiment in 1896 serving in Egypt and India before fighting in the Boer War (1899-1902) for which he was awarded the Queen's South Africa Medal with two clasps, Orange

Free State and Defence of Ladysmith. He was discharged from the army in 1906 and enlisted on 3 September 1914. He served as a Private (9259) with 6th (Reserve) Battalion, Worcestershire Regiment, the 1/Worcesters and 10/Worcesters. He landed in France on 5 November 1914 and was awarded the campaign medals - 1914-15 Star ('*Old Contemptible*'), the British War Medal and the Victory Medal. He was wounded with a GSW to the right hand in January 1915,[521] and although invalided out of the Army in March 1915 he taught himself to shoot and bayonet fight with the other hand and subsequently returned to duty in February 1916. Harry is commemorated on the Gloucester Rugby Football Club Roll of Honour, the Kingsholm Stadium War Memorial, the Gloucester War Memorial and the Roll of Honour at St Mary de Lode Church, Gloucester. Harry played 102 games for the Gloucester Rugby Club as a back row forward between 1902 and 1908, ninety-nine of which were for the First XV.

COOK, Albert (1893-1954) (Rugby player)

Born in 1893 in the parish of St John the Baptist, Gloucester and died on 29 November 1954, Gloucester aged 61 years and buried at Coney Hill Cemetery. Albert, an employee of the Gloucester Railway Carriage and Wagon Company Limited, was the son of James and Jane G. Cook (née Lane) from 84 Alvin Street, Gloucester. He married Kathleen Hannah Nicholls in 1919 and the couple had two children. He enlisted in August 1914 and served as a Private (2504, 240594) in the A Company 1/5th Battalion, Gloucestershire Regiment.[522] He landed in France on 29 March 1915 and was awarded the campaign medals - 1914-15 Star, the British War Medal and the Victory Medal. He was wounded on 23 July 1916 with a GSW to the leg which was subsequently amputated and he was invalided out of the Army. Albert remained convinced throughout his life that he was shot with an exploding bullet.[523] He played sixty-nine games for the Gloucester Rugby Club as a back row forward between 1911 and 1914 of which forty-five were for the First XV. Albert's parents had seven sons, six of whom played rugby for the Gloucester Club and five fought in the Great War; four were seriously wounded. The sixth brother was engaged in a reserved ('starred') occupation.

COOK, Charles ('Ninnie') MM (1887-1959) (Rugby player)

Born in 1887 in St John the Baptist's parish, Gloucester and died on 16 May 1959 at 37 Bibury Road, Gloucester aged 82 years; he was buried at Gloucester Old Cemetery. Charles, an employee of the Gloucester Railway Carriage and Wagon Company Ltd, was the son of James and Jane G. Cook (née Lane) from 84 Alvin Street, Gloucester. Charles married Alice Julia Hoebig in 1921 and had three children. He enlisted at Gloucester on 2 September 1914 and served finally as a Corporal (2752, 240750) in B Company, 1/5th Battalion (TF), Gloucestershire Regiment. He landed in France on 29

---

[521] GSW: standard Army abbreviation, used in documentation for Gun Shot Wound.
[522] Territorial soldiers who enlisted before the end of 1916 have two service numbers. Before the end of 1916 soldiers were assigned service numbers unique to their particular TF unit which lead to some confusion. In 1917 following an Army Council Instruction TF soldiers were given a new 6-digit service number which was unique across all TF units which enabled soldiers to be transferred between TF units without confusion.
[523] Person Communication: Terry Short, grandson of Albert Cook

March 1915 and was awarded the campaign medals - 1914-15 Star, the British War Medal and the Victory Medal. He was also awarded the Military Medal [MM] for gallantry in September 1917 whilst attacking an enemy machine gun emplacement. He was wounded in the head on 4 October 1917 and lost an eye. Invalided out of the army on 24 January 1918; he was awarded a Silver War Badge (317328). He played 183 games for the Gloucester Rugby Club at full back between 1906 and 1921, of which 156 were for the First XV. Charles' parents had seven sons, six of whom played rugby for the Gloucester Club and five fought in the Great War; four were seriously wounded. The sixth brother was engaged in a reserved ('starred') occupation. Charles served with the Home Guard in the Second World War and was awarded the Defence Medal. Charles and Alice's eldest son Lawrence was killed in action in Italy in October 1943 fighting with the 3/Coldstream Guards. Charles' Military Medal and campaign medals are held on display at the Soldiers of Gloucestershire Museum.

COOK, George ('Baggy') (1888-1924) (Rugby player)

Born on 1888 in the parish of St John the Baptist, Gloucester and died on 14 July 1924, Oldham, aged 35 years. George, a Soldier and Professional Footballer with Oldham (Rugby League club), was the son of James and Jane G. Cook (née Lane). George joined the British Army at the end of the Boer War and went on to the Army Reserve in 1906 before being recalled to the Colours in August 1914. He served throughout the Great War as a Private (7688) with 2nd and 1st Battalions, Gloucestershire Regiment. He landed in France on 13 August 1914 and was awarded the campaign medals, 1914 Star with clasp and rose ('*Old Contemptible*'), the British War Medal and the Victory Medal. George was wounded (GSW to the back) and taken prisoner in November 1914 and would remain incarcerated for the remainder of the war; during captivity he underwent several operations over a period of four years for the removal of bone fragments. He died of pneumonia on 14 July 1924 having been caught in heavy rain after taking part in a cricket match nine days previously. He played twenty-seven games for the Gloucester Rugby Club at centre between 1907 and 1908, all of them for the First XV before joining Oldham in the Northern Union. George's parents had seven sons, six of whom played rugby for the Gloucester Club and five fought in the Great War; four were seriously wounded. The sixth brother was engaged in a reserved ('starred') occupation.

CRANKSHAW, Eric Norman Spencer, Sir MBE, KCMG (1895-1966) (Cricketer)

Born on 1 July 1885 at Over Peover, Cheshire and died on 24 June 1966 at Reading, aged 80 years. Eric, a Professional Soldier, was the son of Richard Louis and Emily Crankshaw (née Spencer) and married Winifred Mary Ireland in 1912; the couple had two children. In 1904 Eric was commissioned as a Second Lieutenant in the 4th Battalion the King's Liverpool Regiment, a militia unit but in 1905 obtained a regular commission as a Second Lieutenant in the Royal Fusiliers before being promoted to Lieutenant in 1908. In 1911 he was stationed with 3/Royal Fusiliers at Vacoas on the island of Mauritius. In the Great War he was promoted to Captain (Temp Major) in the Royal Fusiliers although in 1915 he was seconded for a period to the Army Signal Service. He landed in France on 19 January 1915 and was awarded the campaign medals - 1914-15 Star, the British War Medal and the Victory Medal. He was also awarded the Member of the Most Excellent Order of the British Empire (Military Division) (MBE) (June 1919). During his lifetime he would be appointed Companion (CMG) (February 1934) and Knight Commander (KCMG) (June 1939) of the Order of St Michael and St George. He was wounded in his left arm which was subsequently amputated. Eric played one match for Gloucestershire County Cricket Club as a right-hand batsman in 1909. His portrait hangs in the National Portrait Gallery, London.

CUMMINGS, Ernest George (1892-1915) (Rugby player)

Born in 1892 in the parish of St Nicholas, Gloucester and killed in action on 26 April 1915 at Ploegsteert, aged 23 years. Ernest was buried at Ploegsteert Wood Military Cemetery, grave III.D.10. Ernest, a Labourer at an engineering works, was the son of Albert and Eleanor Maria Cummings (née Young) from 21 Union Street, Gloucester. He enlisted in August 1914 and served as a Private (2647) in D Company, 1/5th Battalion, Gloucestershire Regiment. He landed in France on 29 March 1915 and was awarded the campaign medals, - 1914-15 Star, the British War Medal and the Victory Medal. Ernest is commemorated on the Gloucester Rugby Football Club Roll of Honour, the Kingsholm Stadium War Memorial, the Gloucester War Memorial, the 5th Battalion, Gloucestershire Regiment Memorial, Gloucester and the Memorial at St Mark's Church, Gloucester. He played seven games for the Gloucester Rugby Club at scrum half between 1911 and 1913. In 1914 Ernest had enlisted with his father, Albert 'Car' Cummings, a renowned Gloucester rugby player and former soldier who lied about his age, stating that he was 41 years old although he was in fact 45 years old; Ernest joined the Territorials while Albert joined Kitchener's New Army but was soon transferred to the 1/Gloucesters. Albert survived the war.

DENNETT, Edward George ('George') (1879-1937) (Cricketer)

Born on 27 April 1879 at Upway, Dorset and died on 15 September 1937 at Leckhampton, Cheltenham after a long illness, aged 58 years. George, a Professional Cricketer, was the son of Richard and Susan Annie Dennett (née Hoskins) and married Nellie Rumley in 1906; the couple had two children. George enlisted in the British Army on 6 January 1896 at Guernsey and served in the Boer War (1899-1902) from November 1899 until 5 August 1902 as a Sergeant (4569) with B Company, 2nd Battalion, Somerset Light Infantry.[524] He was awarded the Queen's South Africa Medal with five clasps, Cape Colony, Orange Free State, Transvaal, Tugela Heights and Relief of

---

[524] Sergeant George Dennett, 2/Somerset LI, Boer War Service Record

Ladysmith. He was also awarded the King's South Africa medal with two clasps, South Africa 1910 and South Africa 1902. During his time in South Africa he was taken dangerously ill in 1900.[525] On his return to Britain after the end of the war, he spent two months at the Royal Hospital, Chelsea before being discharged from the Army at Netley on 5 August 1902 as unfit for duty with a defective eye as a result of enteric fever contracted during his war service. He enlisted in the Army at the outbreak of the Great War and was appointed as a Quartermaster Sergeant but on 28 July 1915 he was medically assessed as fit only for Home Service or Garrison Duty and awarded a commission as a Second Lieutenant on the General List. On 10 October 1915 he was transferred to the 1st (Garrison) Battalion, East Yorkshire Regiment (Captain) which was assigned to garrison duties at Lucknow, India, in February 1916.[526] George returned home on 28 August 1919 on medical grounds and was discharged from the Army on 2 November 1919. He was awarded the British War Medal. George played 388 matches for Gloucestershire County Cricket Club as a left-hand batsman and slow left-arm orthodox bowler between 1903 and 1926; he played one match for the England XI in 1908.

DIPPER, Alfred Ernest ('Dip') (1885-1945) (Cricketer)

Born on 9 November 1885 at Apperley, Gloucestershire and died on 7 November 1945 at St Thomas' Hospital, Lambeth, London, aged 60 years; he was buried at Manor Park Cemetery, London. Alfred, a Professional Cricketer, was the son of John and Emma Dipper (née Ankret) from Green Farm, Apperley and married Florence Mary Oakley in 1929. Prior to the war Alfred was a member of the Oxfordshire Yeomanry. He enlisted on 29 August 1914; Alfred and **Thomas Gange** (GCCC) were the first professional cricketers to enlist. Throughout the Great War he served with Oxfordshire Yeomanry, Corps of Hussars (Private, 2282, 285442), D Squadron, 1/1st Royal Gloucestershire Hussars Yeomanry (Private, Lance Corporal, 2712) and finally from 31 August 1918 as a Driver in the Army Service Corps (MT). He landed in Egypt in May 1915 and was awarded the campaign medals - 1914-15 Star, the British War Medal and the Victory Medal. He was wounded on three occasions - August 1916, March 1918 and the end of the war (reported in January 1919). Alfred played 478 matches for Gloucestershire County Cricket Club as a right-hand batsman and right-arm medium pace bowler between 1908 and 1932; he played one match for the England XI in 1921. Alfred wrote a book entitled '*Cricket Hints*' (London: Athletic Publications, 1926).

DIX, John William ('Father') (1884-1944) (Rugby player)

Born on 22 November 1884 in St Nicholas' parish, Gloucester and died on 5 January 1944 at Gloucester, aged 59 years. William, an employee of the Gloucester Railway Carriage and Wagon Company Ltd, was the son of Frederick and Fanny Jemina Dix (née Jefferies) and married Ellen Elizabeth Hill in 1907; the couple had two children and lived at 1 Colletts Yard, Gloucester. He enlisted on August 1914 and served finally as a Lance Corporal (11922) with the 8th (Service)

---

[525] *Western Gazette* 18 May 1900
[526] Captain George Dennett, 1st (Garrision) Battalion East Yorkshire Regiment, Great War Service Record TNA WO 339/43229-C595807

Battalion, Gloucestershire Regiment. He landed in France on 18 July 1915 and was awarded the campaign medals - 1914-15 Star, the British War Medal and the Victory Medal. In April 1918 William was taken prisoner near Mount Kemmel and forced to work behind enemy lines and was constantly on the move as the Allies advanced. He was repatriated to Britain in November 1918 from Turnhout near the Dutch border. He played 279 games for the Gloucester Rugby Club at outside half between 1906 and 1924 of which 235 were for the First XV. He was awarded twenty Gloucestershire County caps and was an England reserve for two matches in the 1919-20 season.

Du BOULAY, Arthur Houssemayne DSO, MiD(6) Croix de Guerre (1889-1918) (Cricketer)

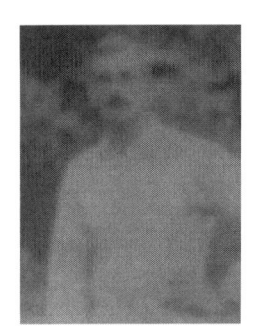

Born on 18 June 1880 at New Brompton, Chatham and died on 25 October 1918 at Fillièvres, France from Influenza whilst on active service, aged 38 years (see Map 2). He was buried at Fillièvres British Cemetery, grave A.36 (Pas de Calais, France). Arthur, a Professional Soldier, was the son of Colonel Woodforde George and Rose Du Boulay (née Hawkins) and married Blanche Kaura Hornung in 1909; the couple had three children and lived at West Grinstead Park, Horsham, Sussex. Arthur attended the Royal Military Academy, Woolwich (1899) and won the Sword of Honour and the Bugle for the Sports Championship. He obtained a commission in 1900 and fought in the Boer War (1899-1902) with the 47th Company, Royal Engineers and was awarded the Queen's South Africa Medal with four clasps, Cape Colony, Orange Free State, Transvaal and South Africa 1902. He was an instructor at the School of Military Engineering (*circa* 1907-1910) and in the Great War served with the Royal Engineers (Captain) and finally as a Major (Brevet Lieutenant Colonel) in the Royal Engineers (A.Q.M.G., Third Army, GHQ). He landed in France in November 1915 and was awarded the campaign medals - 1914-15 Star, the British War Medal and the Victory Medal. He was awarded the Distinguished Service Order (May 1918) for gallantry, Mentioned in Despatches six times, the Croix de Guerre (Belgium) (April 1919), Officier de l'Ordre de Leopold II (avec Palme) (Belgium) (April 1919) and Officer of the Order of Agricultural Merit (France) (June 1917). Arthur is commemorated on the Cheltenham War Memorial, the All Saints Church War Memorial, Cheltenham, the Cheltenham College Roll of Honour, St George's Churchyard Memorial, West Grinstead, the War Memorial at St Botolph's Priory, Colchester and is commemorated on his father's grave, St Peter's Church, Leckhampton and his grandfather's grave (C.H. Hawkins) at St Botolph's Church Cemetery, Colchester. Arthur played three matches for Gloucestershire County Cricket Club as a right-hand batsman and right-arm medium pace bowler in 1908; he played five matches for Kent in 1899. Arthur's brother Hubert was killed in action with the 1/Wiltshires on 3 September 1916.

EDWARDS, Charles William DSO (1884-1938) (Cricketer)

Born on 18 October 1884 at Port Elizabeth, Cape Province, South Africa and died on 22 May 1938 at Earl's Court, London, aged 54 years. Charles, a Professional Soldier served with Royal Army Service Corps (Captain, Major and Lieutenant-Colonel) and landed in France on 9 August 1914. He was awarded the campaign medals - 1914 Star ('*Old Contemptible*'), the British War Medal and the Victory Medal. He was awarded the Distinguished Service Order (DSO) (date after June 1916) for gallantry. Charles played seven matches for Gloucestershire County Cricket Club as a batsman and bowler between 1911 and 1912.

EGERTON, William ('Bill') MiD (1887-1961) (Rugby player)

Born in 1887 in the parish of St Mary de Lode, Gloucester and died on 3 April 1961 at Gloucester, aged 74 years; his funeral was held at St Catharine's Church, Gloucester. Bill, an employee of Messrs Price, Walker and Company Ltd, timber importers, was the son of Henry and Elizabeth Egerton (née Smith) from 9 Bristol Road, Gloucester and married Mabel Edith Mary Gough in 1920; the couple had two children. He enlisted at Gloucester in September 1914 and served in D Company, 1/5th Battalion (TF), Gloucestershire Regiment (Sergeant, 2670, 240697). He landed in France on 25 March 1915 and was awarded the campaign medals - 1914-15 Star, the British War Medal and the Victory Medal. He was Mentioned in Despatches (June 1918); his citation reads, "*240697 Sjt W. Egerton. 1/5th Bn., Glouc.R. (t.F.) was mentioned in a Despatch from General Sir H.C.O. Plumer dated 18th April 1918 for gallant and distinguished services in the Field. I have it in command from the King to record His Majesty's high appreciation of the services rendered. [signed] Winston S. Churchill, Secretary of State for War*". He played seventy-two games for the Gloucester Rugby Club at full back and scrum half between 1906 and 1912 of which thirty-seven were for the First XV. He was a founder of the Nondescripts Cricket Club, Gloucester.

ENGLISH, Ernest Robert Maling DSO, MiD(2), Croix de Guerre (1874-1941) (Cricketer)

Born on 2 December 1874 at Charlton Kings and died on 18 August 1941 at South Kensington, London, aged 67 years. Ernest, a Professional Soldier and Actor, was the son of Major General Frederick and Ellen Sophia English (née Maling) and married Mabel Ilanthe Lardner in 1905; they had one child and lived at 20 Marmion Road, Liverpool. Ernest received a commission as a Lieutenant in 1895, having been an Honorary Queen's Cadet at Sandhurst where his grades in the probationary and final examinations were either very good or exemplary. He went on to serve as a Lieutenant with the 2nd Battalion, Shropshire Light Infantry in the Boer War (1899-1902) and was wounded at Paardeberg in February 1900; he was awarded the Queen's South Africa Medal with six clasps, Paardeberg, Dreifontein, Johannesburg, Cape Colony, South Africa 1901 and South Africa 1902. In 1910 he was promoted to Captain with the 6th (Rifle) Battalion, The King's (Liverpool Regiment). In the Great War he served with 1st Battalion, King's Shropshire Light Infantry (Captain, Major, Lieutenant Colonel). He landed in France on 14 August 1914 and was awarded the campaign medals - 1914 Star ('*Old Contemptible*'), the British War Medal and the Victory Medal. He was awarded the Distinguished Service Order (DSO) (June 1917) for "*…distinguished service in the field…*", Mentioned in Despatches twice and the Croix de Guerre (France) (July 1919). Ernest played one match for Gloucestershire County Cricket Club as a right-hand batsman in 1909. After retiring from the Army in November 1919 with the rank of Lieutenant Colonel, Ernest became an actor (known as Robert English) on stage and screen with thirty-three films over a twenty year career to his credit including *The Four Feathers* (1921), *Waterloo* (1937) and *Mrs Pym of Scotland Yard* (1940).

FARGUS, Archibald Hugh Conway, Reverend MA (1878-1963) (Cricketer)

Born on 15 December 1878 at Clifton, Bristol and died on 6 October 1963 at Eastville, Bristol, aged 85 years. Archibald, a member of the Clergy (ordained 1906 by the Bishop of Winchester), was the son of Frederick John (aka *Hugh Conway*)[527] and Amy Fargus (née Sparks). He married Stella May Clarke in 1909 and they had two children. Archibald attended Pembroke College, Cambridge University from 1898 to 1905 and received a Master of Arts degree. He joined the Royal Navy in 1907 and served on various ships and was on board the cruiser HMS *Europa* on 29 August 1914. He was assigned to HMS *Monmouth* but failed to join the ship after missing his train; HMS *Monmouth* sailed for the Pacific Ocean and was sunk with the loss of all crew. He was awarded the campaign medals - 1914-15 Star, the British War Medal and the Victory Medal. Archibald played fifteen matches for Gloucestershire County Cricket Club as a right-hand batsman and right-arm fast bowler between 1900 and 1901 and won two Blues at Cricket from Cambridge University (1900, 1901). After the war Hugh became Chancellor of St Paul's Anglican Cathedral, Valletta from 1919 until 1922, before moving to a Chaplaincy in Huelva, Spain (1922-25), a Chaplaincy at Thatcham, Berkshire (1929) and finally as Rector of Horfield, Bristol. He played rugby for Clifton RFC between 1901 and 1902.

FOWLER, Theodore Humphrey (1879-1915) (Cricketer)

Born on 25 September 1879 at Cirencester and died on 17 August 1915 at the London County Hospital, Epsom from pyrexia following an operation, aged 35 years. He was buried at Chesterton Cemetery, Cirencester, Row R, Grave 75. Theodore, an Operating Brewer, was the son of Dr Oliver Humphrey and Caroline Fowler (née Slocock). After training with the University and Public Schools Corps, he enlisted on 3 October 1914 in C Company, 1st Battalion, Honourable Artillery Company (Corporal, 2313, 2446). He landed in France on 29 December 1914 and was awarded the campaign medals - 1914-15 Star, the British War Medal and the Victory Medal. He was wounded on three occasions - March 1915, April 1915 (GSW to the head) and June 1915 (Shell Shock). Theodore is commemorated on the Lancing College War Memorial, the Cirencester War Memorial and the [London County] Hospital Memorial. He played forty-six matches for Gloucestershire County Cricket Club as a batsman and wicket-keeper and sometime bowler between 1901 and 1914.

GANGE, Thomas Henry (Harcourt) (1891-1947) (Cricketer)

Born on 15 April 1891 at Pietermaritzberg, South Africa and died on 11 July 1947 at Swansea, aged 56 years. Thomas, a Professional Cricketer, was the son of Thomas Hookway and Henrietta Gange

---

[527] Archibald's father was a novelist who wrote under the name of *Hugh Conway*.

(née McKenzie) and married Edith Kathleen Marion Bishop in 1921; the couple had four children and lived at 13 Beverley Road, Horfield, Bristol. He enlisted on 28 August 1914; Thomas and **Alfred Dipper** (GCCC) were the first professional cricketers to enlist. Throughout the Great War he served with the Royal Horse and Royal Field Artillery (Gunner, Bombardier, Corporal, Sergeant, 1465) and finally as a Sergeant (191479) in the Royal Garrison Artillery. He landed in France on 16 October 1916 and was awarded the campaign medals - the British War Medal and the Victory Medal. Thomas played thirty-seven matches for Gloucestershire County Cricket Club as a right-hand batsman and right-arm fast bowler between 1913 and 1920. He also played rugby for the Cheltenham Football Club.

GRANT, William St Clair MC, Croix de Guerre (1894-1918) (Cricketer)

Born on 8 September 1894 at Bhagalpur, Bengal, India and killed in action on 26 September 1918 at Passchendaele, aged 24 years. He was buried at Gwalia Cemetery, grave II.G.14 (Poperinge, Belgium). William, an undergraduate at Cambridge University, was the son of William St Clair and Camilla St Clair Grant (née Sciortino) from 10 Royal York Crescent, Bristol. He enlisted in September 1914, having joined Clifton College OTC as a Cadet in 1913, and served as a Captain (Adjutant) in the 5th Battalion, Queen's Own Cameron Highlanders. He landed in France on 10 May 1915 and was awarded the campaign medals - 1914-15 Star, the British War medal and the Victory Medal. He was awarded the Military Cross [MC] for gallantry in September 1918 having previously been awarded the Belgium Croix de Guerre (July 1918). He was wounded in 1916 and for two months after recovery was only fit for *"light duty"*. William is commemorated on the war memorials at Clifton College, Bristol and Pembroke College, Cambridge University. He played four matches for Gloucestershire County Cricket Club as a medium-pace bowler in 1914.

GREEN, Michael Arthur (1891-1971) MC, OBE, CBE (Cricketer)

Born on 3 October 1891 at Cotham, Bristol and died on 28 December 1971 at Kensington, London, aged 80 years. Michael, a Professional Soldier, was the son of William Wheeler and Georgina May Green (née Day) and married Muriel Reddall in 1917; they had one child. He served with the 3rd Battalion, Gloucestershire Regiment (Second Lieutenant), the 30th Infantry Brigade (Captain) and finally as a Captain with the 1st Battalion, Gloucestershire Regiment. He was assigned as the Brigade Major for the 30 (Infantry) Brigade. He landed in France on 23 October 1915 and was awarded the campaign medals - 1914-15 Star, the British War Medal and the Victory Medal. He was awarded the Military Cross [MC] for gallantry in July 1918. The citation reads, *"For conspicuous gallantry and devotion to duty. He went forward after a successful attack to reconnoitre and adjust the new line in full view of the enemy and under very heavy artillery and machine gun fire. He showed marked ability in carrying out this work, and obtained valuable information which enabled*

dispositions to be made to ensure the line against immediate counter-attacks" After the Great War he remained in the Army and rose to the rank of Colonel serving in Africa as the Commandant of the Gold Coast Regiment, Royal West African Frontier Force and was appointed by King George VI as a Nominated Official Member of the Legislative Council of the Gold Coast Colony (November 1938). He was appointed an Officer of the Grand Priory in the British Realm of the Venerable Order of the Hospital of St John of Jerusalem (June 1938) and an Officer of the Most Excellent Order of the British Empire (Military Division) (OBE) (June 1938). He also served in the Second World War with the Northamptonshire Regiment and the Royal Air Force Regiment and would attain the rank of Brigadier; in recognition of his "*…gallant and distinguished services in the field..*" he was appointed as a Commander of the Most Excellent Order of the British Empire (CBE) (Military Division) (March 1945). Michael played ninety-one matches for Gloucestershire County Cricket Club as a right-hand batsman between 1912 and 1928; he played two matches for Essex in 1930. He was an all-round sportsman and besides his cricket also played rugby for the British Army and the Harlequins RFC, Association Football for the Army and Surrey and Squash for the Army.

GRIFFITHS, George Henry (1884-1918) (Rugby player)

Born in 1884 in the parish of St Nicholas, Gloucester and killed in action on 4 April 1918 on the Somme, aged 34 years. He is commemorated on the Pozières Memorial, panels 40 and 41 (Missing). George, an Iron Steel Driller at Messrs Fielding and Platt Ltd., Gloucester, was the son of John and Emily Jane Griffiths (née Clarke) and married Kate Cecilia Bishop in 1905; they had three children and lived at 68 St Catherine Street, Gloucester. George joined the 3rd (Militia) Battalion, Gloucestershire Regiment in 1901 but transferred to the 1st Battalion in 1902 and served in Ceylon guarding Boer prisoners. He enlisted in August 1914 and served finally as a Lance Corporal (6392) with Gloucestershire Regiment in the 9th (Service) Battalion, the 2nd Battalion, the 10th (Service) Battalion and the 13th (Service Battalion) (Forest of Dean Pioneers). He landed in France on 20 January 1915 and was awarded the campaign medals - 1914-15 Star, the British War Medal and the Victory Medal. He was wounded once (sprained ankle) in April 1915. George is commemorated on the Gloucester Rugby Football Club Roll of Honour, the Kingsholm Stadium War Memorial, the Gloucester War Memorial and the Newent War Memorial. He played 135 games for the Gloucester Rugby Club as a back row forward between 1907 and 1913 of which 111 were for the First XV; he was awarded two Gloucestershire County rugby caps in 1911-12 season.

GRIFFITHS, James (1892-1916) (Rugby player)

Born in 1892 at South Hamlet, Gloucester and killed in action on 23 July 1916 at Pozières, aged 24 years. James is commemorated amongst the Missing on the Thiepval Memorial, Pier and Face 5A and 5B. James, a Step Maker at Messrs Matthews and Company, Gloucester Docks, was the son of Henry and Annie Griffiths (née Smith). He enlisted in August 1914 and served as a Private (2310, 240490) in A Company, 1/5th Battalion, Gloucestershire Regiment. He landed in France on 29 March 1915 and was awarded the campaign medals - 1914-15 Star, the British War Medal and the Victory

Medal. He is commemorated on the Kingsholm Stadium War Memorial, the Gloucester War Memorial and the 5th Battalion, Gloucestershire Regiment Memorial. He played four games for the Gloucester Rugby Club at second row forward between 1911 and 1914, of which one was for the First XV.

GRIST, Ronald (1868-1918) (Rugby player)

Born in July 1868 at Stroud and died from disease on 15 May 1918 whilst on active service, aged 49 years. He is buried at Rangoon War Cemetery, Myanmar, grave 4.F.10. Ronald, a Bank Manager at the Capital and Counties Bank, Amersham, was the son of Richard and Lucy Grist (née Smith). In July 1916 despite being 47 years old Ronald enlisted as a Second Lieutenant on the General List, Class II National Reserve for home service only. However having passed the test of marching ten miles carrying a rifle and 150 rounds of ammunition he was posted to a Territorial unit and performed garrison duties in India and Burma with the 18th (London) Battalion (TF), Rifle Brigade. He was awarded the British War Medal. Ronald is commemorated on the Kingsholm Stadium War Memorial and the Amersham War Memorial. He played eighteen games for the Gloucester Rugby Club on the wing between 1888 and 1889, all for the First XV.

HALFORD, Jonathan George ('Biddy') (1886-1960) (Rugby player)

Born on 27 November 1886 at Gloucester and died on 30 May 1960 at Tyndale Road, Woodfield, Dursley, aged 74 years; his funeral was held at Christ Church, Gloucester and the Gloucester Crematorium. George, a Blacksmith Striker and Professional Soldier, was the son of Jonathan James and Clara Ann Eugenia Halford (née Manley) and married Martha Jane Dix in 1906; they had six children and lived at 28 New Street, Gloucester. George joined the Gloucestershire Regiment in 1903, having previously been a part-time soldier with the 3rd Militia Battalion, Gloucestershire Regiment. He left the Army in 1905 and went onto the Active Reserve. He served in the Great War as a Lance Corporal (6748) in the 1st Battalion, Gloucestershire Regiment and landed in France on 13 August 1915. He was awarded the campaign medals - 1914 Star with clasp and rose ('*Old Contemptible*'), the British War Medal and the Victory Medal; he is listed amongst the *Old Contemptibles* at Christ Church, Gloucester. He suffered a shrapnel wound to his side in January 1915 and was subsequently declared unfit for further military service in February 1916. By 1919 he had sufficiently recovered to resume his rugby career and in total he played 333 games for the Gloucester Rugby Club at second row forward between 1907 and 1924, of which 320 were for the First XV.

HANCOCK, Walter Henry ('Harry') (1886-1914) (Cricketer)

Born on 4 October 1886 at Gloucester and killed in action on 29 October 1914 at Ypres, aged 30 years. Walter is commemorated amongst the Missing on the Menin Gate Memorial, Addenda Panel 57, Ypres. Walter, a Blacksmith Striker, was the son of Albert and Sarah Jane Hancock (née Moody) and married Mary Ann Eliza Bower in 1909. Walter joined the 3rd Battalion, Gloucestershire Regiment in 1903 and in 1908 he was placed in the National Reserve. He served in the Great War as a Corporal (7140) with the 1st Battalion, Gloucestershire Regiment. He landed in France on 13 August 1914 and was awarded the campaign medals - 1914 Star with clasp and rose ('*Old Contemptible*'), the British War Medal and the Victory Medal. Walter is commemorated on the Gloucester Rugby Football Club Roll of Honour and the Kingsholm Stadium War Memorial. He played twenty-six games for the Gloucester Rugby Club at full back between 1908 and 1911, of which four were for the First XV.

HEALING, John Alfred MC (1873-1933) (Cricketer)

Born on 14 June 1873 at Forhampton, Tewkesbury and died on 4 July 1933 at Caister-on-Sea, Norfolk, aged 60 years. John, a Stock Broker, was the son of William Grafton and Kate Healing (née Ireland) from Gloucester Road, Richmond Hill, Richmond. He served in the Great War with the 4th Battalion, Royal Warwickshire Regiment (Lieutenant), the 20th Battalion, Manchester Regiment (Captain) and finally as a Major and second in command in the 2nd Battalion, Royal Warwickshire Regiment. He landed in France on 29 September 1915 and was awarded the campaign medals - 1914-15 Star, the British War Medal and the Victory Medal. He was awarded Military Cross [MC] for gallantry in June 1917 "*...for valuable services rendered in connection with the war...*". He was wounded in action on 7 October 1917 and demobilised on 22 July 1919 (Special Reserve). John was educated at Clifton College and Pembroke College, Cambridge University. He played ten matches for Gloucestershire County Cricket Club as a left-hand batsman between 1899 and 1906.

HENDERSON, William Douglas (1889-1918) (Rugby player)

Born on 8 December 1889 in the parish of St John the Baptist, Gloucester and died on a training flight crash in a Sopwith Camel on 28 November 1918 at Montrose, Scotland, aged 29 years. He was buried at Gloucester Old Cemetery, grave NG.9246A. William emigrated to Canada in 1911 and was an Auto-Mechanic in Toronto. He was the son of Alexander Cameron and Mary Henderson (née Vance) from Clarence Street, Gloucester. He served with 4th Divisional Ammunition Park, Canadian Overseas Expeditionary Force (Private, 1262244), the Royal Flying Corps (Air Mechanic 3) and the Royal Air Force (Private 2, 68018, Flight Cadet). He landed in Rouen on 19 August 1916 and was awarded the campaign medals – the British War Medal and the Victory Medal. He is commemorated on the Gloucester Rugby Football Club Roll of Honour, the Kingsholm Stadium War Memorial, King's School Roll of Honour at St Mary de Lode Church, Gloucester, the King's School War Memorial, Gloucester and the Canadian Virtual War Memorial (CVWM); William was commemorated in the Roll of Honour published in *Flight* (2 January 1919). He played sixteen games for the Gloucester Rugby Club at second row forward between 1909 and 1910 of which one was for the First XV.

HOLLOWAY, George James Warner Sinclair (1884-1966) (Cricketer)

Born on 26 April 1884 at Stroud and died on 22 September 1966 at Montpellier, aged 82 years. George worked in the family's clothier business and was the son of George John and Emily Catherine Holloway (née Warner) from Hill House, Amberley. In 1920 he married Ivy Sinclair Travis. He trained at the Inns of Court Officer Training Corps (Private, 2215) and gained a commission with the 8th Battalion, Northumberland Fusiliers (Lieutenant, Captain) before he was attached to D Company, 9th Battalion, West Yorkshire Regiment. He landed in Gallipoli in September 1915 and was awarded the campaign medals - 1914-15 Star, the British War Medal and the Victory Medal. He was transferred to the Western Front and was reported as missing in action on 11 August 1916 before being confirmed as a Prisoner of War (10 September). He was held captive for two years at Gütersloh POW Camp and was interned in Holland (12 October 1918) before repatriation to Britain on 19 November 1918. George played ten matches for Gloucestershire County Cricket Club as a left-hand batsman between 1908 and 1911. George's great-uncle, also named George Holloway, a Member of Parliament, was a social reformer and founded the Mid-Gloucester Working Men's Benefit Society, later known as the Original Holloway Benefit Society Limited, which was the first society in Britain to offer disability insurance and a retirement cash sum. A statue was erected to him in Stroud.

HORLICK, James Nockells, Sir BA, MC, MiD(4), OBE (1886-1972) (Cricketer)

Born on 22 March 1886 at Brooklyn, New York and died on 31 December 1972 at Achamore House, Isle of Gighan, Argyll, aged 86 years; he was buried at Kilchatten Graveyard on Gighan. James, a Professional Soldier, was the son of Sir James and Lady Margaret Adelaide Horlick (née Burford) and married Flora Macdonald Martin in 1911; the couple lived at Little Padocks, Sunninghill, Berkshire. He was the 4th holder of the Horlick Baronetcy. In 1907 he joined the Royal Gloucestershire Hussars before joining the Coldstream Guards in 1909 and in the Great War served with the 3rd Battalion (Captain, Brevet Major and Temporary Lieutenant-Colonel) and as a General Staff Officer at HQ 22nd Division (Lieutenant Colonel). He landed in France on 12 August 1914 and was awarded the campaign medals - 1914 Star with clasp and rose ('*Old Contemptible*'), the British War Medal and the Victory Medal. He was awarded the Military Cross (June 1917) "...*for distinguished service in the field*...", was Mentioned in Despatches four times, was appointed an Officer of the Most Excellent Order of the British Empire (Military Division) [OBE] for Services in Salonika (June 1919), a Chevalier, Legion d'Honneur (July 1919), the Military Cross (Greece) (July 1919) and the Order of the White Eagle, (4th Class, with Swords) (Serbia) (January 1920). He was invested as an Officer of the Most Venerable Order of the Hospital of St. John of Jerusalem (O.St.J.) (January 1938). Throughout the Great War he served in France, the Balkans and South Russia and in 1919 attended the Paris Peace Conference where the signing of the Treaty of Versailles officially ended the War. He played twice for Gloucestershire County Cricket Club as a right-hand batsman and slow left-arm orthodox bowler between 1907 and 1910. Between 1923 and 1929 he was the Member of Parliament for Gloucester and in 1963 he was awarded the Victorian Medal of Honour [VMH] from the Royal Horticultural Society for his work with rhododendrons. In 1956 James married

Joan Isabel MacGill. His father and his uncle, William, were the co-inventors of the Horlicks Malted Milk drink.

JAMES, Burnet George (1886-1915) (Cricketer)

Born on 26 October 1886 at Durdham Down, Bristol and killed in action on 26 September 1915 at Langemark, aged 29 years; he was buried at Cement House Cemetery (Belgium), grave XIII.D.37. Burnet, a Tobacco Manufacturer, was the son of Sir Edward and Lady Mabel Amelia James (née Edwards). In 1907 Burnet joined the Gloucestershire Royal Garrison Artillery Volunteers and served for five years. He re-joined the unit, now the 1st South Midland Brigade, Royal Field Artillery (TF) on the outbreak of war before transferring to the Royal Flying Corps [RFC] in July 1915 where he was promoted to a Second Lieutenant in the 7th Squadron. He landed in France in March 1915 and was awarded the campaign medals - 1914-15 Star, the British War Medal and the Victory Medal. Burnet was originally reported as missing on 27 September along with Second Lieutenant Louis Yule before their deaths were confirmed on 1 December 1915. He is commemorated in the Charterhouse War Memorial Chapel, the memorial at St Marys of the Quay, Catholic Church, Bristol, and the Clifton Rugby Football Club Roll of Honour. Burnet played three matches for Gloucestershire County Cricket Club as a left-hand batsman and slow left-arm orthodox bowler in 1914. He also represented Gloucestershire at hockey.

JESSOP, Gilbert Laird (1874-1955) (Cricketer)

Born on 19 May 1874 at Cheltenham and died on 11 May 1955 at Fordington, Dorset, aged 81 years. Gilbert, a Company Director, was the son of Dr Henry and Susannah Jessop and married Millicent Osborne in 1902; the couple had one child. He gained a commission and initially on the General List served with the 14th (Reserve) Battalion, Manchester Regiment (Captain); he was UK-based throughout the war. On 15 June 1916 Gilbert was admitted to the 2nd Southern General Hospital suffering from ruptured muscles and severe lumbago caused by a period of trench digging. He was sent for a mineral water and radiant heat (steam) treatment at Bath but due to a malfunction of the equipment and in the absence of an attendant, he suffered considerably. The excessive steam treatment seriously damaged his heart and he was rendered unfit for active military service. He was appointed as a Second Grade Recruiting Officer and relinquished his commission on 28 August 1918. Gilbert played 345 matches for Gloucestershire County Cricket Club as a right-hand batsman and right-arm fast bowler between 1894 and 1914; he played nineteen matches for England between 1899 and 1912. He won four Blues at Cricket from Cambridge University (1896-99) but after his accident in 1916 he never played cricket again.

JONES, Hugh MC (1888-1918) (Cricketer)

Born on 21 December 1888 at Nass House, Lydney and died on 10 November 1918 at Chatham, Kent from Pneumonia following a wounding in both legs, aged 30 years. He was buried at St Mary's Churchyard, Lydney. Hugh, a Clerk in the family business of Ship Owners, was the son of William and Jane Jones (née Hughes) from 4 Hill Street, Lydney. He enlisted with 12th (Bristol's Own) Battalion, Gloucestershire Regiment (Private, 14898) and on 28 February 1915 gained a commission with the 13th (Service) Battalion (Forest of Dean) (Pioneers), Gloucestershire Regiment (Captain). He landed in France on 4 March 1916 and was awarded the campaign medals – the British War Medal and the Victory Medal. He was awarded the Military Cross (October 1916), "*For conspicuous gallantry during operations. While clearing trenches with his company after an attack, the enemy opened a heavy bombardment. He displayed the greatest courage whilst standing in the open under shell fire for two hours assisting his men to get into safety. Later he went by himself, under heavy shell fire, and fetched two stretchers for his wounded*" He was wounded on three occasions - June 1917, July 1917 and April 1918. Hugh is commemorated on the Lydney War Memorial Cross, the Stained Glass Memorial Window at St Mary's Church, Lydney, the Lydney Cricket Club Memorial, the War Memorial in Wycliffe School Chapel and Wycliffe School War Memorial (on the exterior of the building). Hugh played once for Gloucestershire County Cricket Club as a batsman in 1914 against Worcestershire; opinion was that he showed potential and probably would have played more matches.

KITCAT, Sidney Austyn Paul (1868-1942) (Cricketer)

Born on 20 July 1868 at Charlton Kings and died on 17 June 1942 at Esher, Surrey, aged 74 years. Sidney, a Stockbroker, was the son of Reverend David and Clara Francis Kitcat (née Paul) and married Mabel Hickson (née Greenhow) in 1896 and lived at Warling Dean, Esher, Surrey. Following the death of Mabel in 1922, Sidney was re-married in 1925 to Muriel Maude Antonietti (née Walker). He was a member of a volunteer light infantry unit, the Artists' Rifles, from 1889 until 1895. Rejected as too old in 1914 he managed to serve throughout the Great War as a Lieutenant in the Royal Naval Volunteer Reserve (RNVR), based at the Royal Naval Depot, HMS *Victory VI* (aka HMS *Crystal Palace*). He was awarded the British War Medal. Sidney played fifty matches for Gloucestershire County Cricket Club as a right-hand batsman and right-arm medium pace bowler between 1892 and 1904. Sidney also played hockey for England and played rugby at a minor level.

LANE, Henry William ('Harry') DCM (1884-1918) (Rugby player)

Born on 1884 at South Hamlet, Gloucester and killed in action on 30 March 1918 on the Somme, aged 34 years. He was buried at Bucquoy Road Cemetery (Ficheux), grave IV.K.6 (see Map 2). Harry, a Labourer in Cardiff, was the son of William Henry and Elizabeth Lane (née Randall) and married Louisa Clara Cullis in 1915. Harry joined the Grenadier Guards in 1901 before going onto the National

Reserve. He was recalled to the Colours with the 1st Battalion, Grenadier Guards (Guardsman, 15585) and with the 4th Battalion, Guards Machine Gun Regiment (Lance Corporal, 000205). He landed in France on 8 November 1914 and was awarded the campaign medals - 1914 Star with clasp and rose ('*Old Contemptible*'), the British War Medal and the Victory Medal. He was awarded the Distinguished Conduct Medal [DCM] for gallantry in November 1916 and his citation reads, "*He led his machine gun team forward with great courage and determination, reaching the second objective. Later, he pushed on to the third objective and accounted for large numbers of the enemy*". Harry is commemorated on the Kingsholm Stadium War Memorial, the Gloucester War Memorial, the stone Memorial Screen in St Mary de Crypt Church, Gloucester and the War Memorial in St Mark's Church, Gloucester. He played sixteen games for the Gloucester Rugby Club as a back row forward between 1902 and 1905, of which one was for the First XV.

LEWIS, Alexander Henry Tudor ('Alec') MC and Bar (1887-1941) (Rugby player)

Born on January 1887 at South Hamlet, Gloucester and died on 27 October 1941 at Meriden, Warwickshire, aged 54 years. Alec was cremated at Perry Bar in a service which was accorded full military honours. Alec, an Assistant Master at Tredworth Council School, was the son of Henry Arthur and Susan Lewis (née Browning) from Overton, Deansway, Gloucester and married Elsie Mary Berry in 1922; the couple had two children. He served with C Company, 1/5th Battalion (TF), Gloucestershire Regiment (Lance Corporal, 2693), the 6th (Service) Battalion, Royal Berkshire Regiment (Lieutenant, Captain) and the 4th Battalion, Intelligence Corps (Major). He landed in France on 29 March 1915 and was awarded the campaign medals - 1914-15 Star, the British War Medal and the Victory Medal. He won two Military Crosses [MC] for gallantry in December 1916 and April 1918. His citation for his first MC reads: "*For conspicuous gallantry in action. He assumed command of a company of another unit, reorganised bombing sections and successfully dealt with the enemy and at a critical time. He set a splendid example.*" The citation for his second MC reads, "*For conspicuous gallantry and devotion to duty in carrying out the duties of brigade intelligence officer. During some reconnaisances, made under heavy shell and rifle fire, he gained most valuable information regarding the ground and our dispositions. On one occasion he made a reconnaissance along the front line in close proximity to the enemy and under fire from their snipers*" He was wounded twice, in April 1916 and July 1916. Alec played ninety-three games for the Gloucester Rugby Club at centre between 1908 and 1920 of which eighty-seven were for the First XV. His two brothers, **Melville** and **Tom Lewis** (GRFC) were killed in the attack at Pozières in July 1916, during which Alec was wounded; his brother Percival's brother-in-law, **Sidney Sysum** (GRFC) was also killed in the attack. During the Second World War Alec served with the Birmingham Home Guard and was awarded the War Medal 1939-45 and the Defence Medal.

LEWIS, Melville Edward Lionel (1896-1916) (Rugby player)

Born on 1896 at South Hamlet, Gloucester and killed in action on 23 July 1916 at Pozières, aged 20 years. He is commemorated amongst the Missing on the Thiepval Memorial, Pier and Face 5A and 5B (Missing). Melville, an employee at Messrs Fielding and Platt Ltd, Gloucester, was the son of Henry Arthur and Susan Lewis (née Browning) from Overton, Deansway, Gloucester. He served with C Company, 1/5th Battalion (TF), Gloucestershire Regiment (Corporal, 2694). He landed in France on 29 March 1915 and was awarded the campaign medals - 1914-15 Star, the British War Medal and the Victory Medal. Melville is commemorated on the Kingsholm Stadium War Memorial, the Gloucester War Memorial, the 5th Battalion, Gloucestershire Regiment War Memorial, the War Memorial at St Thomas Rich's School, the Crypt Grammar School War Memorial and the War Memorial in the Lady Chapel at All Saints Church, Gloucester. He played five games for the Gloucester Rugby Club as a back row forward between 1913 and 1914. Melville's brother **Tom Lewis** (GRFC) was killed in the same attack as himself and another brother, **Alec Lewis** (GRFC), was seriously wounded; his brother Percival's brother-in-law, **Sidney Sysum** (GRFC) was also killed in the attack.

LEWIS, Thomas Harry Raymond ('Tom') (1891-1916) (Rugby player)

Born on 1891 at South Hamlet, Gloucester and killed in action on 21 July 1916 at Pozières, aged 25 years. He is commemorated amongst the Missing on the Thiepval Memorial, Pier and Face 5A and 5B (Missing). Tom, a Draughtsman for Messrs Fielding and Platt Ltd, Gloucester, was the son of Henry Arthur and Susan Lewis (née Browning) from Overton, Deansway, Gloucester. He served with C Company, 5th Battalion (TF), Gloucestershire Regiment (Lance Corporal, 2695, 240713). He landed in France on 29 March 1915 and was awarded the campaign medals - 1914-15 Star, the British War Medal and the Victory Medal. Tom is commemorated on the Kingsholm Stadium War Memorial, the Gloucester War Memorial, the 5th Battalion, Gloucestershire Regiment War Memorial, the War Memorial at Sir Thomas Rich's School, Gloucester and the War Memorial in the Lady Chapel at All Saints Church, Gloucester. He played five games for the Gloucester Rugby Club at stand off between 1911 and 1914. Tom's brother **Melville Lewis** (GRFC) was killed in the same attack as himself and another brother, **Alec Lewis** (GRFC), was seriously wounded; his brother Percival's brother-in-law, **Sidney Sysum** (GRFC) was also killed in the attack.

MACKAY, Claude Lysacht (1894-1915) (Cricketer)

Born on 29 October 1894 at Satara, Maharashtra, India and died of wounds on 7 June 1915 at Boulogne, France, aged 20 years; he was buried at Boulogne Eastern Cemetery, grave II.A.31. Claude was the son of Edward Vansittart and Jane (Nina) Mackay (née Whitty). He enlisted on 11 August

1914 and served with 3rd Battalion, Gloucestershire Regiment, 5th Battalion, Worcestershire Regiment, 2nd Battalion, Worcestershire Regiment (Second Lieutenant) and was attached to 2nd Battalion, Manchester Regiment. He landed in France on 7 November 1914 and was awarded the campaign medals - 1914 Star, the British War Medal and the Victory Medal. Claude is commemorated on the Roll of Honour at Corpus Christi College, Cambridge University and Clifton College, Bristol. He played once for Gloucestershire County Cricket Club as a right-hand batsman and right-arm fast-medium bowler in 1914. He was educated at Clifton College and Corpus Christi College, Cambridge University.

MARSDEN, Edmund (1881-1915) (Cricketer)

Born on 18 April 1881 at Madras, India and died from malaria whilst on active service on 26 May 1915 at Myithkina, Myanmar [Burma], aged 34 years. He was buried at Taukkyan War Cemetery, 27.J.2 (Special Memorial). Edmund, a Professional Soldier, was the son of Edmund and Julia Marsden (née Turner). He attended the Royal Military Academy, Sandhurst in 1898 and received a commission as a Second Lieutenant in 1900 with the Indian Army and was promoted to Lieutenant (1902) and Captain (1909); he took part in the Tibet Expedition (1903-04) which entered Lhasa and was awarded the Tibet Medal and clasp (Gyantse) and "...*behaved with the greatest of gallantry in action at Wawang on 28th January* [1915]". Throughout the Great War he was attached to the 64th Pioneers (Captain) from the Indian Army Reserve of Officers. He landed in Burma in 1914 and was awarded the British War Medal. Edmund is commemorated on the Cheltenham War Memorial, the Cheltenham College Roll of Honour and the Memorial in the Chapel of the Royal Military Academy, Sandhurst. He played twice for Gloucestershire County Cricket Club as a batsman in 1909. Edmund was originally omitted from the CWGC database and his name was only added in 2006.

MERRICK, Horace MC (1887-1961) (Cricketer)

Born on 21 December 1887 at Clifton, Bristol and died on 16 August 1961 at Clifton, Bristol, aged 74 years; he was buried at Shirehampton Cemetery. Horace, a School Master at Denstone College, Uttoxeter, was the son of Dr Frank and Phoebe O. Merrick (née Carroll) from School House, Clifton College, Bristol. He served with 4th (City of Bristol) (TF) Battalion, Gloucestershire Regiment (Private, Lieutenant, Acting Captain) and with A Company, 1st Battalion, Gloucestershire Regiment (Captain). He landed in France on 31 March 1915 and was awarded the campaign medals - 1914-15 Star, the British War Medal and the Victory Medal. He won the Military Cross [MC] (June 1917), *"For conspicuous gallantry and devotion to duty. He showed great coolness and bravery when in command of his company and displayed great energy in organising the whole position captured, having had to assume command of the other company meanwhile."* He was wounded once - shot through the mouth - in October 1915. Horace played twelve matches for Gloucestershire County Cricket Club as a right-hand batsman between 1901 and 1911.

MILLARD, Sydney ('Syd') (1884-1916) (Rugby player)

Born on 1884 at Deerhurst, Gloucestershire and killed in action on 23 July 1916 at Pozières, aged 32 years. He is commemorated on the Thiepval Memorial, Pier and Face 5A and 5B (Missing). An Upholsterer for R. James, Northgate Street, Gloucester, he was the son of William John and Alice Millard (née Chandler) from Newton Road, Malvern. Syd enlisted in August 1914 and served with No.13 Platoon, D Company, 1/5th Battalion, Gloucestershire Regiment (Sergeant, 2735). He landed in France on 29 March 1915 and was awarded the campaign medals - 1914-15 Star, the British War Medal and the Victory Medal. Syd is commemorated on the Gloucester Rugby Football Club Roll of Honour, the Kingsholm Stadium War Memorial, the Gloucester War Memorial, the 5th Battalion, Gloucestershire Regiment War Memorial, the War Memorial at Upton St Leonard's Church and the War Memorial in the Lady Chapel at All Saints Church, Gloucester. He played 123 games for the Gloucester Rugby Club as a second row forward between 1909 and 1914, of which seventy-eight were for the First XV. Syd's brother Harold, Devonshire Regiment, died of wounds in October 1917.

NASON, John William Washington (1889-1916) (Cricketer)

Born on 4 August 1889 at Corse Grange, Tewkesbury and killed in action on 26 December 1916 at Vlamertinghe, Belgium, aged 27 years; he was buried at Vlamertinghe Military Cemetery, grave V.B.11. John, a School Master, was the son of Dr Charles St Stephen Richard and Frederica Nason (née Abrahall) and married Dorothea Helen Gawthorne in 1915 He enlisted at Hastings on 28 August 1914 as a Driver (95563) in the 75 Brigade, Royal Artillery. He obtained a commission on 15 November 1914 and from the General List was assigned initially to the 14th (Reserve) Battalion, Royal Sussex Regiment, transferring to the 11th Battalion (Captain) and subsequently in the 46th Squadron, Royal Flying Corps (Captain and Flight Commander) on 12 February 1916; he was appointed as a Flying Officer on 22 September 1916 after completing his course at the RFC Training Centre, Curragh. He landed at Le Havre in March 1916 and was awarded the campaign medals – the British War Medal and the Victory Medal. John is commemorated on the Corse War Memorial, St Margaret's Church, Corse, the Hastings War Memorial, Alexandra Park, and in Ireland's Memorial Records 1914-1918. He played nineteen matches for Gloucestershire County Cricket Club as a right-hand batsman and right-arm slow bowler between 1913 and 1914; he also played twenty-two matches for Sussex between 1906 and 1910. He won two Blues at Cricket from Cambridge University (1909, 1910).

NELMES, William Guy ('Jack') (1889-1916) (Rugby player)

Born on 1889 at Lydney and killed in action on 23 July 1916 at High Wood on the Somme, aged 26 years. He is commemorated on the Thiepval Memorial, Pier and Face 5A and 5B (Missing). Jack, a Tin Plate Catcher at Lydney Tinplate Works, was the son of Guy and Abigail Nelmes (née Criddle) from 21 Albert Street, Lydney. Jack enlisted on 23 September 1914 and served with the 8th (Service) Battalion, Gloucestershire Regiment (Lance Corporal, 13939). He landed in France on 18 July 1915 and was awarded the campaign medals - 1914-15 Star, the British War Medal and the Victory Medal. Jack is commemorated on the Kingsholm Stadium War Memorial, the Lydney War Memorial, the stained glass War Memorial window at St Mary's Church, Lydney and on his mother's grave, Abigail Nelms (1866-1902) in the graveyard of St Mary's Church, Lydney. He played sixty-two games for the Gloucester Rugby Club as a back row forward between 1908 and 1911 of which forty were for the First XV.

PARHAM, William George (1893-1917) (Rugby player)

Born on 1893 at South Hamlet, Gloucester and killed in action on 4 October 1917 at Broodseinde near Ypres, aged 25 years. He is commemorated on the Tyne Cot Memorial, Panels 72 to 75 (Missing). William, a Labourer for a Wireman on the Midland Railway, Gloucester, was the son of William H. and Mary Ann Parham (née Bird) and married Eveline Phyllis Cook in 1916; the couple had one child and lived at 25 Albert Street, Gloucester. William enlisted in August 1914 and served with C Company, 1/5th Battalion (TF), Gloucestershire Regiment (Corporal, 240763). He landed in France on 29 March 1915 and was awarded the campaign medals - 1914-15 Star, the British War Medal and the Victory Medal. He was wounded in the right knee in December 1916. William is commemorated on the Gloucester Rugby Football Club Roll of Honour, the Kingsholm Stadium War Memorial, the Gloucester War Memorial, the 5th Battalion, Gloucestershire Regiment War Memorial and the Roll of Honour at St Mary de Lode Church, Gloucester. He played fifty-one games for the Gloucester Rugby Club as a back row and second row forward between 1912 and 1914 of which thirty-six were for the First XV.

PARKER, Charles Warrington Leonard ('Charlie') (1882-1959) (Cricketer)

Born on 14 October 1882 at Prestbury, Gloucestershire and died on 11 July 1959, at Cranleigh, Surrey, aged 77 years; he was buried at Cranleigh Cemetery. Charlie, a Professional Cricketer, was the son of Leonard and Sarah Jane Parker (née Kitchen) and married Daisy Helena Gardener in 1914; the couple had four children and lived in Bristol. He served with the Royal Flying Corps [RFC] (A.Mech 3) and in the Royal Air Force [RAF] (Clerk 3, 130352). He was awarded the campaign medals – the British War Medal and the Victory Medal. Charlie played 602 matches for Gloucestershire County Cricket Club as a right-hand batsman and slow left-arm orthodox bowler between 1903 and 1935; he represented England once against Australia in 1921.

PEARCE, William James ('Billy') (1884-1917) (Rugby player)

Born in 1884 at Thornbury and killed in action on 2 December 1917 at La Vacquerie, aged 31 years. He was buried at Villers-Plouich Communal Cemetery, Special Memorial 1 (*'Known to be buried in this cemetery'*). Billy, a Manager in the timber trade, was the son of James and Mary Jane Pearce (née Legge) and married Margery Mansell Delany in 1914; the couple had one child and lived at 34 Wellington Road, Bilston. From *circa* 1903 until 1906 he served with the South Africa Mounted Police (Cape Mounted Police). He enlisted in September 1914 and served with 1/5th Battalion (TF) South Staffordshire Regiment (Private, Sergeant, 2963), the 1/5th Battalion (TF), Gloucestershire Regiment (Second Lieutenant) and in the 2/5th Battalion (TF), Gloucestershire Regiment (Lieutenant). He landed in France on 5 March 1915 and was awarded the campaign medals - 1914-15 Star, the British War Medal and the Victory Medal. He was wounded with a GSW to the leg on 23 July 1916. Billy is commemorated on the Gloucester Rugby Football Club Roll of Honour, the Kingsholm Stadium War Memorial, the Gloucester War Memorial, the 5th Battalion, Gloucestershire Regiment War Memorial, the War Memorial at Holy Innocents Church, Highnam, and the War Memorial at Sir Thomas Rich's School. He played forty-two games for the Gloucester Rugby Club as a back row forward and wing between 1906 and 1912 of which thirty-nine were for the First XV. His only child, Monica, founded the St Mary's Hospice, Selly Oak in 1979 and the first hospice in Poland at Gandsk in 1989.

PEPALL, George (1876-1953) (Cricketer)

Born on 29 February 1876 at Cyford, Stow-on-the-Wold and died on 8 January 1953 at Bourton-on-the-Water, aged 77 years. George was the son of Thomas and Susan Pepall (née Dover) and married Mabel Simons in 1907. George had been a Professional Cricketer up until 1911 before becoming a Water Cress Grower and eventually a School Groundsman in 1937. He served in the 4th Battalion, Grenadier Guards (Guardsman, 26470). He landed in France on 19 January 1917 and was awarded the campaign medals – the British War Medal and the Victory Medal. He was wounded on three occasions - trench fever (May 1917), wound to hand (November 1917) and gun shot wound to head (March 1918). George played fourteen matches for Gloucestershire County Cricket Club as a right-hand batsman and right-arm fast bowler between 1896 and 1904.

POPE, Andrew Noble OBE (1881-1942) (Cricketer)

Born on 14 November 1881 at Clifton, Bristol and died on 18 April 1942 at Lansdown, Cheltenham, aged 61 years. Andrew, a Professional Soldier, was the son of John Noble Coleman and Mary Elizabeth Pope (née Eddis) and married Marjorie Lorna Shute in 1911; the couple had two children. Whilst at Oxford University Andrew was granted a commission as a Second Lieutenant (1902) in the 1st (Oxford University) Volunteer Battalion, the Oxfordshire Light Infantry. Throughout the Great War he served with the 2nd Battalion, Royal Fusiliers (Captain), was attached to the 1st Battalion, East

Lancashire Regiment and finally served with the 9th Battalion, Royal Fusiliers (Major); he also acted as the Brigade Major in the 36 Brigade between October and November 1915. He landed in France on 30 May 1915 and was awarded the campaign medals - 1914-15 Star, the British War Medal and the Victory Medal. He was appointed an Officer of the Most Excellent Order of the British Empire (Military Division) (OBE) for his services during the war. He played twice for Gloucestershire County Cricket Club as a batsman in 1911. In October 1922 Andrew was granted the "...*Freedom of this City* [London] *by Patrimony, in the said Company of Grocers because he is legitimate and was born after the admission of his Father into the said Freedom*..."

POWELL, Osman Trevor (1894-1916) (Rugby player)

Born on 1894 at Stonehouse, Gloucestershire and died from Illness contracted whilst on active service on 3 February 1916 at the 1st General Eastern Hospital, Cambridge, aged 21 years. He was buried at Gloucester Old Cemetery, grave 11816. Trevor, a Gas Engine Fitter at Messrs Fielding and Platt, was the son of Trevor Barrett and Ella Charlotte Powell (née Knibbs) from 41 Cromwell Street, Gloucester. He was a pre-war Territorial with the 5th Battalion (TF), Gloucestershire Regiment (Lance Corporal, 1337) and served with A Company, 1/5th Battalion (TF), Gloucestershire Regiment (Private, 1337). Trevor is commemorated on the Gloucester Rugby Football Club Roll of Honour, the Kingsholm Stadium War Memorial and the Gloucester War Memorial. He played thirty-one games for the Gloucester Rugby Club as a wing between 1912 and 1914 of which seven were for the First XV.

PRICE, John ('Jack') (1887-1916) (Rugby player)

Born on 28 June 1887 in the parish of St Nicholas, Gloucester and killed in action on 3 July 1916 at La Boisselle, aged 30 years. He is commemorated on the Thiepval Memorial, Pier and Face 5A and 6C (Missing). John, a Mason's Labourer for Gloucestershire County Council, was the son of Charles David and Emma Price (née Ball) and married Laurel Kean Long in 1913; the couple had one child and lived at 45 Bristol Road, Gloucester. John enlisted in August 1914 and served with B Company, 10th (Service) Battalion, Worcestershire Regiment (Private, 15797). He landed in France on 18 July 1915 and was awarded the campaign medals - 1914-15 Star, the British War Medal and the Victory Medal. John is commemorated on the Gloucester Rugby Football Club Roll of Honour, the Kingsholm Stadium War Memorial and the Gloucester War Memorial. He played twelve games for the Gloucester Rugby Club at back row forward between 1909 and 1911 of which two were for the First XV.

PRIESTLEY, Donald Lacey ('DLP') (1887-1917) (Cricketer)

Born on 28 July 1887 at Tewkesbury and killed in action on 30 October 1917 at Passchendaele, aged 30 years. He is commemorated amongst the Missing on the Tyne Cot Memorial, Panel 153. Donald, a Commercial Traveller and Corn Merchant with Messrs Rice and Sons, Tewkesbury, was the son of Joseph Edward and Henrietta Priestley (née Rice). He married Edith Louie Boughton in 1912. He served with 1/28th Battalion, London Regiment (Artists' Rifles) (Private, 8541 and Lance Corporal, 762550). He landed in France in 1916 and was awarded the campaign medals, the British War Medal and the Victory Medal. Donald is commemorated on the Tewkesbury War Memorial at The Cross, the Memorial in Tewkesbury Abbey, on the Roll of Honour at Tewkesbury Grammar School and on the Memorial in the Wesleyan Church. He played seven matches for Gloucestershire County Cricket Club as a right-hand batsman and right-arm medium pace bowler between 1909 and 1910.

PURTON, Alfred William (1881-1917) (Rugby player)

Born on 1881 at Barton St Mary, Gloucestershire and died of wounds, received at Pilckem Ridge, on 27 August 1917 at No.13 General Hospital in Boulogne, aged 36 years. He was buried at Boulogne Eastern Cemetery, grave VIII.I.18. Alfred, a Deal Porter and Sawyer for Adams and Company, was the son of John and Clara Purton (née Gibbins) from 'Ferness', Tuffley Avenue, Gloucester. He married Florence Louise Bick in 1916. He served with the 4th Battalion, Grenadier Guards (Private, 27506), landing in France in early 1916 and was awarded the campaign medals – the British War Medal and the Victory Medal. He was wounded in October 1916. Alfred is commemorated on the Gloucester Rugby Football Club Roll of Honour, the Kingsholm Stadium War Memorial and the Gloucester War Memorial. He played 109 games for the Gloucester Rugby Club as a second row and back row forward between 1901 and 1907 of which ninety-six were for the First XV.

ROACH, Bernard Arthur Frederick ('Peter') (1890-1914) (Rugby player)

Born on 1890 in the parish of St Nicholas, Gloucester and killed in action on 25 December 1914 at Rue de Cailloux, Essars, aged 24 years. He was buried at Guards Cemetery, Windy Corner, Cuinchy, grave V.E.5. Bernard, a Professional Soldier, was the son of Frederick John and Clara Roach (née Birt) from 33 Edwy Parade, Gloucester. He joined the 2nd Battalion, Grenadier Guards (Private, 16072) in 1911 but remained in the UK after the declaration of war. He was a member of the party which removed the body of Carl Lody from the Tower of London after he had been shot for espionage. He landed in France on 23 November 1914 and was awarded the campaign medals - 1914-15 Star, the British War Medal and the Victory Medal. Bernard is commemorated on the

Gloucester Rugby Football Club Roll of Honour, the Kingsholm Stadium War Memorial, the Gloucester War Memorial, the King's School War Memorial, the King's School Old Boys Roll of Honour at St Mary de Lode Church, Gloucester and the War Memorial at St Mark's Church, Gloucester. He played four games for the Gloucester Rugby Club at centre between 1912 and 1914.

ROBERTS, Francis Bernard (1882-1916) (Cricketer)

Born on 20 May 1882 at Anjini Hill, Nasik, India and killed in action on 8 February 1916 at St Julien, Ypres, aged 34 years. He was buried at Talana Farm Cemetery, grave I.D.1 (Ypres). Francis, a School Master at Wellington College Public School, was the son of Canon Wilson Aylesbury and Ellen Roberts (née Nolan) from Camm. He served in the 9th Battalion, Rifle Brigade (Captain). He landed in France in 1915 and was awarded the campaign medals - 1914-15 Star, the British War Medal and the Victory Medal. Francis is commemorated on the Jesus College, Cambridge University Roll of Honour, the Wellington School Roll of Honour and the marble Memorial Tablet at Camm Church. Francis played sixty-seven matches for Gloucestershire County Cricket Club as a right-hand batsman and right-arm fast bowler between 1906 and 1914. He won Blues at Cricket and Hockey from Cambridge University (1903).

ROBINSON, Douglas Charles MC, Croix de Guerre, (1884-1963) (Cricketer)

Born on 20 April 1884 at Lawrence Weston, Bristol and died on 29 July 1963 at Ham Court Farm, Charlton Kings, aged 77 years. Douglas, a Professional Soldier, was the son of Arthur and Constance Robinson (née Bousey) and married Albertine Clarrisse Pilotelle in 1932 and had one child. Douglas had joined the 3rd (Militia) Battalion, Gloucestershire Regiment in 1902 but subsequently attended the Royal Military College, Sandhurst. He was commissioned as a Lieutenant on 22 May 1906 in the 2nd Battalion, The King's Own (Royal Lancaster Regiment) (Regular Army) and in 1911 was stationed with his battalion at Fort Regent on the island of Jersey. In the immediate pre-war period he served in mainland Britain with the 1st Battalion. He landed in France on 20 August 1914 and was awarded the campaign medals - 1914 Star ('*Old Contemptible*'), the British War Medal and the Victory Medal. He was awarded the Croix de Guerre (France) for gallantry in November 1918 and the Military Cross [MC] in January 1919. He was wounded in the forearm in October 1914. Douglas played 124 matches for Gloucestershire County Cricket Club as a right-hand batsman and wicket-keeper between 1905 and 1926. He also represented an England XI in 1924 and played seven times for the Army between 1912 and 1921. Douglas retired from the British Army in 1924 with the rank of Lieutenant Colonel. He was the cousin of the brothers **Percy Robinson** (GCCC)

and **Foster Robinson** (GCCC). After the war he bred cows at Ham Court Farm near Cheltenham. His brother Eric who worked for E.S. and A. Robinson, was killed in action 16 September 1916.

ROBINSON, Percy Gotch DSO, MiD(2) (1881-1951) (Cricketer)

Born on 21 November 1881 at Sneyd Park, Clifton, Bristol and died on 29 January 1951 at Queen Charlton Manor, Somerset, aged 70 years. Percy, a Professional Soldier, was the son of Edward and Katherine Frances Robinson (née Gotch) and married Gladys M. Davey in 1924 and had three children. Percy gained a commission as a Second Lieutenant in 1900 and throughout the Great War served with Royal Field Artillery (Meerut Division) (Captain, Major, Lieutenant Colonel). He landed in France on 5 October 1914 and was awarded the campaign medals - 1914 Star with clasp and rose ('*Old Contemptible*'), the British War Medal and the Victory Medal. He was awarded the Distinguished Service Order [DSO] for "*...distinguished services in the field...*" in February 1917,[528] the Croix de Guerre (French) (May 1917) and was Mentioned in Despatches three times. Percy played twenty-six matches for Gloucestershire County Cricket Club as a right-hand batsman between 1904 and 1921; he represented the Army once in 1912. He was the brother of **Foster Robinson** (GCCC) and the cousin of **Douglas Robinson** (GCCC). Percy became the join Managing Director, along with his brother, Foster, of the family business E.S. and A. Robinson (Manufacturing Stationers and Printers), Bristol. In 1946 he was appointed as a Deputy Lieutenant of the county of Gloucestershire.

RUSSELL, Arthur Charles BA (1891-1918) (Rugby player)

Born on July 1891 in South Hamlet, Gloucester and died of wounds on 28 October 1918 at Estrun, aged 27 years. He was buried at Dusians British Military Cemetery, Etrun, grave VII.B.40. Alfred, an Assistant Master at Widden Street Council School, was the son of Tom Alston and Ada Elizabeth Russell (née Cole). He trained at the Church of England [Teacher] Training College, Swindon Road, Cheltenham and enlisted on 5 December 1914 immediately after the completion of his studies for which he was awarded a Batchelor of Arts (First Class) Degree from Cheltenham Training College. He served with 3rd (Depot) Battalion, Gloucestershire Regiment (Private, Corporal, 16231), the Army Service Corps [ASC] (Quartermaster Sergeant, R/4/111280), the 6th (Reserve) Battalion, Rifle Brigade (The Prince Consort's Own), after gaining a commission as a Second Lieutenant on 5 November 1917, and the 2nd Battalion, Rifle Brigade (Second Lieutenant). He landed in France in October 1918 and was awarded the campaign medals – the British War Medal and the Victory Medal. Alfred is commemorated on the Gloucester Rugby Football Club Roll of Honour, the Kingsholm Stadium War Memorial, the Gloucester War Memorial, the Crypt Grammar School War Memorial and the Teachers' War Memorial at the Price Memorial Hall, Gloucester Technical Schools. He played ten games for the Gloucester Rugby Club at back row forward between 1911 and 1913 of which five were for the First XV.

---

[528] *Edinburgh Gazette* 20 February 1917 p.425

SAUNDERS, Arthur ('Ronk') MM (1891-1916) (Rugby player)

Born on 31 August 1891 at Lydney and died of wounds on 1 November 1916 near Ovillers, aged 25 years. Arthur is commemorated on the Thiepval Memorial, Pier and Face 5A and 5B (Missing). Arthur, a Labourer at Lydney Tinplate Works, was the son of John James Palmer and Sarah Saunders (née Beard) from 14 Albert Street, Lydney. He enlisted at Gloucester in August 1914 and served with the 8th (Service) Battalion, Gloucestershire Regiment (Sergeant, 13972). He landed in France on 18 July 1915 and was awarded the campaign medals - 1914-15 Star, the British War Medal and the Victory Medal. He won the Military Medal [MM] for gallantry at La Boisselle whilst in charge of a machine gun team on 3 July 1916. The award of the MM was not confirmed until shortly before his death and the medal was presented posthumously to his mother, Mrs Sarah Thorne by Brigadier General Grove at a ceremony on College Green, Bristol, on 11 July 1917 attended by 300 soldiers. He was wounded in September 1916. Arthur is commemorated on the Gloucester Rugby Football Club Roll of Honour, the Kingsholm Stadium War Memorial, the Lydney War Memorial, the stained glass War Memorial Window at St Mary's Church, Lydney and on the grave of his father, John (1857-1896), and his sister, Christina (1893-1923), in the graveyard of St Mary's Church, Lydney. He played forty-nine games for the Gloucester Rugby Club as a back row and second row forward between 1911 and 1914, all of which were for the First XV. His brother, Charles Saunders, Canadian Field Artillery, died of wounds 6 September 1917.

SEWELL, Cyril Otto Hudson (1874-1951) (Cricketer)

Born on 19 December 1874, Pietermaritzburg, South Africa and died on 19 August 1951 at Bexhill-on-Sea, Sussex, aged 77 years. Cyril, a Solicitor, was the son of John Joseph and Annie Christina Sophia Sewell (née Otto) and married Maud Evelyn Maunsell Collins in 1903; they had one child and lived at Clasendon Villa, Stratton, Cirencester. In 1909 Cyril gained a commission as a Second Lieutenant in the 5th Battalion, Gloucestershire Regiment (TF) and was promoted to Captain in October 1914 after he had been transferred to the Oxfordshire and Buckinghamshire Light Infantry. He served in the Great War with 2/5th Battalion, Gloucestershire Regiment (Captain), the 33rd Provisional Battalion (Major) and the Oxfordshire and Buckinghamshire Light Infantry (Major). He landed in France on 10 January 1918 and was awarded the campaign medals – the British War Medal and the Victory Medal. Cyril played 158 matches for Gloucestershire County Cricket Club as a right-hand batsman and right-arm slow bowler between 1895 and 1919. Cyril, born in South Africa, was a member of the first South African cricket side to visit England in 1894 and was the side's top scorer; soon after the tour he moved to England and made his home in Cirencester.

SIMMONS, Percy Marston (1882-1918) (Rugby player)

Born on 1882 at Norton, Gloucestershire and killed in action on 20 October 1918 at St Aubert, aged 36 years. He was buried at St Aubert British Cemetery, grave I.B.16. Percy, an Upholsterer with R. James, Northgate Street, Gloucester, was the son of Alfred Thomas and Ann Simmons (née Williams) and married Violet Madeline Eliza Madelin in 1917 and lived at 21 London Road, Gloucester. Before the Haldane Reforms of 1908 Percy served in B Company, 2nd Volunteer Battalion, Gloucestershire Regiment and was a member of the National Reserve (Class I). He served with A Company, 1/5th Battalion (TF), Gloucestershire Regiment (Private, 2467, Lance Corporal, 240570) and, after gaining a commission, in the 4th Battalion (TF), Wiltshire Regiment (Second Lieutenant). He landed in France on 29 March 1915 and was awarded the campaign medals - 1914-15 Star, the British War Medal and the Victory Medal. He was wounded on three occasions - June 1915 (head), July 1916 and September 1916. Percy is commemorated on the Gloucester Rugby Football Club Roll of Honour, the Kingsholm Stadium War Memorial, the Gloucester War Memorial, the War Memorial Sir Thomas Rich's School, the War Memorial St James' Church, Gloucester and the War Memorial St Mary's Church, Prior's Norton. He played seventeen games for the Gloucester Rugby Club as a back row forward between 1911 and 1913 of which four were for the First XV. Percy's campaign medals, his Death Plaque and uniform are on display at *The Wardrobe*, the regimental museum of the Berkshire and Wiltshire Regiments in Salisbury.

SMITH, Frank (1887-1916) (Rugby player)

Born on 1887 in St Mark's parish, Gloucester and killed in action on 21 April 1916 at Sannaiyat, Mesopotamia (Iraq), aged 29 years. Frank is commemorated on the Basra Memorial, Panel 17 (Missing), Mesopotamia. Frank, a General Labourer in a jam and pickle factory, was the son of Samuel George and Harrlett Ann Smith (née Hall) and married Cecilia Annie Barnes in 1915; they had one child and lived at 9 Watkins Yard, Guinea Street, Gloucester. Frank joined the Gloucestershire Regiment in 1910 and went onto the Reserve in 1914 just prior to the start of the war. He served with 1st Battalion, Gloucestershire Regiment (Corporal, 8310) and with the 7th (Service) Battalion, Gloucestershire Regiment (Sergeant, 8310). He landed in France on 13 August 1914 and was awarded the campaign medals - 1914 Star with clasp and rose ('Old Contemptible'), the British War Medal and the Victory Medal. He was wounded twice - August 1914 and October 1914. Frank is commemorated on the Kingsholm Stadium War Memorial, the Gloucester War Memorial and the War Memorial, St Mark's Church, Gloucester. He played 101 games for the Gloucester Rugby Club as a wing between 1905 and 1910 of which ninety-four were for the First XV. He won three Gloucestershire County caps in 1906-07.

STOUT, Frank Moxon MC (1877-1926) (Rugby player)

Born on 21 February 1877 at South Hamlet, Gloucester and died on 30 May 1926 at The Abbey, Storrington, Sussex, aged 49 years; his last years were spent largely as an invalid due to injuries received during the war. Frank, a Stock Broker in Egypt, was the son of William and Emma Stout (née Adcock). He enlisted in September 1914 and served with Artists Rifles (Private), the Cavalry Reserve (Second Lieutenant), the 20th Hussars (Lieutenant) and in the Machine Gun Corps (Captain). He landed in France in April 1915 and was awarded the campaign medals - 1914-15 Star, the British War Medal and the Victory Medal. He was awarded the Military Cross [MC] (March 1916), *"For conspicuous gallantry and resource. When he heard of an enemy working party in the vicinity, he took a corporal [George Tester] and light machine-gun down a sap, mounted the corporal on his back to enable the latter to fire over the parapet, and opened fire. Later, mounted on the corporal's back, Lieutenant Stout opened fire, although by this time they had been discovered. Next morning fourteen dead enemy were counted and more must have been wounded"*. He was wounded on three occasions. After the Armistice Frank was transferred back to the 20th Hussars which formed part of the Army of Occupation in the Cologne bridgehead. He is commemorated in a stained glass window at St Philip and St James' Church, Hucclecote, where he is depicted as Saint George; the window was commissioned after his death. He played ninety-eight games for the Gloucester Rugby Club at wing forward between 1895 and 1908, all of which were for the First XV. Frank also won fourteen International caps for England between 1897 and 1905 and won seven caps with the British Isles team ('British Lions') on tours of Australia (1899) and South Africa (1903); on the Australian tour he played in all twenty-one matches of the tour. His brother **Percy Stout** (GRFC) was also a Gloucester rugby player.

STOUT, Percy Wyfold DSO, OBE, MiD(5) (1875-1937) (Rugby player)

Born on 20 November 1875 at South Hamlet, Gloucester and died on 9 October 1937 London, aged 62 years; he was buried at Hampstead Cemetery, Fortune Green, London. Percy, a Stock Broker and founder and managing director of the Cairo Exchange Ltd, Egypt, was the son of William and Emma Stout (née Adcock). He married Mary Stone Stout *circa* 1910 at Maadi, Cairo, Egypt; the couple had one child. He enlisted in September 1914 and served in the Cavalry Reserve (Second Lieutenant), the 20th Hussars (Lieutenant), the Royal Naval Air Service [RNAS] (Captain), the Royal Naval Volunteer Reserve [RNVR] (Captain), the Intelligence Department, Cairo; and in the Motor Machine Gun Corps and GHQ (Captain). He landed in France in May 1915 and was awarded the campaign medals - 1914-15 Star, the British War Medal and the Victory Medal. He won the Distinguished Service Order [DSO] for gallantry in August 1917; the citation reads, *"T/Lt (A/Capt). Percy Wyfold Stout, MMG Corps. For conspicuous gallantry and devotion to duty. At a critical moment, when a number of armoured cars were in danger of being cut off, he led the attack to their relief, and after two hours' heavy fighting gained the objective, after inflicting heavy losses upon the enemy."* He was Mentioned in Despatches [MiD] five times, appointed an Officer of the Most Excellent Order of the British Empire (Military Division) [OBE] in January 1919 for *"...valuable services rendered in connection with military operations in Egypt"*. Percy received the Order of the Nile 4th Class from the Sultan of Egypt for *"...exceptional services to the nation"*. He played sixty-five games for the Gloucester Rugby Club as a wing between 1895 and 1899, all of which were for the First XV.

He won five international caps for England between 1898 and 1899. His brother **Frank Stout** (GRFC) was also a Gloucester rugby player.

SYSUM, Sidney (1895-1916) (Rugby player)

Born on 9 June 1895 at St Mary de Lode parish, Gloucester and was killed in action on 23 July 1916 at Pozières, aged 21 years. Sidney is commemorated on the Thiepval Memorial, Pier and Face 5A and 5B (Missing). Sidney, an employee of the Gloucester Railway Carriage and Wagon Co. Ltd., was the son of Charles and Mary Sysum (née Bennett) from 31 St Mary's Street, Gloucester. He enlisted in September 1914 and served with D Company, 1/5th Battalion (TF), Gloucestershire Regiment (Lance Corporal, 2175). He landed in France on 29 March 1915 and was awarded the campaign medals - 1914-15 Star, the British War Medal and the Victory Medal. Sidney is commemorated on the Gloucester Rugby Football Club Roll of Honour, the Kingsholm Stadium War Memorial, the Gloucester War Memorial, the 5th Battalion, Gloucestershire War Memorial and the Roll of Honour at St Mary de Lode Church, Gloucester. He played thirty-three games for the Gloucester Rugby Club at centre between 1913 and 1914 of which twenty-six were for the First XV. The brothers-in-law, **Tom** and **Melville Lewis** (GRFC) of Sidney's sister Eliza, were killed in the same attack as Sidney at Pozières.

TAYLER, Herbert William ('Bert') ('Herbie') DCM, Medaille Militaire, (1887-1984) (Cricketer)[529]

Born on 6 December 1887 at Alsworth, Gloucestershire and died on 17 April 1984 at Dawlish in Devon, aged 97 years. Herbert, a Brewer, was the son of John Osborne and Annie Elizabeth Tayler (née Caddle). He served with Royal Garrison Artillery (Sergeant, 1356) and the Tank Corps (Sergeant, 201523). He landed in France in 1916 and was awarded the campaign medals – the British War Medal and the Victory Medal. He won the Distinguished Conduct Medal [DCM] for gallantry in July 1918; his citation reads, "*He commanded a tank with great success during the whole of an action, fighting it with much skill and the utmost bravery. He destroyed a great many groups of hostile machine guns, and brought away several guns complete with spare parts. On his own initiative he advanced through our protective barrage and patrolled far in advance of the infantry, thus greatly assisting their action. He set an admirable example of cheerfulness and resolute determination.*" In the same action, he was also awarded the French Medaille Militaire. Herbert played twice for Gloucestershire County Cricket Club as a right-hand batsman and right-arm medium pace bowler in 1914 and was described as "*...a great acquisition to Gloucestershire*

---

[529] Photograph of Herbert Tayler courtesy of Alison Steere, Glamorgan Cricket Archives

batting."[530] He resumed his cricketing career after the war, but not for Gloucestershire as he played ten matches for Glamorgan between 1921 and 1927.

THOMAS, Hugh Gareth (1892-1916) (Rugby player)

Born on 1892 at Birkenhead, Cheshire and killed in action on 30 July 1916 at High Wood on the Somme, aged 23 years. Hugh is commemorated on the Thiepval Memorial, Pier and Face 5A and 5B (Missing). Hugh, a Solicitor, was the son of Walter Jeremy and Anne Thomas (née Hughes) from 14 Bayshill Terrace, Cheltenham. He enlisted in August 1914 and served with 6th Platoon, B Company, 1/5th Battalion (TF), Gloucestershire Regiment (Private, Lance Corporal, 2575); 10th (Service) Battalion, Gloucestershire Regiment (Second Lieutenant) and with A Company, 8th (Service) Battalion, Gloucestershire Regiment (Second Lieutenant). He landed in France on 29 March 1916 and was awarded the campaign medals - 1914-15 Star, the British War Medal and the Victory Medal. Hugh is commemorated on the Kingsholm Stadium War Memorial, the Gloucester War Memorial, the Cheltenham War Memorial (East Panel), the War Memorial, Christ Church, Cheltenham and the War Memorial St Mark's Church, Cheltenham. He played once for the Gloucester Rugby Club as a back row forward in 1912 but was primarily a Cheltenham player.

TROUP, Frank Colin (1896-1924) (Cricketer) (1896-1924) (Cricketer)

Born on 27 September 1896 at Mussoorie (now Musuri), United Provinces, India and died on 19 January 1924 at Murray Bridge, South Australia, aged 27 years. Frank was the son of Walter and Francis Orde Troup (née Bigg-Wither) from 10 Windsor Road, Ealing. He served in the Royal Air Force [RAF] (Lieutenant) and was awarded the campaign medals – the British War Medal and the Victory Medal. He played three matches for Gloucestershire County Cricket Club as a right-hand batsman between 1914 and 1921. Frank was an all-round sportsman and also played hockey for Gloucestershire and represented the RAF at Rugby. His father, **Walter Troup** (GCCC), also played for Gloucestershire County Cricket Club.

TROUP, Walter (1869-1940) (Cricketer)

Born on 16 October 1869 at Meerut, Uttar Pradesh, India and died on 14 December 1940 at Isleworth, Middlesex, aged 71 years. Walter, who was employed by the Indian Police Force, was the son of General Colin and Elizabeth Mary Troup (née Birch) and married Frances Orde Bigg-Wither in 1894; the couple had two children including **Frank Troup** (GCCC).[531] He served with Royal Flying Corps (Captain). He played eighty matches for Gloucestershire County Cricket Club as a right-hand batsman between 1887 and 1911. His first-class cricketing career was cut short following an accident.

---

[530] *Cheltenham Chronicle and Gloucestershire Graphic* 22 August 1914
[531] Major Colin Troup was in command of the 68th Bengal Native Infantry when it mutinied in 1857 as part of the Indian Rebellion.

Walter also played one match for an England XI in 1902 and one match for India in 1892.

TRUMAN, Thomas Archibald (1880-1918) (Rugby player and Cricketer)

Born on 29 December 1880 at Newton Abbot, Devon and died from pneumonia whilst on active service on 14 September 1918 at No.1 Canadian CCS, Etrun, France, aged 37 years. He was buried at Duisans British Cemetery, Etrun, grave VI.H.6. Thomas, a Bank Clerk, was the son of Thomas and Catherine Truman and married Margaret Lee in 1908; they had two children and lived at 12 Pendarvis Road, Penzance. He enlisted as an Officer Cadet (1408) in the Inns of Court Officer Training Unit, London in 1916 and subsequently served in the Army Service Corps [ASC], 56th Divisional Train (Second Lieutenant). He landed in France on 27 October 1917 and was awarded the campaign medals – the British War Medal and the Victory Medal. Thomas is commemorated on the Kingsholm Stadium War Memorial, the Penzance War Memorial and St Mary's Church War Memorial, Penzance. Thomas played four matches for Gloucestershire County Cricket Club as a batsman and bowler between 1910 and 1913 and played twice for the Gloucester Rugby Club at centre between 1906 and 1907.

TURNER, Ronald BA (1885-1915) (Cricketer)

Born on 19 June 1885 at Gillingham, Kent and killed in action on 15 August 1915 at Suvla Bay, Gallipoli, aged 30 years. He is commemorated on the Helles Memorial, Panel 144 to 150 or 229 to 233 (Missing), (Gallipoli). Ronald, a School Tutor at St Aubyns School, Rottingdean, was the son of the Reverend Robert Stobbs and Catherine Mary Turner from Dawn House, Rottingdean, Sussex. Between 1907 and 1911 he was a Master at St Aubyns School, Rottingdean (closed 2013) although immediately prior to the war he had tried his hand at fruit farming in British Columbia. He enlisted in August 1914, served with the 28th (County of London) Battalion, London Regiment (Artist's Rifles) (Private, Lance Corporal, 2522) and in the 1st/5th Battalion, Essex Regiment (Second Lieutenant). He landed in France on 22 January 1915 and was awarded the campaign medals - 1914-15 Star, the British War Medal and the Victory Medal. Ronald is commemorated on the Chaceley War Memorial and the Roll of Honour in St John the Baptist Church, Chaceley, the 'War List of the University of Cambridge 1914-1918', Queen's College, Cambridge University, and the Rottingdean War Memorial, St Margaret's Church, Sussex. He played three matches for Gloucestershire County Cricket Club as a batsman in 1906. He won a Blue at Football (Soccer) from Cambridge University (1905) and played Association Football for England.

WALWIN, Oscar Tenison (1895-1916) (Rugby player)

Born on 1895 at St John the Baptist parish, Gloucester and died on 12 November 1916 at a base hospital in Rouen from wounds received at Le Transloy on 2 November 1916, aged 21 years. He was buried at St Sever Cemetery and Extension, Rouen, grave O.I.R.5. Oscar was the son of Walter and Annie Walwin (née Rex) from Upton Lane, Barnwood, Gloucester. He enlisted in 1914 and served with Royal Gloucestershire Hussars Yeomanry (trooper, 3225) and with the 2nd Battalion, Worcestershire Regiment (Lance Corporal, 40219). He landed in France in 1916 and was awarded the campaign medals – the British War Medal and the Victory Medal. Oscar is commemorated on the Kingsholm Stadium War Memorial, the Gloucester War Memorial, the Crypt Grammar School War Memorial, the Royal Gloucestershire Hussars Memorial, College Green, Gloucester Cathedral and the War Memorial at St Lawrence C of E Church, Gloucester. He played three games for the Gloucester Rugby Club at full back between 1913 and 1914 of which one was for the First XV. Oscar's older brother Clifford died from injuries sustained in a rugby match for Bath RFC against Cross Keys on 28 December 1919; as a result the number 13 jersey was withdrawn by Bath.

WASHBOURNE, William Philip Woodman ('Quedge') MM (1891-1977) (Rugby player)

Born on 9 May 1891 at South Hamlet, Gloucester and died on 5 January 1977 at Wickwar, Bristol, aged 85 years. William, an Engineering Fitter at the Gloucester Railway Carriage and Wagon Company Ltd, was the son of Robert Henry and Ellen Victoria Washbourne (née Bearcroft) and married Ellen Alberta Charles in 1917. They had one child and lived at 17 Lady Belle Gate Street, Gloucester. William served with G Company, 5th Battalion (TF), Gloucestershire Regiment from 1910 to 1914 but had left the Army prior to the start of the war. He re-enlisted on 31 August 1914 and served with No.13 Platoon, D Company, 1st/5th Battalion (TF), Gloucestershire Regiment (Corporal, 2726). He landed in France on 29 March 1915 and was awarded the campaign medals - 1914-15 Star, the British War Medal and the Victory Medal. He won the Military Medal [MM] for gallantry in October 1916. He was wounded in November 1916 and after discharge from the Army he was sent as a fitter to a munitions factory in Glasgow (Messrs W. Beardmore and Company Ltd, Parkhead Works). William played 184 games for the Gloucester Rugby Club at wing between 1909 and 1922 of which 167 were for the First XV.

WEST, Ernest Thomas ('Tom') (1882-1915) (Rugby player)

Born on October 1882 at Twerton, Bath, and killed in action on 29 September 1915 near Bois Grenier, aged 33 years. He was buried at Royal Irish Rifles Graveyard at Laventie, grave III.K.18. Tom, an Iron Turner in an iron foundry and a professional rugby player, was the son of Walter and Emma West (née Keates) and married Edith Spencer in 1915. Whilst living in Rochdale he enlisted in 1914 and served with A Company, 10th (Service) Battalion, King's Royal Rifle Corps (Rifleman, R/2812). He landed in France on 21 July 1915 and was awarded the campaign medals - 1914-15 Star, the British War Medal and the Victory Medal. Tom is commemorated on the Kingsholm Stadium War Memorial, the Bath War Memorial, the Twerton War Memorial and the Somerset County Roll of Honour. He played six games for the Gloucester Rugby Club as an "*...extremely fast...*" wing between 1907 and 1908, having previously been a Bath Rugby player; at the start of the 1908-09 season he joined Rochdale Hornets of the Northern League.

WHITE, Alison Kingsley Gordon DSO, MiD(5) (1881-1962) (Cricketer)[532]

Born on 2 January 1881 in Australia and died on 20 March 1962 at Crowborough, Sussex, aged 81 years. Alison, a Professional Soldier, was the son of Reverend William Moore and Eliza Agnes White (née Gordon) and married Violet Seabright in 1921; the couple had two children. A pre-war soldier, he served with the Royal Field Artillery (Captain) and the Royal Artillery (Major) and landed in France on 18 August 1914. He was awarded the campaign medals, 1914 Star ('*Old Contemptible*'), the British War Medal and the Victory Medal. In January 1916 he was awarded the Distinguished Service Order [DSO] for "*...distinguished services in the field...*" and was Mentioned in Despatches [MiD] five times.[533] Alison played eleven matches for Gloucestershire County Cricket Club as a right-hand batsman and right-arm fast-medium bowler between 1912 and 1919. He retired from the Army *circa* 1931 with the rank of Lieutenant Colonel. His son, Flying Officer Lynden Gordon-White, 681 Squadron, RAFNR, was killed in action in Singapore in December 1943.

WICKS, Frank Cowlin (1892-1965) (Cricketer)

Born on 30 January 1892 at Bristol and died on 26 April 1965, Ham Green Hospital, Bristol, aged 73 years. Frank, a Clerk, was the son of George Hosking and Annie Maria Wicks (née Chandler) and married Phyllis Elaine Coulsting in 1916; the couple lived at 10 Belvedere Road, Redland, Bristol. He joined the Bristol University OTC on the outbreak of war and initially enlisted in September as a Private in the 12th (Service) Battalion (Bristol's Own), Gloucestershire Regiment. In January 1915 he gained a commission as Second Lieutenant in the 22nd Battalion, Manchester Regiment and landed in France on 15 November 1915. He was awarded the campaign medals, 1914-15 Star, the British War Medal and the Victory Medal. He was wounded and suffered broken ribs in May 1916, invalided out the Army and awarded a Silver War Badge (1490768). Frank played once for Gloucestershire County Cricket Club as a batsman in 1912.

---

[532] In 1928 Major (Brevet Lieutenant-Colonel) Alison Kingsley Gordon White changed his name to Alison Kingsley Gordon Gordon-White.
[533] *Edinburgh Gazette* 17 January 1916 p.92

WILLIAMS, John Nathaniel ('Nat') (1878-1915) (Cricketer)

Born on 24 January 1878 at Kensington, London and killed in action on 25 April 1915 at Gaba Tepe, Gallipoli, aged 35 years. John is commemorated on the Lone Pine Memorial, Panel 73 (Missing), Gallipoli. John, a Miner with the Waihi Gold Mining Co. Ltd., was the son of Colonel Sir Robert and Lady Rosa Walker Williams (née Simes). Before the war John served in the 4th Dorsets (TF) (Captain) but resigned in 1910 when he went to work in New Zealand. He served with the 6th (Hauraki) Company, Auckland Regiment NZEF (Private, 12/484). He landed in Gallipoli in 1915 and was awarded the campaign medals – 1914-15 Star, the British War Medal and the Victory Medal. John is commemorated on the Memorial at the Church of St Michael, Littlebredy, Dorset. He played three matches for Gloucestershire County Cricket Club as a right-hand batsman in 1908. Before moving to New Zealand John was a Director of an engineering company in Bristol after gaining a Master of Arts degree from New College, Oxford University in 1905

WINTERBOTHAM, James Percival MC, MiD(1) (1883-1925) (Cricketer)

Born on 21 June 1883 at Pittville, Cheltenham and died on 2 December 1925 at Marle Hill, Cheltenham, aged 42 years; he was buried in Cheltenham Cemetery. James, a Solicitor at the firm of Messrs Winterbotham, Gurney and Co., was the son of James Batten and Eliza Hunter Winterbotham (née McLaren) and married Jean Beatrice Ewart Harvey in 1906. The couple had two children and lived at Cranley Lodge, Cheltenham. He enlisted with the Public Schools Corps (Private) and served with No. 7 Platoon, B Company, 1st/5th Battalion (TF), Gloucestershire Regiment (Captain and later Adjutant). He landed in France on 29 March 1915 and was awarded the campaign medals - 1914-15 Star, the British War Medal and the Victory Medal. He was awarded Military Cross [MC] for gallantry in the 1918 New Year Honours' list and was Mentioned in Despatches [MiD] in May 1917. He was wounded on three occasions - 1916 (although he remained on duty), June 1917 (gassed) and August 1917 (hit by a shell fragment in leg); after the latter wounding he was sent to Epsom for an operation and was replaced in his role as Battalion Adjutant. James played once for Gloucestershire County Cricket Club as a left-hand batsman and slow left-arm orthodox bowler in 1902. He was a Cheltenham Town Councillor before the war. After the war he returned to Cheltenham and became a Director in the Cheltenham Gas Company, Georges Limited and the Queen's Hotel Company.

WOOTTON, Edwin Francis (1887-1917) (Rugby player)

Born on July 1887 at South Hamlet, Gloucester, and was killed in action on 25 April 1917 near Senelle Ravine, Salonika, aged 28 years. Edwin is commemorated amongst the Missing on the Doiran Memorial, Salonika, Greece. Edwin, a Stamper at the Gloucester Railway Carriage and Wagon Company Ltd, was the son of William and Sarah Louise Wootton (née Brown) and married Alice Ford in 1911; the couple had two children and lived at 6 Theresa Street, Gloucester. Edwin enlisted at Shire Hall, Gloucester on 28 August 1914 and served with 7th (Service) Battalion, Gloucestershire Regiment (Private, 11325) and with No. 5 Platoon, B Company, 9th (service) Battalion, Gloucestershire Regiment (Lance Corporal, 15505). He landed in France on 21 September 1915 and was awarded the campaign medals - 1914-15 Star, the British War Medal and the Victory Medal. Edwin is commemorated on the Gloucester Rugby Football Club Roll of Honour, the Kingsholm Stadium War Memorial and the Gloucester War Memorial. He played twenty-three games for the Gloucester Rugby Club at scrum half between 1913 and 1914 of which four were for the First XV. Edwin had initially enlisted in August 1914 but after forty-seven days service was discharged as unfit due to knee cartilage damage. He successfully re-joined the Gloucestershire Regiment early in 1915.

WREFORD-BROWN, Oswald Eric ('Eric') (1877-1916) (Cricketer)

Born on 21 July 1877, Clifton at Bristol and died on 7 July 1916, Corbie in France from wounds received at Mametz Wood on 5 July, aged 39 years. Oswald was buried at Corbie Communal Cemetery Extension, plot 1, row B, grave 48. Oswald, a Member of the London Stock Exchange, was the son of William and Clara Jane Wreford-Brown from 62 Quarry Street, Guildford, Surrey. He enlisted in the Inns of Court Officer Training Corps [OTC] and served with the 9th (Service) Battalion, Northumberland Fusiliers (Captain). He landed in France on 15 July 1915 and was awarded the campaign medals - 1914-15 Star, the British War Medal and the Victory Medal. Oswald is commemorated on the Stock Exchange Memorial and the Charterhouse School Memorial. He played once for Gloucestershire County Cricket Club as a right-hand batsman in 1900. Prior to the war, in 1899, he was one of fourteen players who had toured Austria and Germany with the English Football Association team.

YALLAND, William Stanley ('Tough') (1889-1914) (Cricketer)

Born on 26 June 1889 at Fishponds, Bristol and killed in action on 23 October 1914 at Ypres, aged 23 years. William is commemorated on the Ypres (Menin Gate) Memorial, Panels 22 and 34 (Missing). William, a Professional Soldier, was the son of Thomas King and Mary Emily Yalland (née Morgan) from Wellington Lines, Aldershot. William enlisted in the 1/Leicesters *circa* 1908 before gaining a commission in February 1912 with the 3/Leicesters (Second Lieutenant). In December 1912 he was transferred to the 3/Gloucesters and ultimately the 1/Gloucesters and was stationed at Bordon

Camp in August 1914. He served with the 15th Platoon, D Company, 1st Battalion, Gloucestershire Regiment (Lieutenant). He landed in France on 14 August 1915 and was awarded the campaign medals - 1914 Star with clasp and rose ("*Old Contemptible*"), the British War Medal and the Victory Medal. William is commemorated on the Fishponds War Memorial, the Clifton Rugby Football Club Roll of Honour and on the Yalland family grave at St Mary's Church, Fishponds. William played once for Gloucestershire County Cricket Club as a right-hand batsman in 1910. William played rugby for Clifton RFC and Richmond RFC and represented Hampshire as well as the 1/Leicesters XV in the Army's Rugby Cup Competition, reaching four finals between 1908 and 1912.

There were some players briefly mentioned on several occasions throughout the text and information for them is presented below.

GLOUCESTER RUGBY FOOTBALL CLUB (GRFC)

NAME	RANK (Service Nbr)	REGIMENT	POSITION	GAMES
ASHMEADE, H. (F.) (1891-1949)	Private	1/Gloucesters	Wing	11 (1912-1921)
AYLIFFE, Frank (1892-1942)	Lieutenant	8/Gloucesters [wounded]	Back row	242 (1913-1926)
BEARD, Jesse	Lance Corporal 2519	A Company 5/Gloucesters [wounded]	Wing	29 (1907-1909)
COLLINGBOURNE, G.	—	—	Wing	3 (1911-1923)
COOK, Harry	Private (11519)	8/Gloucesters [wounded]	Centre	46 (1911-1914)
CROMWELL, Ernest W. (1893-1952)	Private 2666	5/Gloucesters [wounded]	Back row	8 (1912-1914)
CUMMINGS, Albert E. (1869-1940)	Private 2871	1/Gloucesters	Stand off /centre	73 (1895-1899)
DEANE, Harold	Private (2459)	B Company 5/Gloucesters	Full back	1 (1911-1912)
DOVEY, William (1890-1927)	Lance Corporal 240696	D Company 5/Gloucesters [wounded]	Back row	73 (1910-1920)

Name	Rank/Number	Unit	Position	Matches (Years)
GODDARD, Arthur	Private 19631	D Company 8/Gloucesters	Half back	19 (1898-1905)
GOULDING, Alfred H. ('Fred') (1874-1945)	Lance Corporal 2179	1/Gloucesters [wounded]	Front row /second row	104 (1897-1905)
HALFORD, George (1886-1960)	Lance Corporal 6748	1/Gloucesters [wounded]	Second row	333 (1907-1924)
HALL, Arthur (1886-1966)		Starred Occupation		227 (1913-1928)
HALL, Ernest	Corporal 203050	8/Gloucesters	Three-quarter	108 (1902-1911)
HALL, William	—	—	Half back	156 (1907-1919)
HARRIS, Joe (1890-1963)	Corporal 276100	D Company 5/Gloucesters	Front row	159 (1908-1923)
HAYES, Norman	—	—	Forward	156 (1908-1920)
HUDSON, Arthur (1882-1973)		Royal Navy (Submarines)	Wing	273 (1902-1920)
JEWELL, J.	—	—	Forward	81 (1901-1906)
KINGSCOTT, Hubert (1892-1969)	Private 2690	C Company 5/Gloucesters (Later commissioned into Royal Naval Reserve as Paymaster Sub-Lieutenant)	Scrum half	17 (1912-1914)
LANE, George	Private 2589	D Company 5/Gloucesters	Back row	2 (1913-1914)
LAWSON, Joseph F. (1883-1969)	Second Lieutenant (Act. Captain)	Royal Gloucestershire Hussars [wounded]	Second row	1 (1914) 84 (1914-1922)
LEE, J.	Sergeant	10/Worcesters	Forward	6 (1918-1920)
MANSELL, Frank T.	Private 2448	A Company 5/Gloucesters	Forward	86 (1919-1925)

Name	Rank/Number	Unit	Position	Appearances (Years)
MEADOWS, James (1889-1941)	Sergeant 240002	A Company 5/Gloucesters [wounded]	Second row	90 (1910-1914)
MILLINGTON, Thomas (1892-1960)	Gunner (31546)	Royal Field Artillery [wounded]	Half back	260 (1913-1927)
POLLARD, Harry	Lance Corporal 2702	D Company 5/Gloucesters	Half back	1 (1910-1911)
RIGBY, William H. (1890-1968)	Lance Corporal 240722	5/Gloucesters [wounded]	Scrum half	3 (1912-1913)
ROBINSON, John E. (1885-1951)	Sergeant 30921	1/Gloucesters [wounded]	Centre	2 (1906-1907)
ROMANS, George* (1876-1946)	—	—	Full back /wing	268 (1896-1907)
ROSE, Charles (1872-1949)	Private 3073	1/Gloucesters	Front Row	127 (1893-1899)
SMITH, Hubert (b.1881-1962)	Private 2712	D Company 5/Gloucesters	Full back	110 (1902-1910)
SPECK, Alfred	Corporal	A Company 5/Gloucesters	Scrum half	1 (1900-1901)
STEPHENS, Jim (1875-1936)	Private 2297	B Company 5/Gloucesters	Half back	15 (1897-1907)
SYSUM, William (1887-1966)	Private	8/Gloucesters	Half back	23 (1911-1913)
VEARS, Gordon (1884-1947)	—	Starred Occupation	Front row	295 (1902-1913)
VEARS, Lindsay (1882-1963)	Lieutenant	Royal Field Artillery [wounded]	Wing	73 (1901-1909)
WEBB, C. Fred (1887-1965)	Lance Corporal 240684	C Company 5/Gloucesters [wounded]	Wing	124 (1911-1923)
WEBB, John H. (1890-1953)	Private 2756	B Company 5/Gloucesters	Front row	103 (1913-1924)
WILKES, William G.	Lance Corporal (2776)	B Company 5/Gloucesters	Half back	58 (1911-1914)

*George Romans also played for the Gloucestershire County Cricket Club

GLOUCESTERSHIRE COUNTY CRICKET CLUB (GCCC)

NAME	RANK (Service Number)	REGIMENT	POSITION	MATCHES (Dates)
BARNETT, Charles S. (1884-1962)	Lieutenant	1/5th Gloucesters [wounded]	R-H batsman	108 (1904-1926)
BATEMAN-CHAMPAIN, Claude E. (1875-1956)	Lieutenant Colonel	2/5th Gurkha Rifles	R-H batsman and R-A slow bowler	16 (1898-1907)
BATEMAN-CHAMPAIN, Francis H. (1877-1942)	Captain	Army Ordnance Department (AOD)	R-H batsman and R-A slow bowler	83 (1895-1914)
BATEMAN-CHAMPAIN John N. (1880-1950)	Chaplain		R-H batsman	2 (1899)
BELL, Percy H. (1892-1956)	Second Lieutenant	Royal Flying Corps	batsman	8 (1911-1912)
BELOF, Gerald H. (1877-1944)	Lieutenant	Royal Garrison Artillery	L-H batsman and slow L-A orthodox bowler	11 (1898-1899)
BROWN, William S.A. (1877-1952)	Lieutenant	5/North Staffs	R-H batsman and L-A, M-P bowler	161 (1896-1919)
CHESTER-MASTER, Edgar (1888-1979)	Major	5/Royal Fusiliers	batsman and bowler	1 (1911)
CLARKE, Basil F. (1885-1940)	Lieutenant Colonel	4/Leicesters [wounded]	R H batsman	15 (1914-1920)
CRANFIELD, Lionel L. (1883-1968)	Private GS-111094	Royal Fusiliers	R-H batsman and slow L-A-O bowler	25 (1903-1922)
ELLIS, Francis E. (b.1889)	Sapper WR-150356	Royal Engineers	R-A fast medium bowler	26 (1914-1921)
FORD, Percy H. (1877-1920)	Second Lieutenant	11/Bedfords	R-H batsman and R-A fast bowler	29 (1906-1908)
GILES, Godwin M. (1876-1955)	Lieutenant	Middlesex Motor Volunteer Corps (VTC)	Fast medium bowler	1 (1903)
GODSELL, Richard T. (1880-1954)	Lieutenant	Army Service Corps	R-H batsman	51 (1903-1910)

Name	Rank	Unit	Style	Matches (Years)
GOODWIN, Harry S. (1870-1955)	Major	22/Royal Fusiliers DAD [sic] Royal Engineers	R-H batsman	31 (1896-1907)
HACKER, William S. (1876-1925)	Private 22399	Royal Army Medical Corps	R-H batsman and R-A fast medium bowler	3 (1899-1901)
HEWLETT, Reginald J. (1885-1950)	Corporal 59781	Royal Engineers	R-H batsman	5 (1909-1922)
IMLAY, Alan D. (1885-1959)	Second Lieutenant	Clifton College OTC	R-H batsman	7 (1905-1911)
LEVY Solomon (b. 1886)	Private 14098	7/Gloucesters [wounded]	R-H batsman and R_A off-break bowler	4 (1910-1911)
MAINPRICE, Humphrey (1882-1958)	Captain	6/King's Royal Rifle Corps	R-H batsman and leg-break bowler	15 (1905)
MANNERS, Herbert C. (1877-1955)	Private 636	19/Royal Fusiliers	R-H batsman	5 (1902-1911)
MEAKIN, Bernard (1885-1964)	Captain	Royal Army Service Corps	L-H batsman and leg-break bowler	1 (1906)
MEYER, William E. (1883-1953)	Second Lieutenant	Royal Army Service Corps	R-H batsman and R-A fast-medium bowler	9 (1909-1910)
MILLER, Thomas (1883-1962)	Captain	2/5th Gloucesters	R-H batsman and R-A fast bowler	18 (1902-1914)
MORGAN, Donald L. (1888-1969)	Lieutenant	United Provinces Light Horse (Indian Army)	Batsman	2 (1907)
PENDUCK, Arthur E. (1883-1924)	Corporal	Royal Army Medical Corps [RAMC]	R-H batsman and R-A fast bowler	5 (1908-1909)
PICKERING, Arthur (1878-1939)	Cadet Captain and Adjutant	Merchant Venturers' Cadet Corps (Bristol)	Batsman and bowler	2 (1901-1908)
RATTENBURY, Gilbert L. (1878-1958)	Private 200120	5/Liverpool Regiment [wounded]	R-H batsman and R-A fast bowler	2 (1902-1909)

Name	Rank	Regiment	Style	Matches (Years)
ROBINSON, Foster G., Sir (1880-1967)	Second Lieutenant	3rd Battalion (City of Bristol) Volunteer Regiment	R-H batsman	68 (1903-1923)
ROMANS, George* (1876-1946)	-	-	R-H batsman	11 (1899-1903)
RUST, Thomas H. (1881-1962)	Private 203579	2/6th Gloucesters	R-H batsman	1 (1914)
SALTER, Malcolm G. (1887-1973)	Lieutenant	12 Cavalry	R-H batsman	34 (1907-1925)
SCOTT, Osmund, Hon. (1876-1948)	Lieutenant	Royal Army Service Corps	R-H batsman and slow L-A-) bowler	2 (1905)
SMITH, Harry (1891-1937)	Unknown	British Army (regiment unknown)	R-H batsman and R-A slow bowler and wicket keeper	393 (1912-1935)
STADDON, Ernest H. (1882-1965)	Quarter Master Sergeant 231602	Corps of Hussar	batsman	1 (1912)
TAYLOR, Clifford J., Dr (1875-1952)	Captain	Royal Army Medical Corps	Batsman and bowler	4 (1899-1900)
THOMAS, Edgar L. (1875-1936)	Captain	Dorsetshire Regiment	R-H batsman	27 (1895-1907)
TIMMS, Herbert H.	Private 22027	2/Gloucesters	L-H batsman and R-A fast medium bowler	3 (1911-1912)
TOVEY, Wilson G. (1874-1950)	Lieutenant	4/Gloucestershire Volunteer Regiment	Batsman and bowler	1 (1901)
WATTS, Frederic A. (1884-1968)	Corporal 203051	1/5th Gloucesters	batsman and bowler	1 (1905)
WICKS, Frank C. (1892-1965)	Second Lieutenant	22/Manchesters [wounded]	Batsman	1 (1912)
WOOLLEY, Claude N. (1886-1962)	Corporal 49297	12/King's Own Yorkshire Light Infantry	R-H batsman and R-A slow medium bowler	1 (1909)

*George Romans also played for the Gloucester Rugby Club

R-H=right-hand; R-A=right-arm; L-A=left-arm; L-A-O=left-arm orthodox; M-P=medium-paced;

For Club, King and Country

8

APPENDICES

Appendix A: Exhibition at the Soldiers of Gloucestershire Museum

The soldiers of Gloucestershire Museum will mount an exhibition of rugby during the Great War between September 2015 and April 2016 to coincide with the Rugby World Cup 2015 which will be played between 18 September and 31 October 2015.

Appendix B: Explanatory Notes

NOTE 1: Identification of Players: All of the cricketers who played for Gloucestershire County Cricket Club, regardless of the number of matches, have been identified following a huge amount of effort of trawling through the original county scorebooks and contemporary newspaper reports. This work conducted by Peter Griffiths and his team has been captured in the CricketArchive website (www.cricketarchive.com). Using information from the website and applying the eligibility age limits imposed by the War Office, it was determined that 143 cricketers were eligible for service and eighty five were identified as having served in the Armed Forces. The work to identify the Gloucester Rugby Club players who served in the Great War is not as advanced because the Gloucester Rugby Football Club Community Heritage Project at the Gloucestershire Archives has only been in progress for 5-6 years and the numbers of players involved are greater and the contemporary records are sparse. At present it is estimated that 400-600 players could have been eligible; it should be noted that upwards of eighty players could represent the Gloucester First and Second XVs in a single season.

NOTE 2: Nomenclature of Regiments: A regiment was comprised of a number of battalions. The 1st and 2nd Battalions were the active service battalions (Regular Army) and were supported by one or more reserve battalions which would take the next available numbers e.g. 3rd Battalion, 4th Battalion. In addition there were one or more battalions of the Territorial Force [TF] which would also take the next available battalion numbers, e.g. 5th Battalion, 6th Battalion. Kitchener's New Army Battalions, designated 'Service' battalions, were assigned to the existing regiments and took the next available numbers, e.g. 7th (Service), 8th (Service), etc. In terms of representing the battalions in text, their names can be written out in full or an accepted abbreviation can be used. For example, in full a battalion can be represented as the 1st Battalion, Gloucestershire Regiment or this can be abbreviated either to 1st Gloucesters or to 1/Gloucesters; this applies to all battalions.

NOTE 3: Enlistment Requirements: In August 1914 the Government asked for volunteers between the ages of 18 and 38 years to join the Armed Forces, with no volunteer liable for overseas service until he had reached his nineteenth birthday; there was also a minimum height restriction which was 5' 3" in August 1914 but had been reduced to 5' 1" by February 1915. By May 1915 the age range was extended to 18 to 40 years of age. As it was felt that insufficient numbers of eligible people were enlisting, on 15 July 1915 the Government passed the National Registration Act which required all persons (male and female) between the ages of 15 and 65 years to be registered. This in effect enabled Army recruiters to target all eligible men but as there was no form of compulsion only verbal persuasion was available. On 16 October 1915 Lord Derby introduced the voluntary Derby Scheme which targeted men between the ages of 18 and 40 years and classified them into groups based on age and marital status. These groups were 'called up' in sequential order and it was hoped that men would enlist in the knowledge that they would not be immediately called upon, which had previously been the case; the scheme met with little success. In January 1916 the Government introduced the Military Service Act (1916) which came into force on 2 March 1916. This was conscription and all men between 18 and 41 years of age were liable, by law, to be called up unless they belonged to exempted categories which included married men, men widowed with children and men in reserved occupations. In May 1916 the Act was extended to cover married men (i.e. no longer exempted) and in 1918 the Military Service Act (1918) was introduced which extended the age range of eligibility from 18 to 51 years for all men.

NOTE 4: Artillery Barrages: Prior to an attack the British Artillery would attempt to destroy enemy positions and wire entanglements with a *bombardment* which could last anywhere between ten minutes and seven days. However once the infantry started to move across No Man's Land the artillery would support them with a *barrage*. The barrage often consisted of anti-personnel shrapnel shells which would focus on the immediate objective of the enemy's front line trenches. The shrapnel shell exploded scattering lethal small ball-bearing like projectiles, however because the exploding force travelled forward the attacking infantry could 'lean' on the barrage, i.e. follow relatively close to it. Just before the infantry arrived at the enemy trench the barrage would move on ('lift') to its next objective, which could be the next set of trenches or space between the trenches to prevent an enemy counter-attack. Because the infantry could move quite close to its own barrage the idea was that the infantry would be on top of the trenches before the enemy could react. There remained the problem of shells landing short resulting in casualties caused by 'friendly fire' but it was preferable and less costly in terms of casualties to the alternative which was the infantry moving across No Man's Land unprotected. This was one of the techniques developed as the war progressed. Machine gun barrages were also used which would fire over the heads of the attacking infantry to prevent the enemy bringing up reinforcements.

NOTE 5; Provision for Wives and Families: Early in September 1914 the Government announced that the normal Army separation allowances were to be increased. Wives would get 12s 6d per week which would be increased to 15s for a wife and one child, 17s 6d for a wife and two children, 20s for a wife and three children and 22s for a wife and four children. Many employers announced some sort of pay deal for employees whilst on military service, which was regarded as a patriotic gesture while Local Authorities were instructed by the Government that their employees should be given a leave of absence and retain their full salary adjusted for an Army allowances. These 'pay deals' were put in place at a time when it was considered that the war would be quickly over although as the war progressed employers did try to retain some sort of financial help for wives and families and Government allowances were gradually increased but generally remained insufficient to cover the rapidly rising cost of living.

NOTE 6; Battalion War Diaries: One of the duties of a Battalion's Adjutant was to keep a daily account of the battalion's strength, position and activities throughout the war; the diary entries were approved monthly by the officer commanding the battalion. These diaries, available from the National Archives, provide a detailed account of a battalion's actions and more mundane activities throughout the war and are an essential research source for establishing where individual soldiers were on any particular day and what activities they were likely to be engaged in. In some instances, particularly early in the war, individual soldiers who were wounded or killed were identified by name but with increasing casualty rates this became impractical and only casualty summaries were recorded.

Appendix C: Gallantry Awards

C.1: Medals Awarded for Bravery and Gallantry

Gallantry Medal	Gloucester Rugby Football Club	Gloucestershire County Cricket Club
Distinguished Service Order (DSO)	Captain **Cornelius Carleton**, 2/Welsh (1914) Act. Lieutenant Colonel **Gilbert Collett**, 5/Gloucesters (1918) Captain **Percy Stout**, Motor Machine Gun Corps (1917)	Major **Charles Edwards**, Royal Army Service Corps (1916) Major **Percy Robinson**, Royal Field Artillery (1917) Major **Ernest English**, 6/The King's (Liverpool Regiment) (1917) Major **Alison White**, Royal Artillery (1916) Major **Arthur Du Boulay**, Royal Engineers (1918)
Distinguished Conduct Medal (DCM)	Sergeant **Albert Barnes**, 2/5th Gloucesters (1918) Lance Corporal **Henry Lane**, 1/Grenadier Guards (1916)	Sergeant **Herbert Tayler**, Tank Corps (1918)
Military Cross (MC)	Captain **Alec Lewis**, 6/Berkshires (1916 and 1917) Second Lieutenant **Frank Stout**, 20/Hussars (1916)	Captain **Hugh Jones**, 13/Gloucesters (1916) Captain **John Healing**, 2/ Royal Warwicks (1917) Captain **James Horlick**, Coldstream Guards (1917) Captain **Horace Merrick**, 1/Gloucesters (1917) **Michael Green** (1918) Captain **James Winterbotham**, 5/Gloucesters (1918)
Military Medal (MM)	Sergeant **Hubert Barnes**, 1/5th Gloucesters (1917) Corporal **Charles Cook**, 1/5th Gloucesters (1917) Sergeant **Arthur Saunders**, 8/Gloucesters (1916) Corporal **William Washbourne**, 1/5th Gloucesters (1916)	-

C.2: Mentioned in Despatches (Complete from SoGM database)

Mentioned in Despatches [MiD] (All Ranks) was not a medal but an oak leaf worn on the medal ribbon of the British Victory Medal. It was awarded for carrying out a noteworthy act of gallantry or service; a despatch was an official report written by senior commanders and those written by the Commanders-in-Chiefs were published in the *London Gazette*.

Name (Final Rank and Regiment)	Number of Mentions	Dates
BATEMAN-CHAMPAIN, Captain Francis H.B., Army Ordnance Corps (GCCC)	1	December 1917
BATEMAN-CHAMPAIN, Brigadier General Hugh F.B., Staff Corps (GCCC)	1	August 1918
CARLETON, Captain (Act. Lieutenant-Colonel) Cornelius A.S., 2/Welsh (GRFC)	4	8 October 1914; 20 October 1914; June 1916; May 1917
COLLETT, Temp. Lieutenant-Colonel Gilbert F., 2/5th Gloucesters (GRFC and GCCC)	3	January 1917; December 1917; August 1918
DU BOULAY, Major (Brevet Lieutenant Colonel) Arthur H., Royal Engineers (GCCC)	6	Includes May 1917
EGERTON, Sergeant William, 5/Gloucesters (GRFC)	1	June 1918
ENGLISH, Lieutenant Colonel Ernest R.M., 1/King's Shropshire Light Infantry (GCCC)	2	
HORLICK, Lieutenant Colonel James N., GSO HQ 22nd Division (GCCC)	4	Includes January 1917; July 1917; June 1918
POPE, Major Andrew N., 9/Royal Fusiliers (GCCC)	Multiple	
ROBINSON, Lieutenant Colonel Percy G., Royal Field Artillery (GCCC)	2	January 1916; January 1917
STOUT, Captain Percy W., Motor Machine Gun Corps (GRFC)	5	
WHITE, Major Alison K.G., Royal Artillery (GCCC)	5	
WINTERBOTHAM, Captain James P., 5/Gloucesters (GCCC)	1	April 1917

Appendix D: Statistics

Table 1: Officers and NCOs and ORs

	Officers 1914	NCOs and ORs 1914	Officers 1918	NCOs and ORs 1918
Gloucester Rugby Football Club	7.7%	92.2%	17.7%	82.2%
Gloucestershire County Cricket Club	34.5%*	65.5%	74.6%	25.3%

NCO = Non Commissioned Officer (i.e. Sergeants and Corporals); OR = Other Ranks (i.e. Privates)

*This figure includes Professional Soldiers and those on Officer training courses by the end of 1914. Professional Soldiers account for 20% of the players who fought in the war

Table 2: Average Age of Serving and Enlisted Men in 1914

	Average Age	Percentage Men Over 30 years	Percentage of Men Over 40 years
Gloucester Rugby Football Club	27.3 years	32%	4%
Gloucestershire County Cricket Club	31.7 years	64%	9%

Table 3: Place of Birth

	Bristol	Gloucester	Glo'stershire	Other English Counties	London	Wales	Outside of Britain*
Gloucester Rugby Football Club	0%	75%	20%	5%	0%	0%	0%
Gloucestershire County Cricket Club**	25%	2.4%	26.5%	21.6%	4.8%	2.4%	16.8%

*The countries outside of Great Britain included India, USA, South Africa, Australia, China and the Cape Verde Islands

** From above table 95% of rugby players were born locally (Bristol, Gloucester, Gloucestershire) while 54% of cricketers were locally born

Table 4: The Proportion of Rugby Players and Cricketers Serving (Professional Soldiers and Enlisted Men) in Army Regiments and Royal Navy on Outbreak of War. August-December 1914*

Armed Forces Unit (Regiment/Royal Navy)	Gloucester Rugby Football Club	Gloucestershire County Cricket Club
5/Gloucesters (TF)	54%	5%
Other Battalions, Gloucestershire Regiment	24%	15.5%
Royal Fusiliers	-	10.3%
Royal Army Medical Corps	-	5%
Royal Engineers	-	5%
Royal Flying Corps	-	4%
Royal Artillery	-	9%
Other Regiments	19%	44%
Royal Navy (RN and RNVR)	3%	2%
Total Number of Army Regiments/Units Represented	12	30

*Although not markedly different the pattern had changed slightly by 1918 as men had been transferred to other units,

Table 5: Summary of Facts Regarding Players Who Died During the War

	Gloucester Rugby Football Club	Gloucestershire County Cricket Club
Number	30*	18*
Missing (No Known Grave)	15 (50%)	5 (27%)
Average Age	28 years	30 years
Youngest Player to Die	20 years (Melville Lewis, 23 July 1916)	20 years (Claude Mackay, 7 June 1915)
Oldest Player to Die	49 years (Ronald Grist, 15 May 1918)	39 years (Oswald Wreford-Brown, 7 July 1916)

*Thomas Truman is included in both sets of figures as he played for both GRFC and GCCC.

Appendix E: Snippets

Although not directly relevant to the Great War, some interesting facts associated with the players emerged so rather confine them to the annals of history, some of them are reproduced here.

- In April 1914 **William Grant** (Captain, Cameron Highlanders, 1894-1918) (GCCC) was caught driving a motor-car in Westgate Street, Gloucester at a dangerous speed by two policemen, PC Keeley and Pc Eames who stated in court that they had "...*never seen a car going faster in Gloucester*." William was fined £3 3s with costs of £1 3s 2d for driving between 25 and 30 miles per hour.[534]
- Not all war related deaths were due to enemy action or life in the services. The sister of **Bernard Meakin** (Captain, Royal Army Service Corps, 1885-1964) (GCCC), Mary, had been Commandant of the Stone VAD Auxiliary Hospital, Staffordshire from 1915 till 1919 and been responsible for thousands of wounded soldiers. This situation took its toll on her health and for the last eight or nine years of her life she "... *suffered from nervous trouble brought on by the overstrain of her war work*";[535] her death in April 1932 was attributed to her war work.
- **Hugh Frederick Bateman-Champain** (Brigadier-General, Gurkha Rifles, 1869-1933) (GCCC) had been personally chosen to play cricket for Gloucestershire CCC by W.G Grace. Hugh died in 1933 whilst playing golf. His funeral was attended by many dignitaries, family members and friends including his nephew the Reverend Christopher 'Kit' Tanner, who would make sixty-six appearances for Gloucester Rugby Club on the wing between 1930 and 1938 and would win five International caps for England between 1930 and 1932. Kit Tanner, as the Chaplain on HMS *Fiji*, would die rescuing the crew after the ship was sunk off the Island of Crete on 23 May 1941. He was awarded, posthumously, the Albert Medal for saving life, the only England International Rugby player to do so in the Second World War.[536]
- One of the brothers of Lance-Corporal **Donald Priestley** (1887-1917) (GCCC), 28/London, was Captain Raymond Priestley, a geologist and meteorologist, a member of the Northern Party of

---

[534] *Western Daily Press* 5 May 1914
[535] *Lichfield Mercury* 8 April 1932
[536] Kit Tanner's story is told in "*They played for Gloucester and fought for their country. Gloucester Rugby Football Club: A Place in Military History*" by Martin and Teresa Davies pp.114-17 and pp.237-38. The book is available from the Gloucester Rugby shop and Hudson Sports, Northgate Street, Gloucester.

Scott's ill-fated Antarctic [Terra Nova] Expedition, 1910-13. In the Antarctic there are features named after him, Mount Priestley, Priestley Peak and the Priestley Glacier. Raymond Priestley would survive the war.

- **William Pearce** (1884-1917) GRFC), 5/Gloucesters married Margery Delany on 2 September 1914, eleven days before he left to join his regiment. The couple had one daughter, Monica, born on 20 November 1915 (see Photograph 35). Monica would never marry but would go onto have an illustrious career in nursing in Britain and France. She eventually became the Matron at the Birmingham General Hospital from 1961 until her retirement in 1973. After her retirement she remained active and founded the St Mary's Hospice, Selly Oak, Birmingham, which opened in 1979; for this achievement she was awarded the OBE. Ten years later in 1989 she was instrumental in founding the first hospice in Poland at Gdansk and was subsequently honoured by the Pope John Paul II who was born in Poland. Monica died at St Mary's Hospice in 1993.

Appendix F: The Soldiers of Gloucestershire Museum

Lieutenant Colonel Ralph Stephenson

Trustee, Soldiers of Gloucestershire Museum

The Soldiers of Gloucestershire Museum is situated at the Customs House, in the historic Gloucester Docks minutes away from the Gloucester Quays shopping mall and about a five minute walk from Gloucester city centre. The museum tells the story of the Gloucestershire Regiment and the Royal Gloucestershire Hussars since 1694. Closed for refurbishment in 2013, the museum re-opened in the spring 2014 after being awarded a Heritage Lottery Grant and features new displays, new lighting and interactive screens.

The artefacts of the two county regiments cover silver and art as well as memorabilia from past postings around the world and life size models of soldiers in action create an impression of global conflict. Displays for children as well as a 'dressing up corner' keep the family entertained.

The Museum has a very active web site and will introduce you to the facilities for research, details on the Friends of the Museum as well as news items on Museum activities.

For up-to-date information including open times check the website, www.glosters.org.uk, or telephone 01452 522 682.

Appendix G: Gloucestershire County Cricket Club

Roger Gibbons

Executive Board Member and Honorary Archivist, Gloucestershire County Cricket Club

The earliest reference to cricket in Gloucestershire appears in *The Gloucester Journal* of 16th September 1729. A game was to be played on the following Tuesday for "upwards of twenty guineas" on the Town Ham, an area between the two arms of the River Severn on the outskirts of the city. There is no subsequent reference to any result or even if the game ever took place.

The next reported reference in a Gloucestershire newspaper appears on 29th August 1752 in *Felix Farley's Bristol Journal*. A game was to be played on Monday 31st August on Durdham Down between an Eleven of Bristol and an Eleven of London for a purse of twenty guineas.

During the early years of the nineteenth century there were increasing reports of cricket being played around the county and by the 1850s cricket had developed into a popular pastime. Around this time Dr Henry Mills Grace had been instrumental in the formation of a club in Mangotsfield which in 1846 amalgamated with the Coalpit Heath Club to form the West Gloucestershire Cricket Club. In 1854 William Clarke's All England XI came to Bristol to play a match against XI of the West Gloucestershire Club, a game that the All England XI won by 149 runs. Watching his father play for the West Gloucestershire team was a six year old youngster who went on to become known, amongst other things, as "the Champion Cricketer", William Gilbert Grace.

Over the next few years the influence of the Grace family began to grow with the establishment of a Gentlemen of Gloucestershire XI who played games against, amongst others, the Gentlemen of Devon and in June 1861 at Lord's played and defeated an MCC XI by 134 runs.

The game continued to develop and although there is no written confirmation of the exact date of the formation of Gloucestershire County Cricket Club it is now generally accepted that 1870 was the start with the game against Surrey played on Durdham Down from 2nd to 4th June the first First-class match. Gloucestershire won the game by 51 runs. Later in the year they again defeated Surrey, this time at The Oval by an innings and 129 runs with WG, opening both the batting and the bowling and scoring 143, Gloucestershire's first century and taking eight wickets in the match for 36 runs. The season finished with another victory, this time by an innings and 88 runs against the MCC at Lord's. Again, WG was the outstanding player, scoring 172 and match bowling figures of seven wickets for eight runs!

Apart from that first game, all the early home matches were played at Clifton College although from 1872, one game was played each year at the College Ground, Cheltenham. That number was increased to two in 1878; the Cheltenham Week which still continues, 136 years later as the Cheltenham Festival, the longest running cricket festival at an out-ground. Games were also played at the Spa Ground in Gloucester from 1882.

The club acquired its own ground at Ashley Down in Bristol and established its headquarters there. The current year, 2014, commemorates 125 years at the ground.

The early history of the club was very much tied in with the Grace family; the three sons of Dr Henry Mills Grace, playing a prominent part both on and off the field. All three played in the first game against Surrey. The oldest, Edward Mills Grace captained the side in 1870, played until 1896 and was Secretary until 1902, WG was the first Secretary, played until 1899 and was captain from 1871 whilst George Frederick Grace, "Young Fred" played until 1880 before his untimely death, aged 29 from congestion of the lungs.

Earlier that year all three brothers had played for England against Australia at the Oval in the first Test Match played in England.

Over the ensuing years more than 30 Gloucestershire cricketers have represented England in Test cricket; names include Walter Hammond, Charles Barnett, Tom Graveney and David Allen and in more recent times Jack Russell, David Lawrence, Mike Smith and Jon Lewis and, in One-day Internationals, Mark Alleyne. A similar number of Gloucestershire's overseas players have also represented their countries in international cricket; prominent names in recent years include Mike

Procter, Zaheer Abbas and Courtney Walsh. Interestingly, two nineteenth century players, W.E. Midwinter and J.J. Ferris played for both England and Australia, Midwinter, uniquely, for Australia against England and for England against Australia.

On field success, in the form of trophies has been limited, Since the County Championship was properly established in 1890, Gloucestershire is one of three teams never to have won it, their best seasons being 1930, 1931, 1947, 1959, 1969 and 1986 when they finished second. In One-day cricket they achieved notable success between 1999 and 2004 winning seven different titles, including in 2000 all three competitions.

The club has a strong focus on developing young cricketers; of those who played first team cricket in 2013, nine had progressed through the club's Academy system

In recent years One-day International Cricket has been played at the ground and in 2014 England will take on India, the current 50 Over World Cup holders.

The ground has undergone many changes and in recent years a new pavilion has been built and increased permanent seating installed. Plans are in hand to introduce floodlighting to meet the highest International Cricket Council standards, measures designed to enable the club to continue to host international cricket which will hopefully include World Cup matches when that tournament returns to England in 2019.

The players whose names are recorded in this book are just a few of the 638 who have played cricket for the County – some no more than one or two games – but they all have their place in the history of one of the more famous clubs in the history of County Cricket in England.

Appendix H: Gloucester Rugby Football Club

Simon Devereux

Gloucester Rugby Football Club Player (150 1st XV appearances, Second Row/No.8, 1990 – 1999) and BBC Radio Co-Commentator

I consider myself both fortunate and privileged; Fortunate; to have been born and bred in Gloucester, supporting my home town club from The Shed in my school years and coming through the local rugby ranks with support from my parents. Privileged; to have made around 150 Gloucester 1st XV appearances over a decade which transitioned both the amateur and professional eras, thus playing a small part in the rich heritage and history associated with Gloucester Rugby Football Club and the world famous Kingsholm ground. To me heritage is about the club, which includes the supporters as well as players. Generations have followed from the terraces and played a huge part.

Today, my involvement with the club is co-commentating at Kingsholm matches with BBC Radio Gloucestershire and working after match with the corporate 1873 Club. Fifteen years on from the injury sustained in a Premiership match at Kingsholm which effectively brought a premature end to my professional playing career, the same emotions are stirred every time Kingsholm roars. It never leaves you!

1873 is the year it all began, over 140 years of history and heritage associated with Gloucester Rugby Football Club. The significance of this year for Gloucester Rugby Football Club is still recognised today in the naming of the 1873 Club and 1873 Suite where the players dine after match in the rebuilt Kingsholm Grandstand. Reminders of bygone years and names are prevalent throughout the ground, including the club honours boards with first XV players listed in the bar joining The Shed side of the ground. This is the fabric of Gloucester Rugby Football Club.

Throughout its' history Gloucester Rugby Football club has been an ever present in competing as a top 10 English and Welsh club. Gloucester's legacy has been synonymous with uncompromising forward play and a passionate home crowd at Kingsholm. Ask almost anyone from outside the area what they associate with the City of Gloucester and the response will be rugby, Kingsholm and The Cathedral!

I mention Welsh clubs as arguably, it was these fixtures which formed the highlights of the fixture list for decades and represent a significant part of Gloucester's history. This was pre-professionalism and pre-league rugby, where the measure of success was based on how you performed home and away against the likes of Pontypool, Newport, Cardiff, Swansea and many more. Uncompromising and often brutal fixtures which shaped Gloucester throughout their history.

I have very fond memories of a packed Kingsholm, Wednesday night, under lights, being stood in The Shed with my dad cheering on Gloucester against the legendary International packed Pontypool side. Also being stood on the Pontypool terrace watching the return match where thousands travelled to watch. Nothing at stake, other than pride and passion to play for the Gloucester shirt, and all those who have worn it in the past. A sense of responsibility to protect the heritage of the club.

County rugby was strong in those days and formed the basis of the England team at the time. Gloucestershire were formed of Bristol and Gloucester players and won many County Championships such was the strength of both teams. The local derbies between Gloucester and Bristol were always fierce and that rivalry together with the Welsh fixtures ensured that the County side was strong and competitive and a feeder to the England side. I recall packed Kingsholm matches cheering on the County as well as special trains being laid on and travelling to places like The Vale of Lune in 1980 for the Championship Final where thousands travelled. These were intimate times from a supporter's perspective with a strong empathy with the players they were cheering. Again these players played for the personal pride in what they did and responsibility of carrying the torch for those who had gone before. A sense of not wanting to let the fans down.

Until the onset of professionalism, the path I followed was a familiar one, progressing from the hotbed of local rugby to represent Gloucester. This process was a continuation of the Club's heritage whereby supporters could empathise strongly with the players; everyone knew someone who knew the players or player's family. It created intimacy and passion. This extended to the Club's supporters also. There are many long term supporters who I have met over the years that tell me they were never good enough to play for Gloucester but their father, grandfather and great grandfather had followed the club, passing the baton through generations. This is where their passion comes from and their attachment to the history of the club, something which I hope to pass on to my own young children Grace (7) and Thomas (3) as they grow.

I was always conscious of the Gloucester history and heritage. To go from a fan on the terrace to lining up alongside the players I had been cheering years before at the likes of Pontypool Park, Cardiff Arms Park and Welford Road, to name a few, was special. It was a huge honour to don the Cherry and White, my home town club, representing all those passionate local fans and my heroes from years gone by. Defending the City is one way I would describe it. Defeat at Kingsholm on a

Saturday ruined the week for the working class of Gloucester. I took that personally and it carried a certain responsibility.

Match day, passing out of the changing room of the old compact Grandstand with its narrow corridors surrounded by club honours boards as you turn right and then left before the short walk onto the hallowed turf. I could not help but look at the names of previous players each time as I walked into the cauldron of noise at Kingsholm.

One particular memory from match day was making sure I saw the list of Gloucester players who lost their lives in World War 1 and 2, an emotional driver to perform for those who had gone before me but had made the ultimate sacrifice.

It was during a recent recording I took part in for the BBC World War 1 Series to commemorate 100 years of 'The Great War' that this really struck a chord with me. One of the names and photos on the club walls is of Henry 'Harry' Berry, a well known England player of his time who had played in all the home internationals, re-joined Gloucester for pre-season training, only for the war to commence causing the season to be postponed. Sadly Harry left and never returned.

Mike Kean-Price, a lifelong and fanatical Gloucester fan, who recalled more detail than me about some of the games I had played in, told me how his Grandfather John Price played for the club as a wing forward and died on the Somme on the 3rd July 1916, 2 days after his 30th birthday. We had a photograph session after the recording and a suggestion was to take one on the pitch-side. At this point I was told this was not possible as his father had told him never to walk on the Kingsholm turf unless you had 'worn the shirt'. This was where his passion comes from and attachment to the history of the club. The photograph did not take place. I had a huge amount of respect for that.

Fast forward to the modern game and it was inevitable that the onset of professionalism would bring with it increasing player movement among clubs. Gone were the days when you could reel off the names of each Premiership team from season to season. This challenged the fabric of heritage and clubs needed to work extra hard to generate and maintain a culture which underpinned its' longevity and traditions. New players joining the club must understand the responsibility that comes with it and what the club means to the community, supporters and the players who have gone before. They too will become part of the club's history and what they do today will define them forever. Bonds will be made which last a lifetime.

It remains easy to dismiss heritage in the professional era, which coincides with a more throw-away society, where social media means things are almost out of date before they arrive. However, this presents a dichotomy in that the value of heritage is even more important. Players need an emotional driver to perform, a strong culture and a sense of responsibility to those generations who have played and supported the club before. They need to appreciate the moment and realise it is their time. It will pass in a flash and they too will become names on the honours boards around the ground at Kingsholm for the next generation to reflect, respect and represent.

Appendix I: Maps

1. Theatres of War
2. The Western Front (British Sector)
3. Situation 1 July 1916, Somme Offensive
4. Third Battle of Ypres (Passchendaele) 1917
5. German Spring Offensives, 1918

MAP 1: Theatres of War 1914-1918

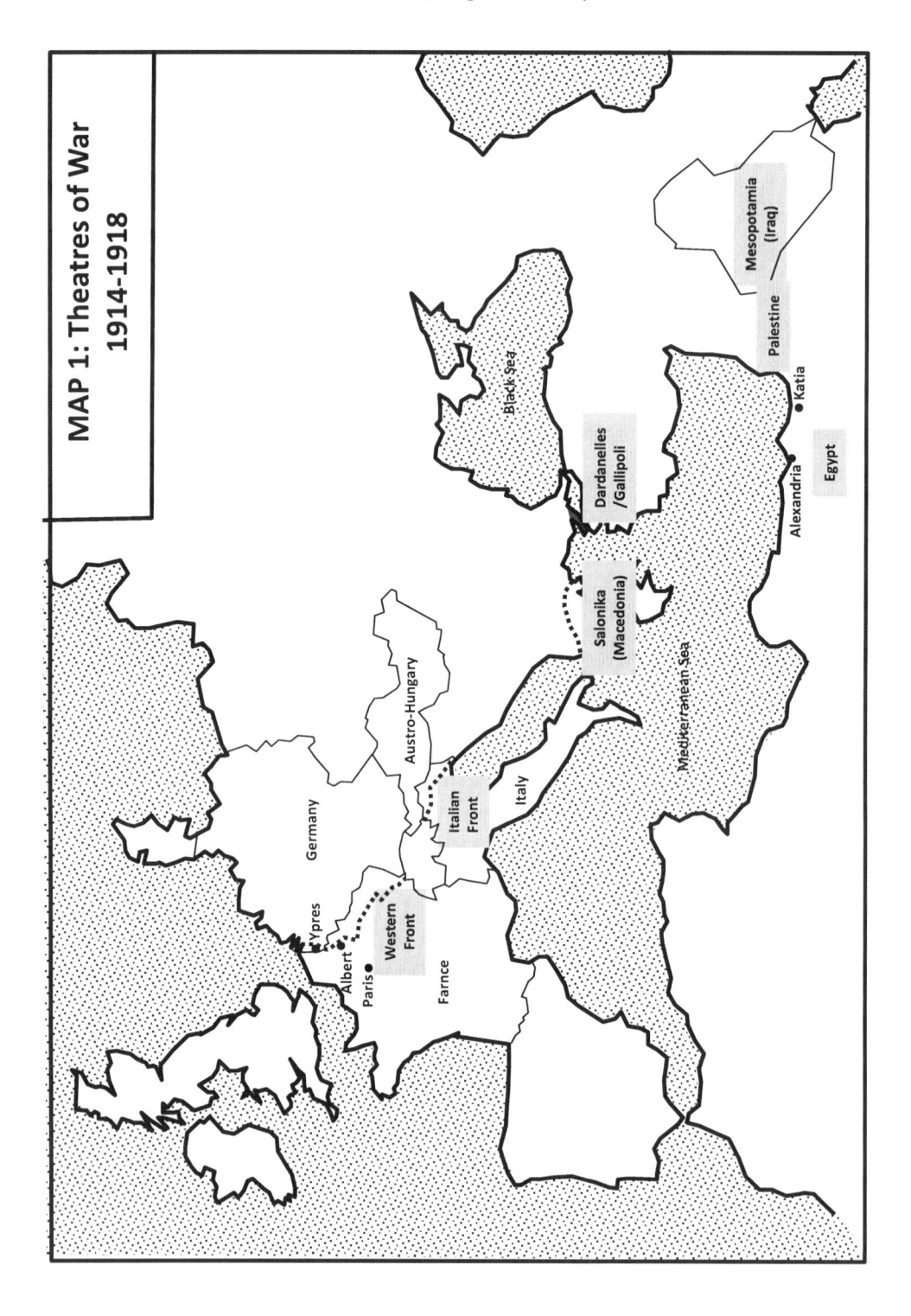

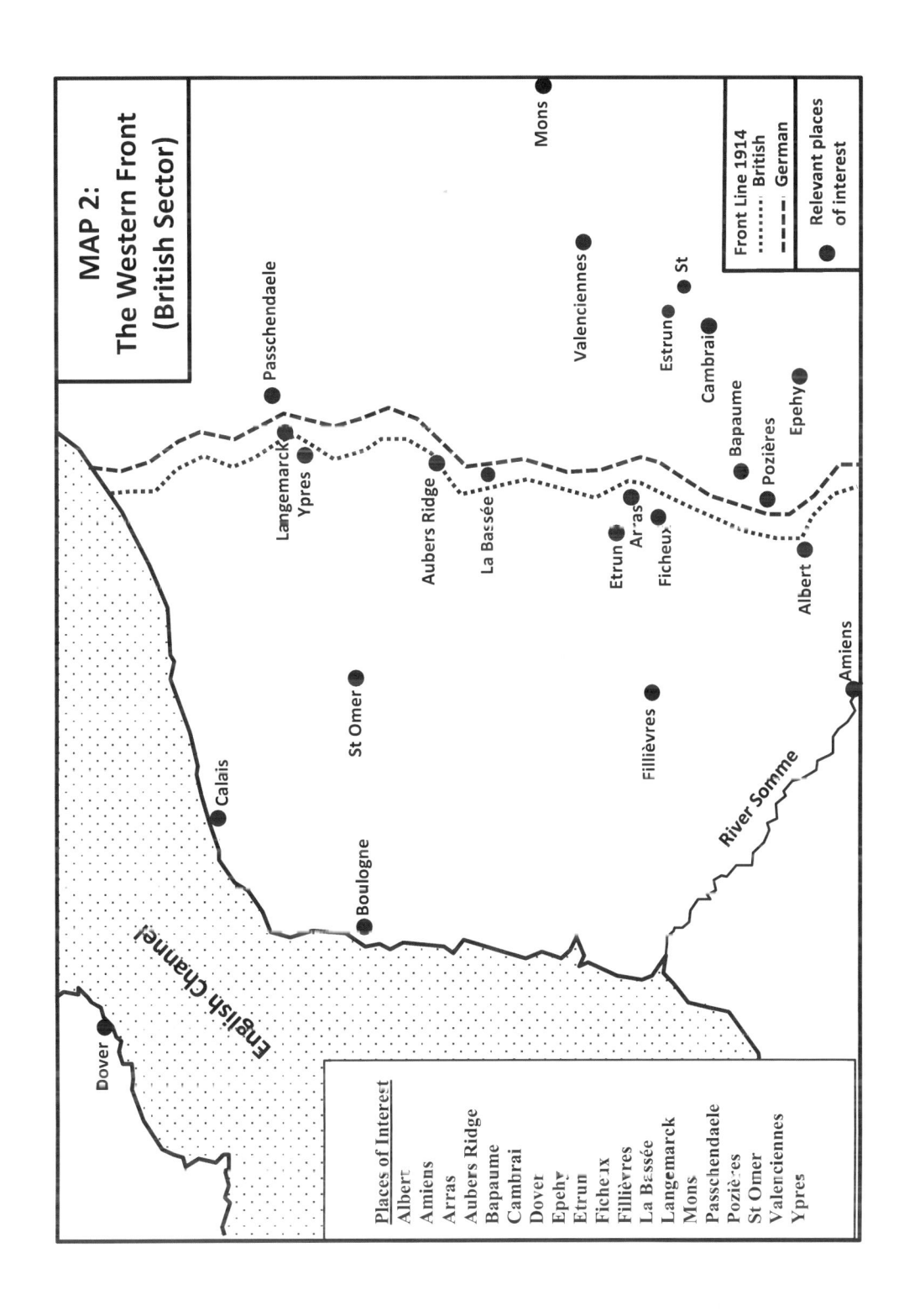

Appendices

MAP 2:
The Western Front (British Sector)

Front Line 1914
.... British
- - - - - German
● Relevant places of interest

Places of Interest
Albert
Amiens
Arras
Aubers Ridge
Bapaume
Cambrai
Dover
Epehy
Etrun
Ficheux
Fillièvres
La Bassée
Langemarck
Mons
Passchendaele
Pozières
St Omer
Valenciennes
Ypres

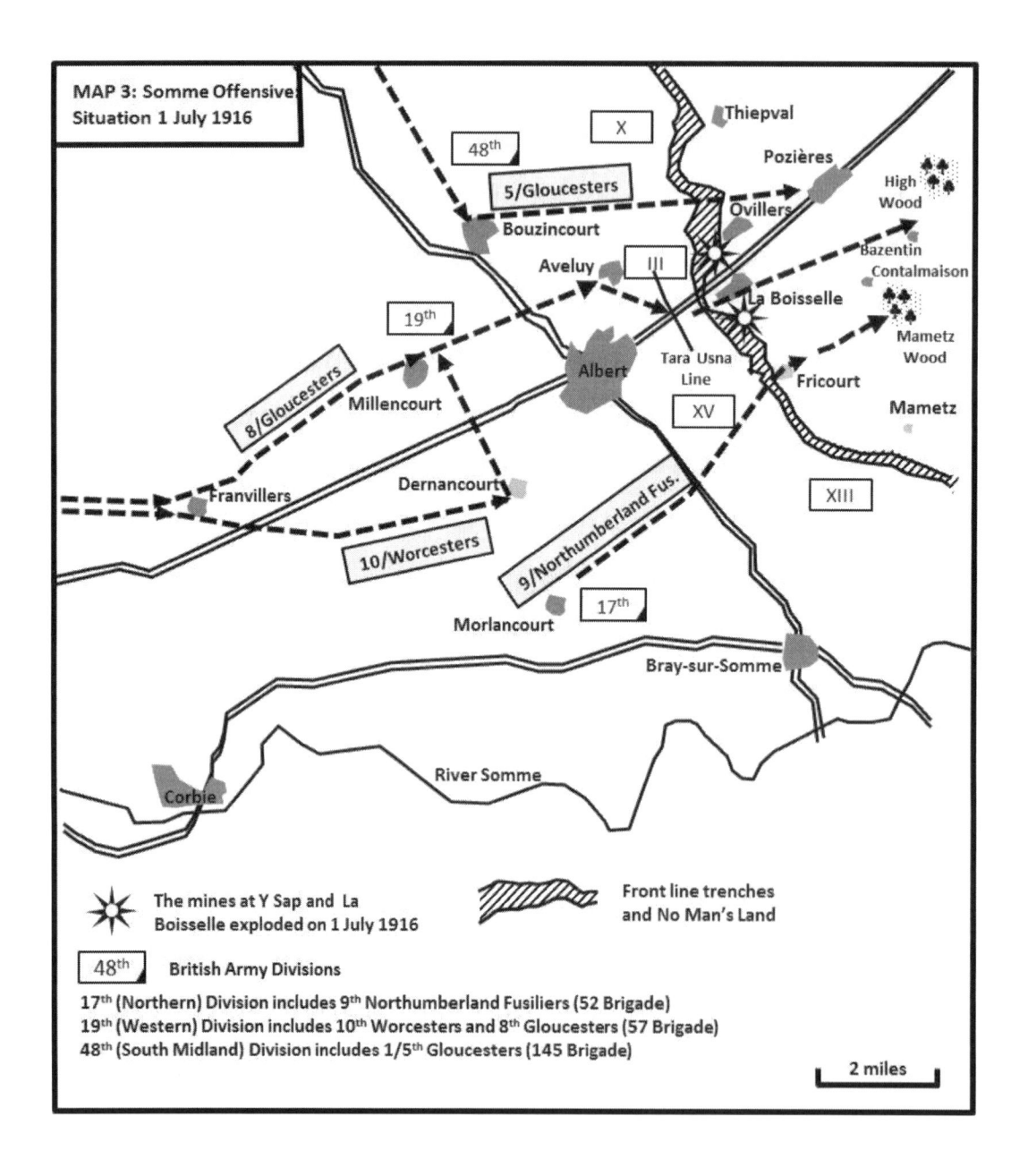

MAP 3: Somme Offensive Situation 1 July 1916

The mines at Y Sap and La Boisselle exploded on 1 July 1916

Front line trenches and No Man's Land

48th — British Army Divisions

17th (Northern) Division includes 9th Northumberland Fusiliers (52 Brigade)
19th (Western) Division includes 10th Worcesters and 8th Gloucesters (57 Brigade)
48th (South Midland) Division includes 1/5th Gloucesters (145 Brigade)

Map 1: Third Battle of Ypres (Passchendaele) (31 July–10 November 1917)

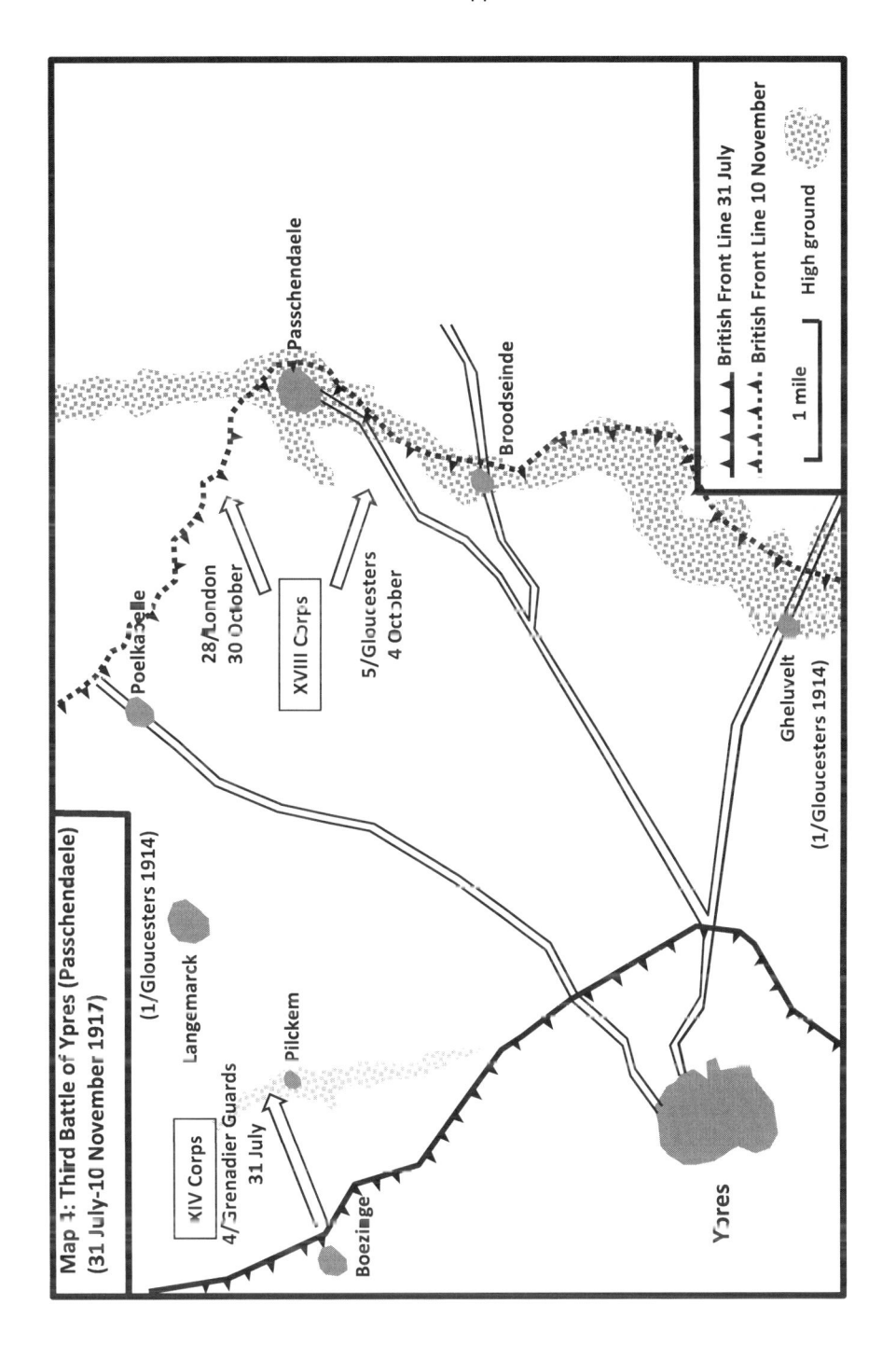

Map 5: The German Spring Offensives 1918

- Calais
- Boulogne
- Ypres
- Mount Kemmel
- Front Line: 29 April
- La Bassée
- Front Line: 9 April

Lys Offensive 9-29 April (Operation Georgette)

- Arras
- Ficheux
- Area occupied by the Guards Division, 30 March
- River Somme
- Bapaume
- Albert
- Amiens
- Le Hamel
- Moreuil
- St Quentin
- Front Line: 5 April
- Front Line: 21 March
- La Fère

Somme Offensive 21 March-5 April (Operation Michael)

Boundary between British Fifth Army and the French Army

German Advances March-July 1918

45 miles

BIBLIOGRAPHY

DAVIES, Martin *Conceal, Create, Confuse. Deception as a British Battlefield Tactic in the First World War* (Stroud: Spellmount, 2009)

DAVIES, Martin and Teresa *They played for Gloucester and fought for their country. Gloucester Rugby Football Club: A Place in Military History*, (Gloucestershire Archives, 2013)

EDMONDS, J. E. *History of the Great War. Military Operations France and Belgium 1916 Vol I: Douglas Haig's Command to 1st July: Battle of the Somme* (London: Macmillan, 1932)

EDMONDS, J.E. *History of the Great War. Military Operations France and Belgium 1914 Vol II Antwerp. La Bassée, Armentières, Messines and Ypres October-November 1914* (London: Macmillan & Co., 1925)

EDMONDS, J. E. *History of the Great War. Military Operations France and Belgium 1917 Vol II 7th June – 10th November. Messines and Third Ypres (Passchendaele)* (London: HMSO, 1948)

EDMONDS, J.E. *History of the Great War. Military Operations France and Belgium, 1918 Vol II March-April: Continuation of the German Offensive* (London: Macmillan & Co.,1937)

Fifth Gloster Gazette. A trench magazine published throughout the Great War by the 5th Battalion, Gloucestershire Regiment. (Now available from Alan Sutton Publishing Limited, 1993)

MARKS, Dean *Bristol's Own. The 12th Battalion Gloucestershire Regiment 1914-1918* (Thatcham: Dolman Scott Ltd., 2011)

WYRALL, Everard *The Gloucestershire Regiment in the War 1914-1918* (London: Methuen, 1931). (Reprinted and available from by Naval and Military Press)

For Club, King and Country

INDEX

'Profile' indicates that a detailed profile of serviceman available (page number); P+number indicates a photograph within the text

Albert, 47, 74, 75,76, 81, 108
Alcock, Arnold, 88
Alderwick, Ernest (GCCC), 98, 137, profile(137)
Amiens, 94, 112
Ashmead, Fred (GRFC), 86, 88
Aubers Ridge, 39, 47, 138, 139
Ayliffe, Frank (GRFC), 74, 122, P1, P14, P39
Bapaume, 108
Barnes Albert (GRFC), 115, profile(137)
Barnes,Herbert ('Harry') (GRFC),11, 20, 48, 50, profile(138)
Barnes, Hubert (GRFC), 61, 93, profile(138), P31
Barnett, Charles (GCCC), 35, 45, 92, 123, 125, 191
Bateman-Champain, Claude (GCCC), 21, 35
Bateman-Champain, Francis (GCCC), 27, 35
Bateman-Champain, Hugh (GCCC), 21, 25, 189, profile(138)
Battalion Cup, 5/Gloucesters, Inter-Company, 34
Battle of Coronel, 31
Bayliss, Stanley (GRFC), 126
Bell, Percy (GCCC), 127
Berry, Henry ('Harry') (GRFC), 10, 11, 20, 21, 47, 48, 50, profile(139), P19
Board, Jack (GCCC), 56. P37
Boer War, 8, 9, 10, 11, 21, 37, 47, 73, 95, 108, 115, 132
Bristol Officer Training Corps, 66
British Army Units:
  XIV Corps, 96
  XV Corps, 74, 75
  XVIII Corps, 96, 101
    Guards Division, 84, 96, 107
    5th Division, 53, 84
    7th Division, 95, 113
    13th (Western) Division, 68
    17th (Northern) Division, 73, 74, 75, 76
    18th (Eastern) Division, 95, 103
    19th (Western) Division ('Butterfly' Division), 73, 74, 113
    26th Division, 94
    48th (South Midland) Division, 5, 12, 46, 60, 73, 77, 95, 98
    63rd (Royal Naval) Division, 101
      1 Guards Brigade, 84
      3 Guards Brigade, 84, 96
      14 Brigade, 53
      22 Brigade, 95
      26 Brigade, 112
      30 Brigade, 111
      39 Brigade, 45, 68

52 Brigade, 73
53 Brigade, 85, 103
57 Brigade, 73, 75, 76
58 Brigade, 113
78 Brigade, 94
143 Brigade, 100
144 Brigade, 12, 78, 93, 95
145 Brigade, 73, 77, 78, 93, 100
  Coldstream Guards, 29, 31, 95
  Grenadier Guards,
    1st Battalion, 51, 84
    2nd Battalon, 36, 107
    4th Battalion, 96
  Scots Guards, 1st Battalion, 30
  ASC, see Army Service Corps
  Army Service Corps, 112, 114
  Artist's Rifles, see London Regiment
  Dorsetshire Regiment,
    3rd (Reserve) Battalion, 27
    4th Battalion, 44, 45
  East Yorkshire Regiment, 1st (Garrison) Battalion, 95, 123
  Gloucestershire Regiment
    1st Battalion, 10, 11, 28, 29, 30, 40, 45, 46, 47, 48, 49, 86, 88, 92, 98, 108, 109, 111, 118, 122, 123
    2nd Battalion, 12, 30, 41
    4th (City of Bristol) Battalion (TF), 12, 13, 71, 81, 95, 119, 132
    1/5th Battalion (TF), 4, 12, 13, 15, 22, 33, 34, 35, 40, 41, 42, 45, 46, 50, 55, 56, 58, 61, 66, 73, 77, 79, 80, 81, 85, 88, 92, 93, 98, 100, 103, 106, 110, 111, 113, 122, 123, 125, 126, 129
    2/5th Battalion (TF), 27, 45, 46, 102, 103, 111, 115, 119
    6th Battalion (TF), 12, 13, 27, 79, 132
    7th (Service) Battalion, 45, 62, 63, 68, 79, 84, 126
    8th (Service) Battalion, 73, 74, 75, 76, 81, 86, 88, 101, 108, 119, 122, 132
    9th (Service) Battalion, 36, 94, 95
    10th (Service) Battalion, 46, 97, 108
    12th (Service) Battalion (Bristol's Own), 15, 84, 132
    13th (Service) Battalion, 15, 45, 82, 83, 84, 108, 116
  HAC, see Honourable Artillery Company
  Honourable Artillery Company, 1st Battalion, 60
  Intelligence Corps, 4th Battalion, 104, 123
  King's Royal Rifle Corps,
    1st Battalion, 31
    2nd Battalion, 92
    10th Battalion, 60
  Leicestershire Regiment,
    1st Battalion, 29
    4th Battalion, 29
  London Regiment, 28th (City of London) Battalion (Artist's Rifles), 36, 59, 81, 101
  Manchester Regiment,
    2nd Battalion, 53, 136
    14th (Service) Battalion, 14, 47, 56, 57, 72
    22nd (service) Battalion (7th City), 15, 52

North Staffordshire Regiment, 5th Battalion, 26
Northumberland Fusiliers,
   8th (Service) Battalion, 117
   9th (Service) Battalion, 73, 74, 76, 137
Oxfordshire and Buckinghamshire Light Infantry, 4th Battalion, 78, 115
Rifle Brigade,
   6th (Reserve) Battalion, 115
   9th (Service) Battalion, 27, 67
   18th (London) Battalion, 110
Royal Berkshireshire Regiment,
   6th Battalion, 85, 103
   8th (Service) Battalion, 109
RFC, see Royal Flying Corps
RGHY, see Royal Gloucestershire Hussars Yeomanry
Royal Field Artillery, 60, 87, 95, 122, 126, 127
Royal Flying Corps, 53, 60, 83, 87, 117
Royal Garrison Artillery, 17, 60
Royal Gloucestershire Hussars Yeomanry, 17, 22, 52, 68, 70, 71, 86, 86, 123
Royal Warwickshire Regiment, 2nd Battalion, 95
South Staffordshire Regiment, 5th Battalion, 103
South Wales Borderers, 1st Battalion, 11, 48, 92
Suffolk Regiment, 11th Battalion, 98, 136, 137
Welsh Regiment,
   2nd Battalion, 24, 29, 92, 109, 113
   6th (Glamorgan) Battalion, 97, 109
West Yorkshireshire Regiment, 9th (Service) Battalion, 82, 117,
Wiltshireshire Regiment, 2nd Battalion, 113, 115
Worcestershire Regiment,
   2nd Battalion, 86, 87
   10th (Service) Battalion, 73, 74, 75, 76, 88
   20th Hussars, 67, 95, 131
British Lions, 20, 68, 131
Broodseinde, 100
Brown, William (GCCC), 26, 123
Brownlee, William (GCCC), 27, 28, 35, 37, 125, profile(139), P3
Bruton, Sir James, 9, 22, 71, 86, 121, 125, 129
Burma, 52, 110
Burns, Tom (GRFC), 122
Cambrai, 75, 92, 93, 95, 101, 102, 113
Canadian Forces Rugby XV, 34
Carl Lody, 36
Carleton, Cornelius (GRFC), 21, 24, 29, 97, 109, 113, profile(140)
Carton de Wiart, Adrian, VC, 75
Charteris, Hugo (Lord Elcho) (GCCC), 22, 35, 52, 69, 70, profile(140), P24
Cheltenham Cricket Festival, 8, 14, 27, 126
Chester-Master, Edgar (GCCC), 21, 35, 61
Churchill, Sir Winston, 10, 14, 40, 43, 55
Clarke, Basil (GCCC), 21, 29, 35, 123
Clifton College OTC, 53, 66, 113
Collett, Gilbert (GRFC), 12, 21, 42, 45, 46, 55, 59, 110, profile(141)
Collett, John Henry, 15, 34, P14

Collins, Henry ('Harry') (GRFC), 10, 21, 75, 76, profile(141)
Colours were left behind for safekeeping, 13
Cook, Albert (GRFC), 15, 22, 46, 80, 129, profile(142), P1, P14
Cook, Charles (GRFC), 20, 34, 46, 61, 91, 97, 99, 100, 119, 122, 129, profile(142), P1, P14
Cook, George (GRFC), 41, 119, 129, profile(143)
Cook, Harry (GRFC), 45, 74, 119, 129
Crankshaw, Eric (GCCC), 21, 35, 123, profile(143)
Cromwell, Walter (GRFC), 50, 61, P2
Cummings, Albert (GRFC), 46, 48
Cummings, Ernest (GRFC), 41, 46, 48, 144, profile(144), P15, P18
Daniels, J. 119
Deane, Harold (GRFC) 34
Dennett, George (GCCC), 10, 21, 35, 95, 123, profile(144), P3, P4, P37
Derby Scheme, 57, 58
Devereux, Simon (GRFC), 192
Dipper, Alfred (GCCC), 17, 22, 27, 35, 52, 69, 123, 125, profile(145), P3, P4
Dix, William ('Father') (GRFC) 20, 74, 108, 119, 122, profile(146), P39
Dovey, William (GRFC), 41, 119, P2, P14, P15
Du Boulay, Arthur (GCCC), 10, 21, 35, 115, 123, profile(146)
Edwards, Charles (GCCC), 21, 35, profile(146)
Egerton, William (GRFC), 41, 55, 59, profile(147), P15
Egypt, 1, 21, 45, 52, 63, 66, 67, 68, 70, 94, 123
Elcho, Lord, see Hugo Charteris
Ellis, Francis (GCCC), 35, 125, P4
English, Ernest (GCCC), 10, 21, 35, 95, 123, profile(147)
FA Cup Final (1915), 17
Fargus, Archibald (GCCC), 31, 35, profile(148)
Fifth Gloucester Gazette, 58, 59
Five Nations Championship, 20, 126
Fowler, Theodore (GCCC), 35, 60, 125, profile(148)
Fricourt, 74, 75, 76
Gallantry and Other Awards:
  Croix de Guerre (France), 123,
  Croix de Guerre (Belgium), 123
  DCM, see Distinguished Conduct Medal
  Distinguished Conduct Medal, 39, 68, 84, 85, 93, 105, 107, 110, 111, 115
  Distinguished Service Order, 24, 68, 85, 95, 98, 109, 110
  DSO, see Distinguished Service Order
  Legion d'Honneur (France), 123
  Medaille Militaire (France), 105, 111
  Military Cross, 55, 67, 82, 85, 95, 103, 106, 111, 113, 116
  Military Cross (Greece), 123
  Military Medal, 76, 85, 86, 91, 93, 95, 99, 100
  MC, see Military Cross
  MM, see Military Medal
  Order of Agricultural Merit (France), 123
  Order of the British Empire, MBE (Military Division), 123
  Order of the British Empire, OBE (Military Division), 123
  Order of the White Eagle (Serbia), 123
  Ordre de Leopold II (Belgium), 123
Gallipoli, 39, 43, 45, 52, 59, 62, 66, 68, 131

Gange, Thomas (GCCC), 17, 21, 27, 35. profile(148), P3, P4
German Spring Offensives, 85, 113
Gheluvelt, 30
Gibbons, Roger (GCCC), 133, 190
Gloucester Football and Athletic Ground Company Limited, 17, 53, 128
Goddard, Arthur (GRFC), 74
Goulding, Fred (GRFC), 10, 21, 46, 48, P19
Grant, William (GCCC), 21, 35, 112, 113, 125, 189, profile(149), P4
Green, Michael (GCCC), 21, 27, 35, 86, 98, 99, 111, 123, profile(149), P4
Griffiths, George (GRFC), 10, 20, 21, 97, 98, 108, profile(150)
Griffiths, James (GRFC), 79, 80, profile(150)
Grist, Ronald (GRFC), 110, profile(151)
Hacker, William (GCCC), 35
Halford, George (GCCC), 11, 14, 20, 40, 71, 88, 120, 122, 125, 126, profile(151), P1, P39
Hall, Arthur (GRFC), 119, P1, P39
Hall, Ernest (GRFC), 74, 88
Hall, William (GRFC), 20, 88
Hamblin, James (GRFC), 14, 15, 22, 34, 46, 55, 56, 59, 61, 120, 125, 126
Hamblin, Lionel (GRFC), 20, 45, P1, P14
Hancock, Walter (GRFC), 11, 28, 30, 37, profile(151)
Harris, Joe (GRFC), 41, 46, 55, 122, P2, P14, P15, P39
Harvey, Will, 58, 59, 82
Healing, John (GCCC), 95, profile(152)
Hébuterne, 77
Helm, George, MC, Reverend, 79, P36
Henderson, William (GRFC), 117, profile(152)
High Wood, 81
HMS Good Hope, 31
HMS *Monmouth*, 31
Holland, Dave (GRFC), 21
Holloway, George (GCCC), 35, 82, 117, 124, profile(153)
Horlick, James (GCCC), 21, 31, 35, 95, 123, profile(153)
Hudson, Arthur (GRFC), 6, 20, 40, 86, 87, 88, 119, 120, 123, P39
Imlay, Alan (GCCC), 28, 66
James, Burnet (GCCC), 35, 60, 61, 67, 125, profile(154)
Jessop, Gilbert (GCCC), 14, 21, 35, 47, 56, 57, 61, 62, 72, profile(154), P3, P22
Jewell, J. (GRFC), 86, 88
Johns, William (GRFC), 6, 20
Jones, Hugh (GCCC), 15, 82, 83, 84, 108, 116, 125, profile(155), P38
Kantara, 52, 68
Katia, 65, 69, 70, 71, 86
Kingscott, Hubert (GRFC), 88, P2
Kingsholm Ground (Stadium), 6, 17, 27, 71, 86, 87, 98, 119, 129, 132
Kitcat, Sidney (GCCC), 35, 36, 83, profile(155)
Kitchener, 1, 3, 10, 14, 18, 22, 24, 37, 45, 46, 62, 65, 72, 144, 184
Kut, 66, 68
La Boisselle, 74, 75, 76, 79, 81, 86, 141, 162, 166
La Vacquerie, 102, 103, 161
Lane, George (GRFC), 41, 88
Lane, Henry ('Harry') (GRFC), 39, 51, 84, 85, 105, 107, profile(155)
Langemarck, 28, 61, 96, 99

Lawson, Joseph (GRFC), 123, P1, P39
Le Touret, 36
Le Transloy, 86, 171
Lee, J. (GRFC), 88, 119, 120
Lesboeufs, 84
Levy, Solomon (GCCC), 15, 35, 84
Lewis, Alec (GRFC), 41, 46, 61, 80, 85, 103, 123, profile(156), P14, P15
Lewis, Melville (GRFC),42, 79, 85, profile(157)
Lewis, Tom (GRFC), 41, 79, 85, profile(157), P14
Lodge, Allen (GRFC), 20
Lody, Carl, 36
Loos, 39, 60, 61, 65
Lovett, Alfred C. 29, 30
Mackay Claude (GCCC), 11, 21, 35, 53, 55, 125, profile(157)
Mametz Wood, 76, 175
Mangotsfield Cricket Club, 1
Manners, Herbert (GCCC), 35
Mansell, Frank (GRFC), 59, 126, P39
Marsden, Edmund (GCCC), 21, 35, 52, profile(158)
Meadows James (GRFC), 12, P14
Meakin, Bernard (GCCC), 189
Merrick, Horace (GCCC), 35, 55, 78, 95, profile(158)
Mesopotamia, 39, 45, 63, 66, 68, 84, 139, 167
Millard, Sydney (GRFC), 41, 46, 59, 61, 79, profile(159), P1, P14, P15, P25
Millencourt, 75, 76
Miller, Thomas (GCCC), 21, 27, 28, 35, 45, P4
Millington, Thomas (GRFC), 123, P39
Mills Arthur (GRFC), 10
Morgan, Donald (GCCC), 21, 35
Morlancourt, 74
Nason, John (GCCC), 35, 87, 125, profile(159), P3
Nelmes, William ('Jack') (GRFC), 74, 81, 101, profile(160)
New Zealand Expeditionary Force, 21, 44
Northern Union, 21, 50, 143
Ovillers, 78, 79, 81, 86, 166
Paish, Arthur (GCCC), 25, 98
Parham, William (GRFC), 34, 61, 97, 100, 101, profile(160), P1
Parker, Charles (GCCC), 123, 125, profile(160), P3, P4
Passchendaele, 75, 91, 96, 101, 112, 149, 163, 195, 201
Pearce, William (GRFC), 80, 102, 103, 125, 189, profile(161), P35
Pegler, Fred (GRFC), 6, 10, 20, 21
Penduck, Arthur (GCCC), 35, 127
Pepall, George (GCCC), 35, profile(161)
Pickering, Arthur (GCCC), 52
Ploegsteert Wood, 40, 43, 46, 144
Pollard, Harry (GRFC), 41, 55, 59, 81
Pont de Nieppe, 46
Pope, Andrew (GCCC), 21, 35, profile(161)
Poulton-Palmer, Ronald, 46
Powell, Trevor (GRFC), 12, 22, 34, 66, profile(162), P2
Pozières, 22, 65, 78, 79, 80, 85, 103, 108, 150, 156, 157, 159, 169

Price, John ('Jack') (GRFC), 22, 65, 75, profile(162)
Priestley, Donald (GCCC), 81, 101, 189, profile(163)
Prince of Wales National Relief Fund, 17
Purton, Alfred (GRFC), 96, 97, profile(163)
Qantara, see Kantara
Qatia, see Katia
Rattenbury, Gilbert (GCCC), 35
Reade, Majorie, 99
Rigby, William (GRFC), 119
Roach, Bernard ('Peter') (GRFC), 36, 37, profile(163)
Roberts, Francis (GCCC), 21, 35, 61, 67, 116, 125, profile(164), P3
Robinson Douglas (GCCC), 21, 31, 35, 123, 125, profile(164), P3
Robinson, Foster (GCCC), 26, 36, 125
Robinson, John (GRFC), 21, 48, 50
Robinson, Percy (GCCC), 21, 26, 35, 95, profile(165)
Robinson, William Leefe, 83, 84
Romans George (GRFC and GCCC), 6, 86, 98
Rose, Charles (GRFC), 48
Russell, Arthur (GRFC), 112, 114, profile(165)
Salonika Front, 94
Saunders, Arthur (GRFC), 74, 76, 81, 86, profile(166), P1
Sewell, Cyril (GCCC), 21, 27, 35, 46, profile(166), P3, P4
Simmons, Percy (GRFC), 61, 77, 80, 113, 114, 115, profile(166)
Smart, Sidney (GRFC), 14, 15, 20, 22, 34, 46, 61, 123, 126, P1, P39
Smith, Frank (GRFC), 11, 45, 62, 68, profile(167)
Smith, Hubert (GRFC), 41, P15
Somme Offensive, 65, 77, 195
Speck, Alfred (GRFC), 34
Spence, Alec (GRFC), 10
Stout, Frank (GRFC), 20, 21, 67, 68, 95, 127, 131, profile(167), P42
Stout, Percy (GRFC), 21, 67, 68, 98, 123, profile(168)
Stroud Football Club, 5, 14, 17
Sumner, Lionel, 59
Sysum, Sidney (GRFC), 34, 41, 46, 55, 59, 79, 80, profile(169), P1, P14, P15
Sysum, William (GRFC), 74
Tayler, Herbert (GCCC), 105, 111, 169, 186, profile(169)
Taylor, L. (GRFC), 119
Taylor, Clifford (GCCC), 181
Tester, George, 67, 68, 168
Thomas, Hugh (GRFC), 45, 74, 81, profile(170)
Timms, Herbert (GCCC), 35
Townsend, Charles (GCCC), 10
Townsend, Frank (GCCC), 10, 95
Troup, Frank (GCCC), 21, profile(170)
Troup, Walter (GCCC), 21, 35, profile(170)
Truman, Thomas (GRFC), 112, 115, profile(171), P37
Turner, Ronald (GCCC), 35, 59, profile(171)
VA Hospitals, 16, 24, 71, 88, 96, 98, 99
Vears, Lindsay (GRFC), 20, 21, 87, 88
Voyce, Thomas ('Tom') (GRFC), 119, 120, 126, P39
Walwin, Oscar (GRFC), 70, 86, profile(171)

War Memorials:
  Bristol War Memorial, 131, P43
  City of Gloucester's War Memorial, 66, 132,
  Gloucester Rugby Football Club Roll of Honour, 121, 129, P40
  5th Battalion, Gloucestershire Regiment's War Memorial, 129, P41
  Helles Memorial, Gallipoli, 59
  Jerusalem Memorial, 70
  Kingsholm Stadium War Memorial, 132, P44
  Le Touret Memorial, 50, P20
  Lone Pine Memorial, 45
  Menin Gate Memorial, 29, 30, P13
  Thiepval Memorial, 80, 81, 108, P30
  Tyne Cot Memorial, 82, 101, P34

Washbourne, William (GRFC), 15, 20, 22, 34, 41, 46, 61, 85, 119, 123, profile(172), P1, P14, P15, P25, P39
Watts, Frederic (GCCC), 35
Webb, Fred (GRFC), 6, 42, 46, 59, 61, 80, 112, 123, 125, 126, P1, P14, P39
Webb, John (GRFC), 34, 45, 119, 120, 123, P2, P39
West, Thomas (GRFC), 60, profile(172)
West Gloucestershire Cricket Club, 1
Westbury, James (GRFC), 45, 52
White, Alfred, 41, P10
White, Alison (GCCC), 6, 21, 27, 33, 35, 52, 123, 125, profile(173)
Wicks, Frank (GCCC), 15, 35, 52, 81, 84, profile(173)
Wilkes, William ('Snowy') (GRFC), 34, 45, P2
Williams, John (GCCC), 21, 35, 39, 44, profile(174)
Winterbotham, James (GCCC), 32, 35, 45, 59, 61, 98, 106, profile(174), P36
Woof, William (GCCC), 10, 126
Woolley, Claude (GCCC), 35
Wootton, Edwin (GFRC), 35, 59, 94, 95, profile(175), P33
Wreford-Brown, Oswald (GCCC), 21, 35, 74, 76, profile(175)
Yalland, William (GCCC), 21, 28, 29, 30, 35, 37, profile(175), P11
Zeppelin, 83

"Do we remember? Why of course we do"

Captain A.F. Barnes, MC, 2/5th Gloucesters